"I came across Billie and Paul's work in a workshop at a queer Christian conference, and it pinged in my spirit as the exact way to describe what I had been experiencing in the Black church. I had been experiencing disgust, but I didn't know what to call it—because it was so subtle and pervasive. We agreed on Blackness. We agreed on the same truth. So, the resistance I was feeling, I didn't know how to name. Encountering their work on disgust and eucontamination was a revelation. It gave me language for what I had been feeling but couldn't articulate. It became a crucial part of my own process of self-actualization and healing from the diseased ways I was taught to move through the world. And as I become more regulated, I'm seeing so much lived manifestation of their deep psychoanalytical, scientific, and theological work. I truly believe that we can infect the world with good. It's working for me."

—**Tamice Spencer-Helms**
Author of *Faith Unleavened: The Wilderness Between Trayvon & George Floyd*

"Drawing on their expertise, experience, and shared commitment to Christ's church, Billie and Paul Hoard have written a book that truly embodies the Way of Jesus. They call followers of Jesus to leave behind a faith marred by disgust theology and embrace eucontamination (contamination for good) as a way to find flourishing for ourselves and our neighbors. This book will leave you thinking deeply and acting boldly. I highly recommend it!"

—**Zach Lambert**
Pastor, Restore Austin

"This book taught me about myself in a way I was not expecting. Paul and Billie are incredibly insightful in teaching us how to navigate societal disgust and shame while demonstrating how joy and love live in tandem with them. An eye-opening read for anyone who wants to learn more about themselves, why we feel disgust and how to navigate our way through this world we all live in. I'm a better person for having read this book."

—**April Ajoy**
Author of *Star-Spangled Jesus*

"Paul and Billie Hoard's remarkable new book offers us a startlingly fresh vision of Jesus, one that is exigent in these times of Christian nationalism and fundamentalism. Rather than just being a figure of love, Jesus becomes a force that compels us to act against our own inherent tendency toward disgust. Under the Hoard siblings' radical new vision, Jesus calls us to embrace what disgusts us. It's no longer just 'love your enemy' but 'love the disgusting.'"

—**Todd McGowan**
Professor of Film Studies, University of Vermont

"'For God so loved the world that he contaminated it with his Son . . .' Rather than being repulsed by or excluding the other, siblings Paul and Billie Hoard demonstrate that Jesus's Way of love dares us to reimagine division, separation, and exclusion as the very things which Christ expels. This book guides us to see and feel every loving relationship is a contamination for good—a eucontamination—and that any disgust response just may be a Holy Spirit nudge to practice loving God and neighbor as we learn to love ourselves. I highly commend this book to you . . . it's infectious!"

—**Dwight J. Friesen**
Professor of Practical Theology, The Seattle School of Theology and Psychology

"I have been waiting for this book! Working with kids on the street for over thirty years taught me that beauty, community, and justice always revealed themselves in mutual transformation. Billie and Paul thoughtfully illuminate the impediment of toxic forms of false purity and the psycho-social illusions of moral superiority, introducing the reader to the relational aspect of divine love found in the perceived other. They lead us towards a truth that is greater than objective and subjective platitudes—a truth that is deeply relational."

—**Ron Ruthruff**
Associate Professor of Theology and Culture, The Seattle School of Theology and Psychology

"The central insight of this creative, well-researched, and highly sophisticated book is that the human disgust reaction has been overpowerful yet underexamined in shaping some of the most destructive expressions of traditional Christianity, including, crucially, its historic contempt toward LGTBQIA+ people. The authors coin the term eucontamination to name what is actually a quite prominent theme in the New Testament—God's grace in Christ is contamination for good. This is why we need not live out of a fearful purity ethic. They also offer reflection on church practices that can train us in seeing and living this way in the world. I highly recommend this breakthrough work."

—**David P. Gushee**
Distinguished University Professor of Christian Ethics, Mercer University

"Differences that challenge our identity often evoke fear or anger. Paul and Billie Hoard brilliantly argue that underneath much of the hostility and division that fuels our polarized debates is the unaddressed presence of disgust. Disgust guards the edges of our fragility and soaks the other with self-serving righteous contempt. This compelling and troubling tour de force will rock you. You may differ with some conclusions or implications. Still, their honesty, humanity, and depth of reflection invite a stellar engagement with truth, love, and the wild, disruptive presence of Jesus."

—**Dan B. Allender**
Professor of Counseling Psychology, The Seattle School of Theology and Psychology

"In this provocative work, Paul and Billie offer a critical examination of the evangelical purity culture contending that such a framework fosters binaries, advances marginalization, and creates hostility toward those deemed 'other,' and is a misrepresentation of the gospel. Contrary to purity culture's emphasis on separation and exclusion, they introduce the concept of eucontamination—a sacred undoing, a holy reversal where the impure is made pure not through separation, but through direct contact with the other. Purity is brittle. It hides, it protects, it fears. But eucontamination is wild, embodied grace—it is messy, alive, and unafraid. It reaches into the muck. It touches. It heals. It loves. Billie and Paul invite us in—to step into the ache of the world. They challenge the church to abandon fear, soften our boundaries, to live in the blur and imagine a gospel capacious enough, tender enough, bold enough to hold the other in love. This book strikes with a force, awakening and unsettling your understanding of the gospel."

—**Roy Barsness**
Founder, Contemporary Psychodynamic Institute

"In this theologically and psychologically sophisticated book, Hoard and Hoard use the psychology of disgust to explain some of our worst human behavior. But then they subvert disgust—helping us see the way, truth, and life of Jesus as a form of contamination (eucontamination) which has the power to transform individuals and communities away from othering, exclusion, and dehumanizing to Christ's way of love. This book is not only accessible but practical for a church desirous to embody a different way. Christendom needs this book for these times."

—**Brad D. Strawn**
Evelyn and Frank Freed Professor of the Integration of Psychology and Theology,
Fuller Theological Seminary

"I love reading books that rouse me from intellectual slumber and invite me to reimagine my thinking, categories, and meaning—particularly when the authors speak from inside my tradition and cultural history. Written with penetrating erudition and clarity, siblings Paul and Billie Hoard engage our gut, our visceral imagination of what it means to be Christian. Drawing broadly from theology, psychoanalysis/psychology, literature, philosophy, current events, and popular culture, Paul and Billie have written an enormously interesting, engaging, and provocative confrontation of how disgust and contamination infuse and distort our spiritual and relational lives. How do we live and love as Christians with those we are different from? How do we acknowledge our own contributions to the fracturing of our world? How do we identify the damaging discourses of our faith that counteract the work of God? How do we reverse the contamination of sin, not with fear, but with engaging the transformative power of Christ's messy, engaging, infectious love? This book makes a critically significant contribution to answering these questions."

—**Earl Bland**
Professor of Psychology, Biola University

"From the moment I first heard the Hoards discuss eucontamination, I was captivated. Their insights into disgust, its entanglement with shame, and the possibility of its playful subversion on behalf of the way of truth and life are nothing short of transformative. This is a powerful book. One that just might change how you view the world."

—**Matthias Roberts**
Author of *Beyond Shame*

"One of the defining features of the modern world is that it embodies a type of purity culture. We constantly split the world into the clean and the unclean, seeking one and avoiding the other. Increasingly we seek only the same and stay away from the other. In *Eucontamination* we encounter a wonderful invitation to step out of the sterile and dangerous environments we increasingly inhabit. While purity cultures set boundaries—between the good and the bad, the sacred and profane, the inside and outside—*Eucontamination* offers the vision of something much messier. It is a celebration of porosity, transmission, excess, and hybridity. It is a call to remove our hazmat suits and get dirty in a vibrant and chaotic world."

—**Peter Rollins**
Author of *Insurrection*

"One of the most important books to read this year. Billie and Paul's work on disgust theology doesn't just break new ground—it breaks open the systems that fuel dehumanization in our politics and religion. It is an eye-opening read that brings disgust to forefront, an often-invisible force animating so much of the division and hatred we see today. But what I love most is that they don't stop at naming what's wrong—they offer a better path forward rooted in the life of Jesus and a reframed understanding of sin and purity. Billie and Paul expose how disgust and contamination shape our theology—and how the teachings of Jesus flip our understanding of both on its head. *Eucontamination* is where theology meets psychology in a way that is bold, brilliant, and necessary for Christians to meet the call of our historical moment."

—**Tim Whitaker**
Founder, The New Evangelicals

Eucontamination

Eucontamination

Disgust Theology and the Christian Life

Paul Hoard *and*
Billie Hoard

CASCADE *Books* • Eugene, Oregon

EUCONTAMINATION
Disgust Theology and the Christian Life

Copyright © 2025 Paul Hoard and Billie Hoard. All rights reserved. Except for brief quotations in critical publications or reviews, no part of this book may be reproduced in any manner without prior written permission from the publisher. Write: Permissions, Wipf and Stock Publishers, 199 W. 8th Ave., Suite 3, Eugene, OR 97401.

Cascade Books
An Imprint of Wipf and Stock Publishers
199 W. 8th Ave., Suite 3
Eugene, OR 97401

www.wipfandstock.com

PAPERBACK ISBN: 979-8-3852-1372-6
HARDCOVER ISBN: 979-8-3852-1373-3
EBOOK ISBN: 979-8-3852-1374-0

Cataloguing-in-Publication data:

Names: Hoard, Paul, author. | Hoard, Billie, author.

Title: Eucontamination : disgust theology and the Christian life / Paul and Billie Hoard.

Description: Eugene, OR : Cascade Books, 2025 | Includes bibliographical references.

Identifiers: ISBN 979-8-3852-1372-6 (paperback) | ISBN 979-8-3852-1373-3 (hardcover) | ISBN 979-8-3852-1374-0 (ebook)

Subjects: LCSH: Aversion. | Purity (Ethics). | Purity, Ritual—Biblical teaching. | Hospitality—Religious aspects—Christianity. | Christian ethics.

Classification: BJ1533.P97 .H36 2025 (paperback) | BJ1533.P97 (ebook)

VERSION NUMBER 07/21/25

To the Tooch! May you be remembered in all our gatherings.

Contents

Acknowledgments | ix
Introduction | xi

1. On Disgust and Purity | 1
2. Disgusted Distortion | 18
3. Eucontamination | 37
4. The Poetry of Truth | 54
5. Prophetic Heresies | 74
6. Shame Faced | 95
7. Recovering Joy | 116
8. Yuck Walks and Desire: The Way of Jesus | 136
9. Of Flames and Ashes | 160
10. Further Up and Further In! | 183

Appendix: Liturgy of Eucontamination | 205
Bibliography | 211

Acknowledgments

A BOOK LIKE THIS is never born from just our minds alone. From the start our conversations and understanding were "infected" for good by countless conversations, shared experiences, and the love and support of many who have walked this journey with us.

First and foremost, we extend our deepest gratitude to our families. Mary and Ashley, your unwavering love and encouragement have sustained us through this entire process. You have endured so much with patience and grace—thank you. To our children—Liam, Ruth, Oz, John, Iris, and Bea—you are our inspiration and motivation. Through you, we have learned the profound connections between love and disgust.

We are also deeply grateful to our parents, Andy and Cathryn, for the home they created, the love they poured into us, and the faith they modeled so beautifully. To our siblings, Joanie and Sam, thank you for challenging, questioning, and pushing us toward deeper understanding. And to our grandmother, Ruth (Billie) Hoard—we miss you dearly. We are who we are because you loved us.

A special thanks to Lauren Peiser and Dwight Friesen for your invaluable contributions to the practice of *eucontamination*. Your vision and *shalomic* imagination are woven into the very fabric of this work. We are humbled by your insight and deeply grateful for your belief in this project. Kat Coffin, thank you for shaping our words into something clear and comprehensible—we truly do not understand commas!

Finally, to our readers, conversation partners, faith communities, peers, and students—thank you. This book is the result of the wisdom we have gathered from and alongside you. The ideas within these pages were born out of our shared journey, and now, we offer them back to you.

With gratitude,
Billie and Paul

Introduction

THIS IS A BOOK about disgust and contamination. And Jesus. We would dare to assert that few if any other texts on theology and the Way of Jesus spend as much time talking about poop as the one you are reading. However, if you are willing to move towards your disgust, we hope you just may find Jesus in the last place you expect, but the very place he said he would be.

This book comes from countless hours of discussion between us as siblings reflecting on our childhood in the evangelical church. Something about othering, fear, and a felt need to protect faith kept making its way into our conversations. We couldn't shake the sense that all of these dynamics were related, but it wasn't until we started talking about the psychology of disgust that the pieces started snapping into place. Disgust psychology gave us a way to talk about what was living in our bodies and seemed to be fueling the division, fear, and protectiveness we had been struggling to account for. Over several years, we kept talking, reading, and arguing from our respective positions. Paul as a mental health counselor was diving much deeper into psychoanalytic theory while Billie was exploring and developing her theological understanding, but we always returned—as a dog returns to its vomit[1]—to disgust. It was the underexplored yet somehow always present dynamic behind so many of the social, religious, and even political problems we encountered.

Richard Beck's writing in his book *Unclean* explores the relationship between disgust, purity, and biblical imagery.[2] He invites his readers to consider how the psychology of disgust can help us better understand the

---

1. Prov 26:11.
2. See Beck, *Unclean*.

life and actions of Jesus—particularly around communion. His thinking, and our shared experiences, prompted the discussions which eventually (after hundreds of hours of conversation, reading, research, and more conversation) culminated in this book on disgust theology. It is an interdisciplinary work that leans into our wondering around how the psychology of disgust might help us understand the Way of Jesus.

We are both third culture kids, having grown up in Turkiye to American parents. As white evangelicals, living in a Muslim majority country, we were often asked about the *other*. Whether that be from American friends reacting to 9/11 or Turkish friends responding to the first or second Gulf War, we were often positioned as representatives of an *other*. Many of these conversations revolved around a sense of fear: fear of foreigners, fear of empire, fear of moral or religious corruption. And we found that we ourselves often identified with those *others* both in America where we were sometimes bemused, sometimes horrified to hear what our fellow citizens thought (or assumed) about our friends and neighbors—our community—back in Turkiye, but also in Turkiye trying to defend or account for the actions of our friends, family, and country back in the States. Our liminal position left us in a near-permanent tension between *us* and *them*.

But what if there was more than fear behind this tension? As we explored the nature of disgust, and the role of unconscious (or preconscious) processes, the limitations of the fear paradigm started to show. No matter how much reason or clear argumentation we employed, minds and hearts never seemed to change. What we found most impactful in this space of being the other was our friendships and not our arguments. But that didn't make any sense. Being friends with a random kid from the US makes no impact on the threat the American military poses. Knowing two siblings from Turkiye has no rational bearing on the felt risk of terrorist activity, but on an affective, somatic level, somehow it did. Friendships seemed to change people's perception of reality.

When we moved back to the US, finished college and graduate school, got married, and began attending churches, we found a similar process at work. As tensions around gay marriage, deconstruction, and the relationship between the white evangelical church and the Republican party intensified, so did the antagonism between fellow Christians on either side of these arguments. Once again, we found ourselves often representing the other in different spaces. Once again, fear seemed to be the dominant frame. "What will it say about us if we let *them* into our midst?" "What worldview does this come from?" "What if this leads to back-sliding?" "I'm afraid you are losing your faith." And once again, it was friendships and community that seemed to change minds and not arguments.

This all began to make more sense once we started exploring the psychology of disgust and then applying it to the life of Jesus. We aren't so much afraid of one another as disgusted—a much harder truth to face. We don't resist the foreigner, orphan, and widow out of fear for our lives and well-being so much as out of a fear that they will contaminate us—change us into something we do not want to become. It's a very human and very normal reaction but not one that Jesus seemed to follow. The Way of Jesus runs in the opposite direction of the exclusion that disgust instigates: it welcomes instead of rejecting, integrates instead of segregating, and loves instead of fearing. As we hammered our ideas, reflections, and experiences out in countless conversations over commutes, dog walks, and pandemic zoom calls, something more seemed to be at work theologically and not just psychologically. We needed a term, a concept, to represent this anti-disgust way of engaging the other that Jesus modeled. This book is where we have landed—for now.

Throughout the rest of this book, we want to invite you on the theological and psychological journey that we have been on for the past several years. The works of C. S. Lewis and Jacques Lacan feature heavily as some of our primary theological and psychological guides. We start with an exploration of disgust in chapter 1 and then highlight its disastrous misapplications in chapter 2. Chapter 3 explores the theological concept of *eucontamination* or a contamination for good—our answer to Jesus's puzzling relationship with disgust. From there, we dive directly into the life and teaching of Jesus through the verse in John 14:6 where Jesus says, "I am the way, the truth, and the life." How might each of these: way, truth, and life, be vectors of eucontamination—contaminants to our self-understanding and social realities that lure us back to Christ? This is where the rest of the book goes, exploring each of these concepts through both an individual and a communal lens. Chapters 4 and 5 look to truth as more than fact and a real beyond our imagination—truth that refuses to leave our individual (chapter 4) or communal (chapter 5) selves content. The following two chapters look at life as a eucontaminant, questioning the role of shame and joy in the formation of our identity as individuals (chapter 6) and as communities (chapter 7). We look to the Way last as we wanted to end with an application and ethic, grounded in understanding. Moving too quickly to action can often be a form of defense and avoidance. In chapters 8 and 9, we explore the nature of desire and love around an ethic of freedom in Christ, through the sacraments of the church. As a reader, we invite you to move towards the liturgies of the church, with a full awareness of the resistance and disgust that they ought to induce, but in the context of a community bound together by Christ's love. We end in chapter 10 with an acknowledgment of our own limited thinking and the dare to continue recklessly pursuing Christ by continually asking "what if there's more?" as we journey together "further up and further in."

1

On Disgust and Purity

Litany of the Table

One: Who is welcome at Christ's table?
Many: **All are welcome and loved by G-d!**
One: Even me?
Many: **Yes. Even you!**
One: But I'm so hungry, and thirsty, and weary.
Many: **Come as you are, this table is lovingly prepared for you, and for all.**
One: But I feel so I afraid, and lonely . . . I ache.
Many: **At Christ's table you are not alone. It is here we discover communion.**
One: Then let's welcome each other.
Many: **Yes, let's become a welcoming people! Cheers to the open table Christ sets!**

—Litany by Dwight Friesen

THERE IS A STORY often told in evangelical churches of a father who bakes his kids a surprise tray of brownies. He carefully combines all the ingredients: the flour, sugar, and cocoa powder with the milk and eggs, then he adds an extra special secret ingredient. He patiently waits as the brownies bake while his children sit glued to whatever movie or show has caught their attention this week. Once the toothpick comes out clean, he pulls the tray from the oven and sets it to cool (not too much) before cutting big servings of brownie onto individual plates, adding a big scoop of vanilla ice cream, and walking them over to his kids.

"Surprise! I made brownies; who wants one?" he announces and his children come running while he holds the tray full of plates high in the air. "Before you get any, these are my super special brownies; I made them with my secret ingredient; are you sure you can even handle these brownies?"

"Daaaaaad," the kids laugh, "We're sure we can handle them. Give us the brownies." But Dad isn't ready to hand them over just yet.

"Don't you want to know about the secret ingredient?"

"We don't even care," they assure him, "those smell soooooo good; can we please have them???"

"Well," Dad replies, the brownies still held aloft and out of reach of hungry hands, "let me at least tell you what it is first; it might make a difference."

Sensing that Dad has some point to make and that brownies will not be forthcoming until he has had his say, the children decide to humor him.

"OK, what is your secret ingredient?" they ask.

Now adequately prompted, the father makes his announcement: "Dog poop! The secret ingredient is dog poop!"

Immediately, the kids recoil. "What? No way! Gross!" But Dad will not be deterred.

"Oh, it's just a little bit, less than a tablespoon; it adds flavor and a little texture, really brings the whole thing together, sort of spices it up." He adds a chef's kiss for emphasis. At this point, the children are backing away and shaking their heads vigorously.

"No. Ewwww. You are so gross; we aren't eating that!"

"Then why were you watching those shows? You know that there is some pretty sinful stuff in there: cursing and violence and sex. If you don't want to eat these delicious brownies because they have disgusting dog poop in them, why are you willing to watch shows with sin? Don't you know that sin is even more disgusting than dog poop?"

In countless stories like this, disgust is marshaled as a powerful tool to impart knowledge, enforce behavior, and shape values in evangelical circles. It is certainly a powerful tool but, like so many powerful tools, it can be misused as easily as it can be used well. In this book, we will be highlighting some of the ways in which disgust has been leveraged to cause harm within the church.[1]

SIN AND DISGUST

Western society has long prized reason and rationality over emotion, pitting the head against the heart.[2] However, psychologists, neurologists, sociologists, and any parent of a toddler can tell you that reason does not hold the final say. Actually, our reasoning is much more about making up reasons for what our intuition is pushing us toward. In other words, why you think you do something is usually only the excuse your conscious mind has conjured up for why that thing is so important or right. This means that impacting one's behavior is much less about the sound argumentation that many of us were taught to believe in school. Instead, influence and change is rooted in our gut or heart, not our head. Think about therapy for a moment; if knowledge and reason were enough to change people, self-help books could replace therapists, but as everyone who's failed a New Year's resolution can attest . . . they don't. This is what makes disgust such a powerful tool. Disgust reaches beyond our conscious minds and witty rationalizations to motivate us on a visceral level. You don't have to know *why* you think something's disgusting in order to avoid it—just that it's gross.[3]

Because it is so powerful, parents and preachers have used disgust to warn or train their children and congregations away from sin. Theologically, we are often told that sin is any action or inaction, thought or attitude which turns us away from God; sin is a failure to *meet the mark* or to really live as Jesus tells us to. But just knowing something rarely seems to be enough to keep anyone from falling into sin; they need to be helped to *feel* the right way about sin as well. Certainly a fear of sin is frequently deployed to this purpose—the loneliness or suffering of hell is an obvious go-to with this approach—but even more useful (if somewhat less noted) is disgust. If children and congregants can be made to feel that sin is disgusting, surely that will keep them away from it.

1. Hoard and Hoard, "Eucontamination."
2. For more information on the history of Western reliance on logic and reason at the expense of emotion, experience, and other forms of knowing, see Smith, *You Are What You Love*; and Caputo, *Philosophy and Theology*.
3. Haidt, *Righteous Mind*.

There are parts of the Bible which have proved to be very useful material in training Christians to be disgusted by sin. The language of purity is a common theme in both the Old and New Testaments, and there are a few images and colorful phrases (particularly in the works of St. Paul) that play on disgusting imagery to make their points. And disgust is not antithetical to the Christian life, nor is it a *bad* part of the human experience (though often unpleasant). But it is powerful and, as such, can be used for both helpful and instructive as well as very harmful, controlling, and insidious ends. It is not disgust in itself that we want to address in this book, but rather its use and misuse.[4]

With this in mind, we want to highlight the ways that disgust has been horribly overused and abused by the church in America. More than that, we want to put forward another model for Christians thinking about the language of holiness, sin, purity, and disgust.

WHAT IS DISGUST?

Disgust may have been the most surprising emotion included in the Pixar film *Inside Out* as it is one that we don't often consider.[5] In most people's minds disgust is usually tied more closely to physical reactions than internal emotions. However, disgust is a really significant, though regularly hidden, architect of our lives, selves, and social world. Disgust helps secure the border between what is me and what is not me. It is all about our boundaries and sense of self.[6]

Consider your reaction to being asked to spit into a sterile cup and then drink your own saliva—a famous hypothetical used in disgust studies. Rationally this should be fine, but as most participants reported—and most of you reading this are viscerally aware—that's disgusting. But why? You are currently swallowing saliva. Nobody likes dry mouth after all. So what happens to that saliva when you've spit it into a cup? It's the same spit. But now that it has left your body, it holds a more ambiguous relationship to you—is it you or not you anymore—and so disgust steps into clarify and delineate between what's you and what's not-you.

---

4. For a thorough exploration of how the Bible uses purity, contamination, and disgust language, see Beck, *Unclean*.

5. Doctor, *Inside Out*.

6. Rozin and Fallon, "Perspective on Disgust."

Importantly, disgust does not seem to be something that infants are born with; rather it is tied directly to our social world. Babies just don't seem to get grossed out. Instead, children are socialized to find their excrement gross. If you've ever had the pleasure of toilet training a child, you have most likely been a part of helping to develop disgust within that kid. Children actually often find their feces fascinating, like a homemade finger paint, and it is only through the experience of their caregivers' reactions that they internalize the "no, icky."[7]

But disgust does much more than help us learn what our social group thinks is nasty. Disgust helps us establish and maintain our sense of self. Lacanian psychoanalytic theory posits the significance of what is termed the *mirror stage* for children.[8] It is around the time when a child is 6–18 months old that they begin to develop a sense of themselves as a whole, bounded thing—often by visually seeing themselves as a complete unit either in the mirror or in the eyes of their caregiver. Suddenly they are a *me* that exists in the world as opposed to disjointed and fragmented sensory experiences. This binding and capturing of the self as a unit creates a sense of stability and predictability, but it also means that *not-me* also now exists in the world. It's important to note that this sense of self is just that: a *sense* of self. So what is forming in this stage is not the physical, bodily presence of me (that happened earlier) but the psychological, conscious experience of *me*—or in terms that may be more familiar—the ego or self-image. Whereas an infant may not be able to recognize their primary caregiver as separate (when pre-birth, in many cases, they were quite literally the same body), with the development of the ego, the budding toddler starts to live in a world with difference and differentiation. As soon as *I* exist, suddenly everything else is *not-I*. The existential ponderings of the emo college student of "who am I" actually begins way back in infancy with the subjective experience of oneself as a self.[9]

However, the self-image that is generated in the mirror stage is just an image, a *me* from a third-party, external perspective. I see my reflection *as if* I can see me from the outside. This means that the very beginning of

---

7. See Boothby, *Sex on the Couch*.

8. Jacques Lacan was a prominent, French psychoanalytic thinker whose influence has been mostly felt in non-Anglophone countries. He is known for his reinterpretation of Freudian ideas through modern linguistic theory. We will use many of his frameworks throughout this text.

9. See Boothby, *Freud as Philosopher*; Žižek, *How to Read Lacan*; Fink, *Lacanian Subject*.

my sense of self includes both dislocation and externalization. This *I* or ego is experienced from the outside; so a fundamental split occurs. The feeling, sensing, experiencing subject of the infant is suddenly split off from the *me* that has just been born. What I experience as *me*, is only a piece of my total self—I am a split subject with my conscious ego on one side and my unconscious on the other. This means that there is always more to you than you think there is, and it is at the point of this split where disgust comes in. Disgust helps maintain that *sense of self*, keeping out the split-off experiences in order to maintain a sense of stability and unity. Disgust protects your ego.[10]

This self-image, while a psychological creation, is also intimately tied to your body. It is the image of your body as a whole, complete unity that fuels the genesis of the ego, leading to the body becoming one of the first metaphors on which our ego is constituted. This helps to explain why the defense of that ego is such a visceral experience. Threats to the body are threats to the ego. The magic of the Band-Aid for little children's cuts is less about their healing power and more about their ability to cover over a literal tear in the unity and wholeness of the body.[11]

As such, what becomes part of the body and what is expelled from the body are intimately interconnected with what can and can no longer be part of me. Eating and eliminating are the early, inherently ambiguous actions right at the border of the body that therefore intersect most directly with disgust. What I eat will become me; what I pass is no longer part of me. I must lower my disgust response to allow that broccoli to be incorporated into my body. Or once I have expelled something from me, I am revolted by it. It can't be me any longer.

This returns us to the hypothetical about spitting in cups. Once the saliva leaves your body, it stops being *you*. Disgust helps you keep a very clear *me* in the face of uncertainty.[12]

Additionally, as we grow out of toddler-hood and into adolescence and adulthood, so too does our sense of self and the complexity of individual and group identity.[13] Romantic and sexual attraction highlights this through intimacy. Consider the contradictory response to another

---

10. See Boothby, *Sex on the Couch*.

11. See Boothby, *Freud as Philosopher*; Tyson and Tyson, *Psychoanalytic Theories of Development*.

12. See Rozin and Fallon, "Perspective on Disgust"; Beck, *Unclean*; Haidt, *Righteous Mind*.

13. See Siegel, *Developing Mind*.

person's saliva in kissing versus spitting. The same substance is either vile or acceptable depending on the relational context. In intimacy the differentiation between me and you becomes less rigid and far more permeable on a physical and emotional level as our bodies and feelings intermingle. Intimate relationships are able to find play in the contradiction of simultaneously blurring identities while maintaining individuation. I am able to be connected to you without losing myself in us. This could be a traumatic, destabilizing, and ego-threatening experience, but in healthy relationships it is life giving. In codependency and enmeshment, however, it can be extremely damaging. Sexuality and sexual behavior, then, is a form of "intimacy embodied."[14] In sexual play, the physical boundaries between people are blurred and in healthy relationships, far from being a disgusting event, this sexual union is a beautiful, transcendent experience of connection. The strict delineation of me is able to be played with in connection to you, but it is not disgusting due to the presence of intimacy. This emotional intimacy thus facilitates a transcendence as opposed to disgust.[15]

Beyond bodily fluids, disgust also operates on the social level, influencing group identity and morality. Our sense of self and self-image is intimately tied to our social circles. We develop and maintain identity through how we are seen in the eyes of others—remember the ego is first formed through an experience of being seen by an *other*. Also, identity is not just captured in individuals. Identity is social.[16] Being a *me* is relevant insofar as it implies a *you* who is different. Consider the different identity markers you carry: race, gender, sex, sexuality, age, education, height, ability, vocation . . . each of those exists within a social imaginary and context.[17] For Paul, being a straight, white, cisgender male is relevant insofar as those identities are at least implicitly connected to separate, different identities; on the individual level, those identities tell Paul something about who he is and how he operates in the world. At a social level, they explain much of how he *fits* (or doesn't) into society within the context of his culture; those identities tell us a lot about how the world will relate to him as a human: what opportunities will be made available

---

14. See Celenza, *Erotic Revelations*, 16.

15. See Atlas, *Enigma of Desire*; Celenza, *Erotic Revelations*; Bader, *Arousal*.

16. See Watkins and Shulman, *Toward Psychologies of Liberation*; Siegel, *Developing Mind*; Leupin, *Lacan Today*.

17. See McGowan, *Universality and Identity Politics*; Fors, *Grammar of Power*; Allen and Ruti, *Critical Theory*.

to him or will be withheld, and how he will be perceived by the thousands of people who pass him on the street. On a relational level, those identities have a lot to do with shaping the interactions and expectations between Paul and whoever he is interacting with. In other words, who *you* are is also deeply embedded in who *we* are. And, when we engage the social sphere, we are also now engaging systems of power and privilege. When disgust becomes entangled with power, it begins to create nausea and the forces that lead to expulsion; and at that point we are at great risk of dehumanizing one another.[18]

Disgust operates on this social level in profound ways to, as with the individual, maintain boundaries. Disgust helps a community differentiate who is part of *us* (in whatever social sphere we are talking) and who is a *them*.[19] This mechanism was embraced by the Trump campaign during the last months of the 2024 presidential race in the form of the "Kamala is for they/them. President Trump is for you" ads.[20] This ad campaign simultaneously deepened the perceived us/them distinction between "regular Americans" (the undefined "us") and transgender people, while casting Harris as a partisan of the "other"—*them*. However, while some forms of disgust on the individual level can be helpful in developing a sense of self, at the group level, disgust is often much more dangerous and potentially dehumanizing, particularly when systemic power is able to be used. This is often accomplished through what is called *projective disgust*, wherein one group projects all of the bad, gross parts of themselves onto an *other*. Like with the formation of the individual ego, an identity is formed through a splitting off of aspects of ourselves. Those parts that aren't able to be metabolized into the imagined identity of the group are projected outwards. As Nussbaum writes, "projective disgust involves a double fantasy: a fantasy of the dirtiness of the other and a fantasy of one's own purity. Both sides of the projection involve false belief, and both conduce to a politics of hierarchy."[21] We form groups that feel safe and call it *us* only by choosing some other portion of humanity and designating it *them*. Once that has happened it becomes a threat to *us* for even one of *them* to enter into our space.[22]

18. See Serano, *Sexed Up*.
19. See Haidt, *Righteous Mind*.
20. See Tomlinson, "Two Sentences."
21. See Nussbaum, *From Disgust to Humanity*, 17.
22. See Girard, *Things Hidden*; McGowan, *Racist Fantasy*.

We see this in the all too familiar association of disgust-adjacent words like "dirty," "filthy," and "gross" for marginalized groups. The groups with more social power and privilege in society often use that power to maintain an image of themselves as pure and good while labeling members of the outgroup as disgusting. For example, projective disgust was at play in the historic racist stereotype of Black men as sexual predators in the US despite the actual rates of sexual violence showing that white men committed far more.[23] White people projected the split-off reality of themselves as predators onto the racial other, using the existing systems of power to enforce their fantasy on reality and hide from the truth of themselves.[24] This use of disgust was then used to justify all sorts of horrific, oppressive, racist policies. Or in recent examples, we can also see this projective disgust on full display in the anti-trans movements. Using the rhetoric of fearing sexual perpetration and violence, anti-trans activists often then engage in sexual and physical violence on transgender individuals.[25] What we can't tolerate in ourselves we project into others so we can justify crushing it.[26]

Trans author and theorist Julia Serano has pointed out that disgust as an emotion and reaction, when shared widely enough, has the effect of stigmatizing the object of the disgust. People are stigmatized when they are marked by characteristics and identities that some significant part of society has deemed disgusting, and those who are stigmatized are conceptualized in certain ways that are peculiar to disgust. In Serano's words:

> This fear of contagion is not rooted in our contemporary understanding that germs may cause infections and disease but rather relies on pre-modern "magical thinking" that adheres to the following formula: 1) a *transfer of "essence"* occurs when two objects come into contact with one another; 2) *negativity dominance*: Bad qualities are more potent than, and inevitably trump, any positive qualities an object may have; 3) *dose insensitivity*: Even extremely brief or minimal contact is sufficient to thoroughly spread the contagion; and 4) *permanence*: Once the contagion is contracted, its effects are irreversible.[27]

---

23. See Cone, *Cross and Lynching Tree*; Alexander, *New Jim Crow*.
24. See Hoard, "Beyond Fragility."
25. See Serano, *Sexed Up*.
26. See McGowan, *Racist Fantasy*.
27. Serano, *Sexed Up*, 196.

Social disgust, then, stigmatizes its object and will effectively mark individuals as bodies which must not be incorporated into the *us* lest their "bad" essence be transferred to the social body. The stigmatized individuals' positive qualities, often regardless of the standing they might otherwise have in the community, will always be insufficient to "make up for" their stigmatized traits. Further, it justifies (or seems to justify) exclusion of minority individuals who will be seen as a threat despite even overwhelmingly lower numbers due to negativity dominance. And the expulsion of the stigmatized individual from the group is likely to be accomplished in a way that is final and extreme as social contamination by the stigmatized body will be seen to irrevocably mark the social body as *other* also.[28]

What this amounts to within the church is the creation of a church culture based in the conviction that purity is fragile and must be protected from contamination, and that people—those who are marked by their variance from the cultural, theological, political, and sexual norms of the church—are the vectors or sources of that contamination. The church, by *misinterpreting* scriptural purity metaphors, stigmatizes and projects disgust onto whole populations of our fellow human beings and often onto our siblings in Christ.[29]

Biblically, an example of projective disgust can be found in the story of King David's rape of Bathsheba and murder of her husband in 2 Sam 11–12. In response to David's violence, God sends the prophet Nathan to rebuke him. Nathan uses the parable of a rich man stealing the beloved sheep of a poor man as a way to illustrate to David what he had done. David's inability to see where Nathan was going with the story and David's own exaggerated emotional reaction to the parable underline David's psychological state. He can't see himself as he is, but projects his dissociated feelings of disgust and guilt onto the rich man in the story as the text writes, "David burned with anger against the man and said to Nathan, 'As surely as the LORD lives, the man who did this must die! He must pay for that lamb four times over, because he did such a thing and had no pity'" (vv. 5–6). David's rage is excessive; it is projective. What he is defended against finding in himself, he projects onto this character. However, Nathan's response "you are the man" (v. 7) cuts past David's

---

28. If you are queer or possess any other quality which has been stigmatized by a church body you were once a member of, this process will be familiar.

29. Hoard and Hoard, "Eucontamination."

defenses.[30] Nathan then clearly articulates all that David was unable to admit about himself. Projective disgust thus functions as a way to protect our egos from a reality about ourselves that we can't yet metabolize into our self-image.

Just recently one of the de facto wardens of evangelical purity, The Gospel Coalition (a conservative, complementarian organization deeply invested in maintaining the purity of evangelical culture), wrote an article complaining about a Christian musician who released a song celebrating gender diversity and fluidity.[31] The author recounts having "a strange mixture of disgust, pity, and clarity . . ." while watching the singer putting on drag in the video. He goes on to argue that by emphasizing inclusion, love, and acceptance of the marginalized (in this case trans people and drag queens) the singer is bringing heresy into the church. The author argues that the singer and those like him need to be excised, saying, "Like cancer, these values-run-amok bear the genetic imprint of their native body. But unrestrained by the ultimate function and purpose of that body, they mutate into something deadly and difficult to contain." In other words, disgust, entangled with power, begins to create nausea and to build up a force that leads to expulsion and dehumanization.

THE LOGIC OF DISGUST

So how does the logic of contamination function, and what are the ways it can be used to foster community instead of contempt? Firstly, remember that we don't like to think about disgust. Also, why we think we do something is never the full story. We are split-subjects as Jacques Lacan termed it.[32] Consider the last time you were in a fog or didn't quite feel like yourself. For many people, talking with a trusted friend in those times can help us recognize aspects of ourselves that we hadn't realized, recognize that we are more than we had thought. As you speak, you learn through your own words. One of the funny aspects of being a therapist is that while most people go to therapy thinking they want to be told something, a lot of therapy actually involves the therapist shutting up. Change comes less from hearing something new, than by recognizing more of

---

30. It is worth observing that today the claim that David had raped Bathsheba is often met with hostility from an audience less open to the conviction of the Holy Spirit than David seems to have been.

31. Morris, "Heresy at the Heart of Derek Webb's 'Boys Will Be Girls,'" lines 1–45.

32. See Fink, *Lacanian Subject*.

what was already there—more of ourselves that had been split-off. Those other parts of you are always there; we just work hard to make them look more appropriate for everyone else. The work we do to hide them is what we call psychological defenses: the ways we hide the things that don't fit our self-image (ego) from ourselves.[33]

The implications of all this for disgust is that we have nicer ways of talking about disgust so as not to face it directly. In the US, fear seems to be a much more palatable response to something than disgust. A few minutes on any news program will typically be enough to incite a nice jolt of fear into any viewer. Jobs are dwindling, the economy is failing, *they* are coming to make things worse, and so on. But if we dig under the surface a little, we can find that often mixed in with that fear, or under the guise of it, is actually disgust.

Disgust operates in a few important ways that can help us recognize it and differentiate it from other feelings like fear. Both fear and disgust are responses to threats. Both help protect us from dangers. As such, they often blend into each other and interact in complex ways. Fear tends (though not entirely) to be more rational than disgust. Fear helps you recognize a danger and then activates your brain and body to react. You may remember learning about fight/flight/freeze/faint in health class. What this means, though, is that if you can recognize that the thing you thought was dangerous is actually harmless, your fear tends to dissipate. When going to the zoo, you may be confronted with scary, dangerous animals, but your trust in the park's security and fences that separate you from the predators keeps you calm and happy. Disgust doesn't work as simply as that. Think back to the spit-in-the-cup example. The knowledge that the saliva is sterile wouldn't change most people's resistance to drinking it. Disgust doesn't respond to reason.[34]

Disgust is visceral. Disgust helps us navigate not so much the world of our five senses, but the seemingly supernatural world beyond them. Evolutionary theory suggests that disgust came about to help with the omnivore's dilemma: If humans are able to eat most things, but some are deadly poisonous, how are we to differentiate? Prior to an understanding of bacteria and germs, how were humans to keep themselves safe from disease? Disgust was the answer. Disgust helped us stay away from rot and other potential contaminants, like waste and poisons. This means

---

33. See McWilliams, *Psychoanalytic Diagnosis*.
34. See Haidt, *Righteous Mind*.

that since disgust is attuned to protecting us from threats that can't be understood through our senses, it often overlaps with the spiritual and supernatural as well as the superstitious. As the previous Serano quote illustrates, it operates less on logical lines of physical transmission and more on lines of association, like poetry.[35] In other words, if I associate an object with something gross, I will often find that object itself to be gross as well. For example, few people would have trouble eating a chocolate bar, but if that bar were to be melted slightly and shaped to resemble feces, most of us would have a much harder time eating it, even if we consciously knew it was the very same bar. Or, as a cruel joke to play on someone, ask them to think about defecating when they are in the middle of eating peanut butter. Nothing at all changes about the peanut butter, the texture, the taste, smell—any of the five senses of the experience. However, the association between peanut butter and feces in that moment is enough to ruin the experience.[36]

This brings us to another important aspect of disgust—its logic. The logic of disgust operates in a binary. If something is gross, or a contaminant, then it is actually incredibly powerful. The logic of disgust works so that it is the small, microscopic entity that can pollute and contaminate anything. Size doesn't matter. Quantity doesn't matter. When disgust is operant, anything greater than zero is too much. How much urine do you tolerate in your drinking water? What this leads to is an inversion of most understandings of power. Where most of the time we see the big as powerful and the small as weak, once disgust enters the picture, the weak becomes the more powerful of the two.[37]

A scene in the *The Sword in the Stone* illustrates this well.[38] The film is loosely based on the Arthurian legend with Arthur and Merlin as the main characters. At one point in the film, Merlin the wizard battles Mad Madam Mim in a wizard duel. Both characters assume more and more powerful forms in an attempt to destroy the other until Mim transforms into a dragon. In response, Merlin takes the form of a germ that Mim catches. In this way, Merlin illustrates the power of a contaminant. His little germ infects Mim so that he wins the duel.

35. See Rozin and Fallon, "Perspective on Disgust."
36. An important caveat to keep in mind here is that individuals will all have different levels of disgust tolerance and sensitivity. What I find gross may not be gross at all to you and vice versa.
37. See Beck, *Unclean*.
38. See Reitherman, *Sword in the Stone*.

Another aspect of this disgust binary is the inversion or negation of disgust, namely purity. The logic of disgust assumes the incredible fragility of purity against even the smallest contaminant. Something is pure only insofar as not a single element of the contaminant is present. Purity is less the presence of a thing than the absence of impurities; meaning that for something to be pure, something else must be impure. Purity requires the disgusting. Also, once something has been made impure, it is very difficult if not impossible to purify it. We burn germs and throw away contaminated food. We may know that a filtration system is almost perfect, but would still feel gross knowing that the water was recycled sewer water. In fact, many religious liturgies are careful ways to try to make something holy, pure, or sacred. While at their best these rituals can act in a *good magic* mode, countering the general permanence of stigma and disgust—think about Christianity's emphasis on "being made new," being "born again," and being cleansed of sin—at their worst, they can reify our stigmatization of the other as those unwilling to accept cleansing. It seems worth noticing how often we think of baptism, particularly as a cleansing or purifying of our sins, and how rarely we think of it, per the ancient baptismal formula, of joining Jesus in death.[39]

DISGUST AND SHAME

This binary of disgust, its role in the boundary-enforcing aspects of the self, and the advent of the split-subject, brings us to where we can start moving our discussion closer to a more common experience for many people in noting the connections between disgust and shame. Shame, like guilt, is a painful emotional experience that is connected to behavior and group belonging. Shame and guilt are both related to our senses of right and wrong and living within the strictures of the given social authority. Shame, however, has been theorized to be more about one's sense of self, who you are, whereas guilt is more connected to what you have done. Consider the difference between saying "I did something bad" versus "I am bad."[40]

---

39. See Beck, *Unclean*. We will also say more about baptism and other Christian sacraments in later chapters.

40. For more on the nature and impact of chronic shame, see DeYoung, *Chronic Shame*; for more on the nature of social authority to induce guilt and shame in individuals, see Žižek, *How to Read Lacan*; McGowan, *Enjoying What We Don't Have*; Hoard and Bland, "'How Am I Responsible?'"; and Pfaller, *On the Pleasure Principle*.

So we can map the distinction between fear and disgust onto the one we've just drawn between shame and guilt. I fear doing something that would make me feel guilty, whereas I am disgusted by things that would cause me to feel shame. Fear can stay rational and connected to actions. Disgust is about our essence. Once we've come into contact or been associated with an object of disgust, we feel the shame of having been contaminated, which helps to highlight the power of disgust to impact behavior. When disgust is marshaled, it brings shame along. Disgust is able to influence our behavior because it is not just an unpleasant experience that we are avoiding, but also the shame of having been contaminated by whatever was labeled disgusting. This helps to explain why disgust is such a powerful motivator and so often used by those in authority to enforce boundaries and behaviors. For example, telling teens not to do something is often a great way to actually increase their desire for it, but make them feel disgusted by it, and you are utilizing all of the powerful, affective motivations of shame and group identity (primary concerns for most adolescents).[41]

Moreover, on the spiritual plane, disgust regulates something that the psychologist Richard Beck calls "the divinity dimension in human experience."[42] It is a metaphorical, vertical hierarchy of beings with the divine, spiritual, and holy at the top and the more physical and animal at the bottom. Saints and sinners, then, are organized along this dimension with saints being closer to God and angels, while sinners are kept separate in their lower status. This somewhat neoplatonic[43] differentiation leads to disgust when things that are higher are mixed with the lower. Toilet talk, for example, is usually considered taboo in a church sanctuary as that would be contaminating the higher, spiritual, with the lower realities of the human body and waste. Shame and disgust help maintain this hierarchical structure threatening the contamination and social exclusion of anyone who would violate the community's purity.

In more conservative, religious circles in the US, this disgust-shame combo was widely used in what has been labeled purity culture.[44] Dis-

---

41. Just imagine the difference in effect between telling a teenager "X is bad" and telling them "X is cringe." For more on the development and psychology of adolescents, see Berzoff et al., *Inside Out and Outside In*; and Boothby, *Sex on the Couch*.

42. Beck, *Unclean*, 150.

43. In an earlier draft we described this differentiation as "gnostic" but on reflection realized that describing things as gnostic has become cringe.

44. See Sellers, *Sex, God, Conservative Church*.

gust-inducing metaphors were associated with certain (if not all) sexual behaviors as a way to motivate members of the church or congregation to abstain from those behaviors. Many female-identifying youth in church were told that they would be like chewed gum if they were to have sex, with the metaphor sometimes being stretched to caution that each sexual encounter would represent another person "chewing that gum." The disgusting image of chewed gum evokes strong, visceral reactions in most and then conjures up the threat not just of having performed something against the rules, but of being something gross, a source of shame.[45] The brownie story we opened with was and is frequently deployed with sexual content represented by the "poop in the brownies." Other popular analogies include an apple that is bruised and/or has had multiple "bites" taken out of it by each sexual partner, a glass of clean water to which various contaminants are added with each sexual encounter, a cookie that the rest of the youth group has already touched, or a lollipop that has already been licked. In all of these, the message is clear: there is something irredeemably disgusting about the person who is contaminated. Gum can't be unchewed, apple bites put back, or poop baked out of brownies. The best you can do is throw it away.

While we hope that the negative aspects of this kind of coercion are obvious enough, we want to highlight just a few to underscore their significance. Remember, disgust is about parts of ourselves we've split off and operates via association not necessarily through standard logic. Therefore, when we are told that we are like chewed gum for having sex, it is not a far leap to recognize that some part of me does want to have sex and therefore I must be bad for wanting something so gross.[46] So now even if I haven't engaged in the behavior that my youth pastor was trying to highlight, I still experience shame as if I did. This leads to a withdrawal from community, if not physically, then at least in authentic engagement, because now I run the risk of my shame being seen by others. The best I can do is work hard to hide that from everyone else. I am now feeling a greater and greater distance between my ideal self that I present to my church and the internalized, shame-ridden self-image that I carry around. Thus, in turning to disgust to enforce behavior, many churches

---

45. See Welcher, *Talking Back*.

46. Lacan actually argues for the centrality of the death drive in motivating everyone towards the very things that we find disgusting. For more on the role of the death drive and prohibition in eliciting desire, see McGowan, *Enjoying What We Don't Have*; and Boothby, *Death and Desire*.

and leaders (like the dad above) have further entrenched and induced feelings of shame and loneliness in their members, encouraging false personas: the very antithesis of a healthy community. Jesus in Matt 23:27 accused the religious elite in his day of being "like whitewashed tombs, which outwardly appear beautiful, but within are full of dead people's bones and all uncleanness."

Returning to the case of the poop brownies, the dad has effectively helped to develop a deeper feeling of shame in his children for the desire they feel to watch the shows. Now they are less likely to connect with him honestly about their desires or behavior for fear of that shame being exposed and heightened (who wants to admit they like the taste of poop in their brownies or the sin in their shows?). The most likely outcome of his anecdotal lesson is that they will continue to watch the shows he finds sinful and disgusting, but do it behind his back—deepening their own disgust of themselves and resentment of him in the fear that he will further shame them. So he can now further exert his fantasy of a world where his children avoid such "disgusting filth" while actually fostering a greater divide between himself, his children, and reality.

All this highlights that for the church, disgust is a really big problem. The overuse and misapplication of disgust logic has led to a church that is more *of* the world than *in* it—hiding from imagined contaminants while projecting the worst parts of itself onto those Christ called us to love. So this brings us to an important question: how can we use these insights into disgust and purity to re-imagine what it means to be a follower of Christ? As we will explore in the rest of the book, we believe that the logic of disgust in dialogue with the life and the teachings of Jesus, can help us re-form our personal and collective identities. By working to more faithfully embrace the disturbing and disruptive implications of what Jesus means in calling himself the Way, the Truth, and the Life and trusting in his power to contaminate us with love so that we can love others, the church can hopefully move closer to becoming the Bride of Christ.

2

Disgusted Distortion

But God has so arranged the body, giving the greater honor to the inferior member, that there may be no dissension within the body, but the members may have the same care for one another. If one member suffers, all suffer together with it; if one member is honored, all rejoice together with it.

—1 Cor 12:24b–26 NRSVUE

THROUGHOUT THIS BOOK, WE will explore just some of the ways that an overuse and misapplication of disgust has damaged Christian practice. But of course, "Christian practice"—however that is understood by individual Christians—doesn't exist without reference to Christian theology. Christian practice, or praxis, and Christian theology operate in a mutually informing loop. We get our understanding of how Christians ought to behave from our Christian theology; at the same time the theology we accept and affirm is shaped by our experience as Christians. While this is circular and can, at its worst, spiral into a knot of self-affirmation, it is not *necessarily* a closed circle. New ideas, information, perspectives, and experiences are all able to enter the system and influence it in different directions when we are open to them. Psychologist Richard Beck writes of this intersection between our beliefs and our selves in that "the interplay between theology and psychology is interactive and dynamic.

Theology—good or bad—affects how we experience the world, psychologically speaking. And psychological factors can affect and constrain theological reflection."[1]

A counseling patient of mine (Paul) once told me that he thought the hardest con to pull was conning yourself. I respectfully (though I'm not sure how therapeutically) disagreed. We first and foremost deceive ourselves and hide from the reality of who we are. One way to think about therapy is helping someone become more aware of what they already know. If you want to learn what someone actually believes and cares about, asking them will give you one answer, while watching them will give you a totally different answer. It's important to analyze our beliefs, but it's also important to face our actions. The gap between the two is far greater than most of us care to admit.

For this reason, we need to closely examine both our experiences as well as our explicitly and implicitly held theologies, and in so doing, spend time reflecting on how our theology has shaped us and how we have shaped our theology in turn. We need to listen for the conversations that have been going on just beyond our awareness. The church, we argue, has a theological disgust problem which has been shaped by and in turn reinforced the church's praxeological disgust problem. In other words, disgust has contaminated both our beliefs and our actions because those two are inherently linked and mutually reinforcing.

To explore this, we need to talk about *contamination* and *stigma* as they speak to the ways disgust is worked out in the interpersonal and social realm. *Contamination* is "the process of making something dirty or poisonous, or the state of containing unwanted or dangerous substances."[2] In relation to disgust, contamination is the process of making a thing disgusting insofar as it makes something unacceptable for incorporation into our body. Meanwhile, *stigmatizing* is a social term for being perceived as socially contaminating. This means that on a social level, stigma is how we navigate the contaminating impact of others on ourselves—stigmatizing those who threaten to contaminate us. In *The Cultural Politics of Emotion* philosopher and sociologist Sara Ahmed explains that disgust is not so much a category of things (or persons) as it is a reaction to those things which we have designated as stigmatized or contaminated and contaminating. She writes, "to name something as

---

1. See Beck, *Unclean*, 4–5.
2. Cambridge English Dictionary, "Contamination."

disgusting is to transfer the stickiness of the word 'disgust' to an object, which henceforth becomes generated as the very thing that is spoken."[3] In other words, we make things disgusting—we are disgusted by them—when we perceive them as contaminated. Disgust is not so much about inherent qualities of an object, person, or group, but about the concern they create around contamination. Nothing is *inherently* disgusting.

Fear, remember, is often used as the guise for disgust because it is more socially accepted and less an affront to our sensibilities. I'm not supposed to be disgusted by my neighbor, but I can justify my fear of them. Being a part of the family, the in-group, necessitates the exclusion of the other. We aren't just us, we are also specifically NOT them.

This means that disgust is relational. It involves both the object of disgust (them) and one who is disgusted (us). It is connected to our actions and posture towards that object (or group). We use disgust to protect us from the perceived contaminant. Disgust is about both our beliefs and what we see as contaminating, as well as our actions with how we react to disgust. On the social level, this phenomenon is seen through the use of stigma. We mark people as disgusting—we are disgusted by them—when we perceive them as stigmatized. So, it is in the intersection of these two facets of belief and action that we need to look for the implications and dangers of disgust.

Contamination in turn has a counterpart concept: purification—as we mentioned in chapter 1. Whenever contamination is being referenced or invoked, the concept of purification is also present—even if only implicitly—and vice versa. The relational dynamic of disgust demands something pure and something contaminating—something fragile and something dangerous. While holiness and all that is associated with God are frequently presented and perceived as pure, sin is presented and perceived as contaminating. In contrast to sin or contamination, purity is generally associated with (or even is a stand-in for) Holiness; and on one level this works really well. Holiness is good for us; holiness is opposite to sin and death—both of which are frequently represented as contaminants. But following this logic too far leads us to the theologically catastrophic conclusion that holiness is also something fragile, at risk of being overpowered by sin.

---

3. Ahmed, *Cultural Politics of Emotion*, loc. 2187.

DISGUST ON DISPLAY

On Thursday, the fifteenth of February 2024, there was a funeral for Cecilia Gentili held at St. Patrick's Cathedral in New York. It was an unusual funeral for the cathedral because Cecilia was an unusual person. She was a transgender woman, who had come to America as an undocumented immigrant from Argentina before eventually being granted asylum. She was a sex worker and an actress, and lived her life as an outspoken activist for transgender rights and for the rights of sex workers. She had, at best, a complicated relationship with religion. In 2023 in an interview with *Interview* magazine, she summarized her experience of God saying:

> Yeah, I have been reexamining my relationship with religion for a long time. I went to treatment for drug use for 17 months. At the time, I was sleeping with men, and there was no direction on how to treat a trans woman. Sometimes it was fun, but it was not the best thing for me. I am now in a harm reduction approach to drugs, but at that time, I was in abstinence, so I was also going to NA groups. In NA, it's a lot about your relationship with God. Even if you go to the agnostic ones, I felt like I couldn't do the program because I didn't have a god. I just never had opportunities to experience a faith that was fully embracing of me. Religion is such a complicated issue for most queer and trans people. I used to go with my grandmother to the Baptist church, and they didn't want me there. They made it very clear. I used to go to the Catholic church, too, and both were such traumatic experiences for me as a queer person. So I came to identify as an atheist, but I know that so many trans people have been able to find a relationship with faith in spaces that include them.
>
> . . .
>
> But I come from a family of so many different faiths, so I didn't feel attached to any of them. I had so many choices, but none of them felt right because I was queer. At the time, there was no openness. Nowadays, some churches have queer pastors or rabbis or imans. I remember I had a friend when I was starting my transition as a teenager. She would invite me to pray with her. And I was like, "What are we praying to?" And she'd say, "No, we are praying. There's a lot of power in the act of just praying." It was therapeutic.[4]

At the funeral, Gentili's community filled the building. Actors and advocates testified, sang, and chanted to show their respect for her.

---

4. Nevins, "Cecilia Gentili," para. 34.

According to the write up of the service on CNN, attendees were asked to honor her by "serv[ing] their best looks" and they did not disappoint, showing up in the brightest, most dramatic fashion the cathedral has likely ever seen.[5] A later CNN article summarized the sentiment at the funeral saying, "Funeral organizers told CNN that they chose to honor Gentili at St. Patrick's Cathedral because they felt its grandeur was a fitting tribute to her legacy—she was remembered at her funeral for championing the most marginalized peoples in society."[6]

It caused a scandal. At one point in the ceremony, a friend and fellow advocate praised Cecilia as "This whore, this great whore . . . St. Cecilia Mother of all whores." Less than 48 hours afterwards, the New York Archdiocese condemned the event. Conservative groups called it "unbelievable and sick," "a mockery of the Christian faith," "revolting," "blasphemous and sacrilegious."[7]

Two days later, the pastor of St. Patrick's Cathedral announced that they had held a Mass of Reparation at the Cathedral. A *Mass of Reparation* is a specific liturgy intended to cleanse or purify a worship space in the wake of scandal, injustice, or egregious sin. Catholic churches in the US have, for instance, recently held masses of reparation in response to clergy sex abuse scandals.[8]

The story of Cecilia Gentili's funeral gives a powerfully illuminating example of how disgust and purity frequently operate in the American church. Accounts are divided, but the specific scandal that prompted the Archdiocese of New York is thought to range from the simple fact of having held a funeral service for a transgender woman, for a former sex worker, for an advocate for sex workers and/or transgender people, for having had such a great number of "unrepentant whores" and transgender people in the building, for the immodest outfits that were worn by some attendees, for the use by someone at the front of the building (they were not at the altar) of the word "whore" in both English and Spanish with a sense of approval rather than condemnation, for reported substitution by attendees (though not officiants) of Cecilia's name for St. Mary's in the closing hymn, or for some other form of (real or perceived) sin. Or maybe it was some, all, or none of the above. Whatever the cause, something about Cecilia Gentili's funeral caused the Archdiocese to

5. Kaur, "Trans Icon Cecilia Gentili," para. 32.
6. Kaur, "Archdiocese of New York," para. 9.
7. Stack, "N.Y. Archdiocese," para. 6.
8. Brinker, "Mass of Reparation Atones."

conclude that the Cathedral itself had been contaminated and needed to be spiritually purified before Sunday morning when the faithful would gather there for Sunday Mass.

From a traditionalist perspective formed by disgust theology, this is all logical if, at most, a little embarrassing, given the appearance of transphobia. God, we know, is holy and good and cannot abide the presence of sin and evil. The Eucharist is served at mass and therefore to hold a mass in a space or building contaminated by sin would itself bring scandal to the very body and blood of Christ. And that cannot be allowed—the purity and the sanctity of the Eucharist has got to be preserved.

But when we look at it all from another perspective, a very different picture emerges. Here you have a community of marginalized people, the very types of people Jesus loved spending time with and teaching, and for a moment they felt welcomed into a church where they grieved the loss of someone who had cared for them and seen them as full persons with real dignity. They commemorated Cecilia Gentili in their own idiom and with language and music that made sense in their culture and within their value systems. In showing up to her funeral in their most flamboyant and finest, they were honoring a woman who had delighted in them and told them that they had worth, dignity, and beauty. In calling her a whore, they were saying that she knew their experience; in calling her a saint they were using the language and values of Christianity to communicate to one another and to the world how much they appreciated her sacrifice, work, and love on their behalf.

And when the Archdiocese of New York condemned the service and then held a special mass to purify the church of their expression of love, honor, and respect and their grief at the loss of Cecilia, they saw the church telling them that they themselves are a contaminant to the church. They saw and heard "sick... revolting... blasphemous and sacrilegious" thrown at what they had brought in good faith, and the message was clear: "You are disgusting to us and we say that you are disgusting to God. God will not be here until all traces of your presence are destroyed."

Take a moment and ask yourself: regardless of your theology of sex work and of transgender identities, are those people more or less likely to seek God today than they were before Cecilia's funeral? This specific incident is unique to the Catholic Church, but its resonance in protestant and broader Christian circles speaks to the ubiquity of the response.

The church has a disgust problem.

CHRISTIAN NATIONALISM

Politics in the US is another place where we can see the impact of this disgust theology and praxis on display. As was mentioned in chapter 1, disgust often hides itself behind the mask of fear because it is far less threatening to our senses of self and far more acceptable in public to say that something is dangerous than to admit that it repulses us. Think about how different it feels to say that someone scares you rather than they disgust you. Christians in particular know that we aren't supposed to be disgusted by other people—but we can fear them (to say nothing about what perfect love is supposed to do to that fear, but that's for another chapter). Parties from across the political spectrum have long utilized fear in varying degrees to manipulate and control populations. Politicians regularly lean on the fear of what the *other* will do to galvanize their base into voting in elections and supporting themselves as candidates. However, much of what passes as fear in political rhetoric is, when examined closer, a more polished and socially acceptable form of disgust. The most egregious example of this in America today can perhaps be seen in the union of white evangelical and conservative Christians with the political right in the rise of Christian Nationalism.[9] The theology and politics of this movement are a direct outworking of disgust eroding the message of Jesus in the church. It's worth exploring, then, what this movement is and how it's related to disgust.

On February 8, 2023, PRRI released the results of an extensive poll asking over 6,000 Americans to weigh in on certain core tenets of Christian Nationalism.[10] Unsurprisingly, one of the key findings from this survey showed that adherents of Christian Nationalism endorsed statements connected to contamination and purity far more than the general American public. Statements like the following:

> "The American way of life needs to be protected from foreign influence"
>
> "Jewish people hold too many positions of power"
>
> "The values of Islam are at odds with American values and way of life"
>
> "We should prevent people from some majority Muslim countries from entering the U.S."

---

9. See Cooper-White, *Psychology of Christian Nationalism*.
10. PRRI Staff, "Christian Nation?"

Think about those statements for a moment and what they say about who is an "American" in the mind of someone who would endorse them. Each of them either explicitly or implicitly denotes an *us* and a *them*, casting *them* in the position of threat or contaminant—stigmatizing. They indicate an inclination towards exclusion over embrace for the sake of protecting an illusion of purity.[11] Andrew Whitehead, associate professor of sociology at Indiana University-Purdue University, writes that one of the key elements of Christian Nationalism includes "a desire for strict boundaries around national identity, civic participation, and social belonging that fall along ethno-racial lines. A 'Christian nation' is generally understood to be one where white, natural-born citizens are held up as the ideal, with everyone else coming after."[12]

In order to identify the extent of Christian Nationalistic ideology and adherence, the PRRI survey asked the respondent for answers ranging from "Completely disagree" to "Completely agree" to five statements:

1. The US government should declare America to be a Christian Nation.
2. US laws should be based on Christian values.
3. If the US moves away from our Christian foundations, we will not have a country anymore.
4. Being Christian is an important part of being truly American.
5. God has called Christians to exercise dominion over all areas of American society.

Notably, the fourth question measures the person's commitment to the idea that a non-Christian is less American than a Christian is. It is a question that gets at the idea of purity because affirming the statement requires a belief that non-Christians diminish or contaminate the country making America less American by their presence and participation in our shared political system. Using those five statements, researchers organized respondents into four categories:

Christian Nationalism Adherents . . . These Americans overwhelmingly either agree or *completely* agree with the statements in the scale. This group includes 10 percent of Americans.

11. For more on the theology of exclusion versus embrace, see Volf, *Exclusion and Embrace*.
12. Whitehead, *American Idolatry*, 29.

Christian Nationalism Sympathizers . . . A majority of these Americans agree with the statements in the scale but are less likely to *completely* agree. This group includes 19 percent of Americans.

Christian Nationalism Skeptics . . . A majority of these Americans disagree with the statements in the scale but are less likely than rejecters to *completely* disagree. This group includes 39 percent of Americans.

Christian Nationalism Rejecter . . . These Americans *completely* disagree with all five statements in the scale. This group includes 29 percent of Americans.[13]

In other words, according to this survey, almost 30 percent of Americans would be considered Christian Nationalism adherents or sympathizers. That's a lot of people.

Turning specifically to those who identify as some form of Christian, the findings become even more stark. White evangelical Protestants contained the highest numbers of Christian Nationalist adherents (29 percent) and sympathizers (35 percent). Regular religious service attenders were significantly more likely (50 percent) to be adherents or sympathizers than sporadic attenders (36 percent) or non-attenders (18 percent) were. So white evangelical Protestants who regularly attend church are the highest demographic of Americans who either adhere to or sympathize with Christian Nationalism. Whitehead's own research on the topic confirms these findings as he writes, "just under seven in ten white Christians are at least favorable toward Christian nationalism."[14] This demands the question: what is happening in these churches? How are the followers of Jesus the ones who are most likely to exclude?

Additionally, the poll revealed a surprising discrepancy between our beliefs and labels. When those whose beliefs would classify them as Christian Nationalist sympathizers were asked directly about their view of the term "Christian Nationalism" 47 percent—almost half—didn't know, hadn't heard of it, or just didn't answer; while another 14 percent were somewhat or very unfavorable towards the term. The scary thing here is that it means almost two-thirds of those who endorse Christian Nationalistic beliefs have no idea what they are really promoting. We deceive ourselves first.

---

13. Whitehead, *American Idolatry*, 29.
14. See Whitehead, *American Idolatry*, 34.

Let the numbers from this survey sink in for a moment. Remember that almost two-thirds of white evangelical Protestants qualified as either Christian Nationalist adherents or sympathizers and that higher rates of church attendance correlate with a greater embrace of Christian Nationalism. For students of American Christianity, this should come as no surprise, as it is in line with consistent critiques from BIPOC theologians.[15] Empirically, the white evangelical church in America is significantly made up of people whose attitudes towards non-Christians and non-white people can be accurately characterized as one of disgust.[16] The white evangelical church has listened to their own disgust reactions, rejecting Jesus for the sake of protecting a sense of purity.

Within a week of Cecilia Gentili's funeral, news broke of Nex Benedict, a 16-year-old non-binary student in Oklahoma who had died the day after being beaten up in the bathroom by three students at their school.[17] Several days later, at a public forum in Talequah, Oklahoma, the audience began asking a panel of Republican state senators and representatives about the problem of bullying in schools. According to the *Talequah Daily Press*, at one point a woman named Cathy Cott asked the panel, "Is there a reason why you won't answer about the 50 bills targeting the LGBTQ community in the state of Oklahoma? If you are ashamed of those bills, they shouldn't be there." In his response to Cott, Oklahoma State Senator Tom Woods said that his "heart goes out" in regards to Nex's death, but continued saying,

> We are a religious state and we are going to fight to keep that *filth* out of the state of Oklahoma *because we are a Christian state—we are a moral state.* . . . I'm going to vote my values, and we don't want that in the state of Oklahoma.[18]

Whether by *filth* he was referring to Nex, to non-binary students, to queer people generally, or to queerness, transness, or non-binaryness in the abstract, the language is horribly revealing. Senator Woods justified his use of *filth* as a descriptor of a recently deceased child by claiming that his job was to defend the purity of a *Christian* and *moral* state. When a state

---

15. See Charles and Rah, *Unsettling Truths*; Jennings, *After Whiteness*; Gafney, *Womanist Midrash*; Cone, *Cross and the Lynching Tree*.

16. For more on the intersection of white evangelical theology and white body supremacy, see Hoard and Bland, "'How Am I Responsible?,'" 653–70; Jones, *White Too Long*.

17. Hennessy-Fiske, "Okla. Nonbinary Teen Died After School Fight," para. 2.

18. Guthrie, "Senator Calls LGBTQ+ People 'Filth,'" para. 11 (emphasis ours).

senator can call on Christianity to characterize a dead child as *filth* and to say that his Christian and moral values lead him to seek the expulsion of similar people from his state, Christianity has a disgust problem. But of course, disgust based language like that has been modeled "from the top" by the leader of Senator Woods's party, Donald Trump. Recall that Trump inaugurated his first campaign for president by characterizing immigrants as "murderers and rapists" and campaigned on the promise to construct a physical barrier to prevent them from entering into "our" country—the space of our national body. Since then, he has routinely used disgust based language to describe those whom he wants to distance himself or the nation from. "Shithole countries"[19] and the more recent "poisoning the blood of our country" (a phrase lifted directly from Hitler)[20] being two of the better known examples.

We learn what is disgusting from one another and, when someone as influential and well respected (within his own political ecosystem) as a president uses disgust language to talk about a group of people, the predictable consequence is that people are going to begin developing disgust reactions to members of those groups. If unchecked, these reactions establish a vicious cycle in which disgust begets deeper disgust until, in the final stages, violent expulsion of the targeted group will grow to seem routine and normal.

If this feels par for the course for Christianity or for evangelicalism, if it is what you expect from white American evangelicals, then think for a moment how wildly different all of this is from the example and teachings of Jesus who was derided as a "friend of sinners,"[21] who touched the diseased,[22] drank with the stigmatized,[23] and chose to carry "the sins of the world."[24]

And, while we believe that the distorting impact of disgust is most thoroughly embraced by the politics and politicians of the right, the left is not immune to it either. In times of heightened fear and especially when facing an identity crisis, disgust based thinking and exclusion becomes a temptation for anyone. We saw this dynamic on display in the weeks immediately following the 2024 election. As white Democrats wrestled with

19. Dawsey, "Trump Derides Protections," para. 2.
20. Arnsdorf, "Trump Makes Demonizing Immigrants," para. 2.
21. Matt 11:19.
22. Matt 8:1–4; Mark 1:40–45; Luke 5:12–16.
23. Matt 9:9–13; Mark 2:13–17; Luke 5:27–32.
24. Matt 8:16–17; 1 Pet 2:24–25.

their loss and tried to negotiate unpalatable facts about what the election meant about what sort of a people Americans are, many turned inward to see what elements of their own platform and which communities within their "big tent" were responsible for their loss.

The GOP and the Trump campaign spent over $215 million on anti-trans advertising during the campaign, attacking Harris for supporting the rights of incarcerated transgender people while the Harris campaign did almost nothing to push back.[25] Despite having hardly engaged the topic at all, much less going to bat against the anti-trans narrative, in the immediate wake of the 2024 election, several prominent democrats and liberal commentators jumped to the conclusion that they had lost the election because they had gone too far in supporting transgender rights. In response to a $215 million dollar effort by the Republican party and Trump campaign to cast transgender people as a contaminant, frightened Democrats struggling to integrate the fact of their loss with an image of themselves as resurgent supporters of "the common man" ended up accepting the designation of trans people as disgusting and began advocating for our ejection from their party platform as a way of regaining their lost identity.[26]

Both within and without the church, designations of disgust often originate at the top with leaders or influencers, but not always. Sometimes those "at the top," whether politicians or pastors, find that designations of disgust have gotten out ahead of them. An overapplication of the purity metaphor and disgust rejection of other people is so blatantly contrary to the lived and taught example of Jesus, that it is not uncommon for pastors and church leaders to find themselves at risk of being "contaminated" by association with, or even just sympathy for, those their own congregations have learned to experience as disgusting. When this happens, leaders can be faced with the decision of whether to join their followers in designations of disgust or to risk stigma and the loss of influence.[27]

When our Christian practice is shaped by disgust, the consequences are grim.

---

25. See Serano, "Should Democrats Throw Trans People Under the Bus?"
26. See Lavietes, "Some Democrats."
27. For one example of a pastor wrestling in this way and ultimately overcoming, see Wilson et al., *Letter to My Congregation*.

WHEN A METAPHOR GOES TOO HARD

An important point of reflection here rests on the role of metaphor in our lives. Metaphors are deeply significant in shaping how we experience the world and our own consciousness. Lacanian psychoanalytic theory, for example, looks at an individual's use of metaphor as one of the significant factors in diagnosis. The philosopher and chess grandmaster, Jonathan Rowson, writes that "metaphor is less like a comparison to think about, and more like a psychoactive lens through which we see, creating patterns that shape how we feel and think."[28] In psychotherapy, a large part of the work with patients involves reframing the metaphors they have been using in life to help them find more adaptive ways to see their world and situation. We reframe thoughts, stories, and histories so as to allow for new and more flexible ways of metabolizing experiences. Finding the right metaphor for something is a necessary step to fully perceiving so as to understand it.

Part of what makes metaphors so generative is the distance between them and reality. The very fact that our minds are not computers is what allows us to use the metaphor of a computer as a helpful way to consider and reflect upon how our minds do work. Taking a metaphor too literally forecloses the beauty and possibilities within the distance between the metaphor and reality. Additionally, when experienced uncritically, metaphors implicitly shape our frame and interpretations of reality in ways that blind and control instead of illuminating and freeing. Consider the term "surgical strike" for a type of military intervention. By using the metaphor of medicine, the term brings with it an implicit framing of the event that indicates care and healing—hiding the violence and carnage involved in the actual act. "It's not an act of war, it's a medical intervention," the metaphor quietly whispers. In this way politicians, leaders, and marketers are often incredibly skilled in their use of metaphor to associate positive ideas and images with themselves or their product. This is why every car ad is seemingly all about sex and says very little about the car. So it is incredibly important to be mindful of our metaphors and how they are shaping our realities.

Our theological metaphors are no different. They are necessary in helping us develop ways of relating to God, one another, and creation. Metaphors are everywhere in the Bible, pointing us beyond the material

---

28. See Rowson, *Moves That Matter*, 13.

world and what we think we see to a reality beyond us, as Lewis pointed out in *Mere Christianity*:

> There is no need to be worried by facetious people who try to make the Christian hope of "Heaven" ridiculous by saying they do not want "to spend eternity playing harps." The answer to such people is that if they cannot understand books written for grown-ups, they should not talk about them. All the scriptural imagery (harps, crowns, gold, etc.) is, of course, a merely symbolical attempt to express the inexpressible. Musical instruments are mentioned because for many people (not all) music is the thing known in the present life which most strongly suggests ecstasy and infinity. Crowns are mentioned to suggest the fact that those who are united with God in eternity share His splendour and power and joy. Gold is mentioned to suggest the timelessness of Heaven (gold does not rust) and the preciousness of it. People who take these symbols literally might as well think that when Christ told us to be like doves, He meant that we were to lay eggs.[29]

Biblical metaphors help us see the Divine in the mundane as the glory of God is shown throughout creation. Metaphor points beyond itself and biblical metaphor is no different. But just as they can illuminate—uncritical, misused, and overapplied metaphors can have disastrous consequences.[30]

Purity is certainly used as a metaphor for holiness in the Bible, but the purity/disgust metaphor can be misinterpreted and taken too far. In the Bible, Jesus is referred to as the Lamb of God,[31] a central and beautiful metaphor for our understanding of the role he plays in the salvation of the world. Jesus is also referred to as the Lion of the Tribe of Judah, another powerful metaphor (especially for all of us who grew up reading the Narnia books) that expands our understanding of the Second Person of the Trinity. Critically though, we need to know how far to take these metaphors *and where to stop*. As the Lamb of God, slain from

---

29. Lewis, *Mere Christianity*, 106.

30. Theologians like to describe two ways of thinking about God: cataphatic and apophatic. Cataphatic theology explores the language we use for God, recognizing that all words and statements about God are ultimately metaphorical and do not describe God with perfect fidelity but work to explore those metaphors and see how we might use them to know God *better*. In contrast (or perhaps in a complementary way) *apophatic* theology focuses on the fact that all words about God are insufficient and therefore concerns itself with denying their accuracy.

31. E.g., John 1:36; 1 Cor 5:7.

the foundation of the world,[32] Jesus is the central figure in breaking the power of sin and death through his self-sacrifice, death, and resurrection. But, being the Lamb of God does not for a second mean that Jesus grows wool, is unintelligent, or has cloven feet. Trying to wear a sweater made from Jesus's hair would be a disappointing—if singular—experience.

Jesus is the Lion of Judah,[33] but it would be ridiculous to conclude that Jesus has a mane or eats raw meat after stalking his prey all day. Jesus is the True Vine,[34] but nobody ever tried to pick grapes off of his elbow; he is our Cornerstone,[35] but if you want to build a house you probably don't want to plant him in your basement; he is the Bread of Life,[36] but he isn't baked in an oven.[37] Jesus used the metaphor of a hen to talk about himself,[38] but we don't expect to find him molting or laying eggs. Of course it is ridiculous to take these metaphors that far and we generally don't. But how far is too far? One of the great challenges of theology is working out answers to that question. If Jesus is the Lamb of God, Lion of Judah, Bread of Life, True Vine, Cornerstone, and so much more, the critical interpretive question is "in what way?" *In what way* is Jesus the Lamb of God? *In what way* is Jesus the Lion of Judah? *In what way* is Jesus the Bread of Life, the True Vine, the Cornerstone?

Or for our purposes, *in what way* is holiness a form of purity and *in what way* is sin a form of contamination? If we allow the "purity as holiness; contamination as sin" metaphor to play too strongly, we risk giving the impression (explicitly or implicitly communicated) that holiness operates by the same rules—the same logic—that purity does, and that sin operates by the logic of disgust. That would lead to treating sin both as sticky and as more powerful than holiness in the same way that a contaminant is sticky and is more powerful than purity. Remember, in the showdown between a pure substance and a contaminant, the contaminant is powerful while the pure is fragile. When your drinking water and something disgusting come into contact, your drinking water is the one at risk of being contaminated by the foreign substance. If we make

---

32. Rev 5:6.
33. Rev 5:5.
34. John 15:1.
35. Eph 2:20.
36. John 6:35.

37. This is not a criticism of the doctrine of transubstantiation; the bread which becomes the body of Christ was still only bread when it was being baked.

38. Matt 23:27.

the mistake of overinterpreting the metaphor of holiness as purity and sin as contamination, we will end up thinking of holiness as something threatened by exposure to sin.

In terms of Christian praxis, we have already seen some of the disastrous implications of an overapplied purity/disgust metaphor, but let's dig a little deeper. For many who were raised in a Western, individualistic culture, disgust is usually focused around the individual body and independent identity. I am disgusted by things that don't fit nicely into my view of myself—everything from germs and disease to bad food or inappropriate thoughts. However, as has been noted in psychological, cultural, biological, and neurological discourses (among others), this concept of the individual self is far more fiction than fact.[39] There is a lot to unpack in that statement that we will develop in a much more robust way in future chapters. For now, though, we just want to note that where we draw the lines of *me versus not me* is much less straightforward than we'd often believe. Acclaimed psychiatrist and interpersonal neurobiology researcher Dan Siegel uses the term MWe to talk about the interconnectedness of humans. He writes, "who 'we are' is both a me and a we, an us, a set of interconnected, interdependent, interrelationships that involve our body and its brain, yes, and also our being interconnected with something broader than the brain and bigger than the body. Our relationships are *also* who we are [emphasis in original]."[40] In other words, you are both *you* and you are *us*. Your felt sense of being a singular *me* is somehow simultaneously true and a complete fiction, as Siegel writes that the mind is both a noun and a verb. In order to protect against this paradox and to reinforce the cultural value of individualism, we implicitly marshal disgust as a defense against this more complex, interconnected reality of our identity. Put another way, disgust offers clarity in the face of our own uncertainty.[41]

Taking this even further, from the perspective of psychoanalytic theory, what we experience as *other* is also an aspect of ourselves. The beginning of consciousness splits self and other in a fictive but functional way—not in a reflection of reality. It's pragmatic, not true. From the advent of that mirror stage that we discussed in the previous chapter, our

---

39. See Cooper-White, *Braided Selves*; Siegel, *Developing Mind*; Watkins and Shulman, *Toward Psychologies of Liberation*; Leupin, *Lacan Today*; Croasmun, *Emergence of Sin*; Fernandez, *Reimagining the Human*; Menakem, *Quaking of America*.

40. Siegel, *Developing Mind*, 497.

41. Sartre relates the ambiguity of what is me and what is not found in the interaction with slime to our disgust reaction to stickiness.

ego identity is only ever an imaginary ego. It is distinctly not the real—as the fullness of who we are cannot be contained in language. It resists symbolization. This means that our ego is under constant threat of being exposed as insufficient. The emperor of who you think you are is actually totally nude and lacking—you are so much more! We require rigid defenses to protect ourselves from the vulnerability of our fragile egos. Disgust is a powerful weapon in this arsenal, as it not only activates our physiological response to distance ourselves from anything that would threaten to expose the truth of our ourselves, but also provides the necessary justification to maintain the segregation it demands. In other words, disgust gives us the energy and impulse to get away from something gross and helps us believe it really is contaminating so that we continue to avoid it in the future.

The notorious Stanford Prison Experiment highlighted this extremely well. In this experiment, regular college students were randomly assigned the position of guard or inmate in a mock prison. The experiment was canceled early and became a case study in the ethical dangers of using human subjects in psychology research due to the abusive behavior of the guards against their fellow classmates who were cast in the role of inmate. One of the justifications the guards used for their abuse came in the form of a belief that a clear distinction existed between the guards and inmates—even though they were randomly assigned from the same pool of research subjects. As the guards limited the hygiene opportunities of the inmates, the resulting smell was then used as part of the rationalization for why the inmates were inherently bad—they were gross. Zimbardo, the principal investigator of the study who was also the fake prison superintendent, writes, "blaming the victims for their sorry condition—created by our failure to provide adequate shower and sanitation facilities—became common."[42] In this way, disgust was used to protect the fiction of difference from the reality of their shared humanity and overrode their normal sensibilities. One of the dangers of reading about a study like this is to assume that we would do anything differently. On the contrary, as Nathan said to David, "You are [that] man" (2 Sam 12:7). We have a disgust problem.

From a theological perspective, this use of disgust is disastrous. Where our individualist society has deployed disgust as a means to preserve the illusion of our individuality, Christianity teaches us to break

---

42. See Zimbardo, *Lucifer Effect*, loc. 2120.

down, to dissolve, those same barriers. From Jesus claiming identity with the poor, naked, prisoner, and hungry,[43] to St. Paul's description in 1 Cor 12 of the church as one body with many parts, orthodox Christianity demands that we recognize and embrace the MWe-ness of ourselves and the church—in fact with all who are "the least of these." Contrast what we saw with the Stanford Prison Experiment with St. Paul's words:

> The eye cannot say to the hand, "I have no need of you," nor again the head to the feet, "I have no need of you." On the contrary, the members of the body that seem to be weaker are indispensable, and those members of the body that we think less honorable we clothe with greater honor, and our less respectable members are treated with greater respect, whereas our more respectable members do not need this. But God has so arranged the body, giving the greater honor to the inferior member, that there may be no dissension within the body, but the members may have the same care for one another. If one member suffers, all suffer together with it; if one member is honored, all rejoice together with it.[44]

Allowing an overinterpreted disgust/purity metaphor to shape our understanding leads to blaming the poor for their poverty, the disabled for their disability, the oppressed for their oppression, and the marginalized to their marginalization. Where Christ calls us to clothe those we think less honorable with greater honor, our disgust reactions—defending our fragile individual egos and the ego of our church as a place of holiness set apart from contamination by "the world"—push us to expel, stigmatize, and marginalize. A church formed by disgust is a church which is going to invest in maintaining the illusion of its independence from society and from the wider body of Christ. A church which has bought into an overapplied disgust/purity metaphor is going to see itself not as salt and light, but as something fragile and delicate. A disgust-formed church will be concerned not with who it can welcome in but with who needs to be kept out. In St. Paul's idiom, a disgust-formed church is a church made up entirely of hands determined not to be contaminated by any ego threatening association with eyes, feet, or genitals.

Ultimately, to ascribe to sin the power of disgust is to teach in direct contradiction to the power and gospel of Jesus Christ. We believe that this is a mistake that the white evangelical church in particular makes all

43. Matt 25:31–46.
44. 1 Cor 12:21–26 NRSVUE.

too often with disastrous consequences for the church's theology and for her witness in the world. It has driven us to pull back, create boundaries, and exclude when we should have embraced, mingled, and joined. We believe that the Bible offers a counter narrative and teaches life-giving practices to help us reform ourselves in defiance of disgust's fragility. In this book, we want to explore these liberative narratives and practices to help reimagine the life and role of the church community in our pursuit of Christ as the Way, the Truth, and the Life.

3

Eucontamination

Christ is the Son of God. If we share in this kind of life we also shall be sons of God. We shall love the Father as He does and the Holy Ghost will arise in us. He came into this world and became a man in order to spread to other men the kind of life He has—by what I call "good infection." Every Christian is to become a little Christ. The whole purpose of becoming a Christian is simply nothing else.

—C. S. Lewis, *Mere Christianity*

In 2013, Thabiti Anyabwile wrote a now infamous piece for *The Gospel Coalition* in which he argued in favor of "your gag reflex when discussing homosexuality."[1] In this, Anyabwile is explicitly arguing in favor of Christians having a disgust reaction to gay marriage. Anyabwile believes that gayness is sinful and chooses to argue that Christians would therefore be well served in strengthening their disgust reactions to it. As we said in chapter 2, even if Anyabwile were right about gayness,[2] his willingness to deploy disgust in service of protecting the "purity" of his fellow Christians and the society they live in relies on a belief in the fragility of holiness. By accepting and embracing the logic of disgust, Anyabwile

1. Anyabwile, "Importance of Your Gag Reflex."
2. He is not.

is encouraging his readers to recapitulate the world's defensive posture towards "outsiders," to believe that the love and goodness of Christ are weaker than the threat and allure of sin,[3] and to engage in the violent expulsion and rejection of those marginalized by the world.

But what if there's more? What if the Way of Jesus was about a radically different relationship with ourselves, our bodies, and one another? In response to the problems we have been outlining around the power and logic of disgust, we offer a reinterpretation of how Jesus models and invites us to be in the world. By consistently violating the accepted social norms of his day and moving towards—making contact with—the outcasts, contaminants, and disgust-inducing others, Jesus inverts the power of contamination and dares us to trust in the power of love. Instead of protecting a fragile purity within us, we are instead called to be the contaminants in a world that cannot overcome the Spirit. It is this simple but subversive notion of a contamination for good—a *eu*contamination—that can help us boldly move towards embrace instead of fearfully excluding.

The church has a disgust problem and we see it in our praxis—in the way the church participates in the world and, as a result, is perceived by the world. And, as we said in the previous chapter, praxis and belief are linked in a circular relationship that can spiral like Dante's Inferno, down into the depths of Hell or, like his Purgatorio, up towards the heavens. These days, for many Christians in the United States, that spiral—fueled by an overdetermined metaphor of purity and sin—seems to be headed downward towards ever more exclusionary theology and practice. This is alarming for many "exvangelical people"[4] in particular who express concern that exclusionary and othering dynamics may be inextricably linked to fundamental Christian belief. That concern is both real and reasonable.[5]

But we believe that the Bible and Christian tradition offer a counter-logic to the disgust logic that has justified and driven so much exclusionary Christianity. Right from the outset Jesus seems to have taken a completely inverted view of purity and disgust from the approach we explored in chapter 2—an approach that is both counterintuitive and revolutionary.[6] Throughout his ministry, Jesus never acted as though he

---

3. Though, of course, he is wrong about what is and is not sin.

4. Those who have left evangelicalism behind for either some other form of Christianity or have chosen to renounce Christianity altogether.

5. For more on the destructive effects of exclusion, see Volf, *Exclusion and Embrace*.

6. While Jesus certainly taught and modeled this counterintuitive and revolutionary approach, in doing so he was developing and working in conversation with a

was at risk of being contaminated. He was perpetually interacting with the sinful (both those perceived as sinful and the really sinful) as though contact and association with them was powerless to contaminate him. In the idiom of the Gospels, Jesus acted like someone who could not be made unclean by any external force. Indeed, he explicitly taught as much in Matt 15 saying, "Don't you know that it is not what goes into a [person's] mouth that defiles them but what comes out of it" (Matt 15:11) and clarifies it a few verses later explaining that it is what comes out of someone's heart that defiles them. And we should note that the whole discussion was prompted by some teachers complaining to Jesus that his followers were eating without washing their hands first—a rather disgust-inducing oversight.

In other instances, Jesus ate with people whom his society, and most notably his religious contemporaries, saw as sinful and therefore contaminating. When he was confronted about it, his argument (it is the sick, not the well who need a doctor)[7] highlighted his conviction that there was something about him which was not only immune to contamination but which could itself purify the already contaminated. Why then have so many Christians, now and throughout history, been so taken with the logic and expression of disgust? What is so enticing about disgust?

OF GODS AND MONSTERS

Disgust is directly tied to our sense of self and to what goes into, or must be kept out of, our mouth and body (the common facial expression of disgust is of someone close to gagging and vomiting). Food is a common locus of disgust, circling around our willingness and capacity to allow various things to become parts of our body. So, while we are eating, we are in a direct confrontation with the border guards of disgust (how many seconds do you allow for your chips to be on the ground and still be edible?). This is a part of why eating with others is such an intimate and social act. On an individual basis, the act of eating questions what is and can become me; eating with others extends this question and asks now who can be considered *us*. High school lunchrooms can be fraught with social meaning and personal value—students are navigating who they are

---

revolutionary and liberative stream that exists throughout the Prophets and the full Hebrew Bible. See Howard-Brook, *"Come Out My People!"*; and Brueggemann, *Prophetic Imagination*.

7. Matt 9:12.

and where they belong. We eat on dates, we share tables with friends, we feast together in mourning or celebration. Eating and socializing, connecting with others, is an important part of human cultures. To eat with others and share a meal with them invites a level of relationship or connection that in many ways helps to expand our sense of self and take in the others as now part of *us*. The contrast of this was seen graphically in the *Game of Thrones* episode "The Rains of Castamere,"[8] where an entire family is slaughtered at a feast, having been invited under the auspices of a truce, where in fact the offer to "share bread and salt" had been extended as a promise of peace. The violence and betrayal is underscored by its adjacency to and manipulation of intimacy.

And beyond Jesus's interactions during his ministry, the incarnation itself is a deep repudiation of any disgust logic as applied to sin and holiness. In the incarnation, God joined God's self eternally and fundamentally to humanity. To quote the Athanasian Creed:

> [Jesus] Who although he is God and Man; yet he is not two, but one Christ. One; not by conversion of the Godhead into flesh; but by assumption of the Manhood into God. One altogether; not by confusion of Substance [Essence]; but by unity of Person. For as the reasonable soul and flesh is one man; so God and Man is one Christ.[9]

Jesus, the God-man, is, in Christian theology, both fully God and fully human. God (the only One who is pure good) is now also part of God's fallen world, joined to a world marked by sin and death, but somehow at no point does this remotely threaten God's holy pureness. To the contrary, the joining of human and divine in the person of Jesus of Nazareth is the broken boundary through which holiness has infected a fallen world and has gone to work at making it whole again. In the creedal formulation, because of the incarnation, humanity is assumed into God and in that process, instead of contaminating God's holiness, humanity "puts on" divinity. The whole disgust process is working in reverse.

St. Paul is also very clear on this point, writing that "just as through one man (Adam) death entered the world, the resurrection of the dead also comes through one man (Jesus Christ). For as all die in Adam, so all will be made alive in Christ" (1 Cor 15:22 NRSVUE). For St. Paul, Adam's sin is described in conventional contaminating terms but in a shocking

---

8. Nutter, *Game of Thrones*.
9. "Athanasian Creed," 771.

reversal, so is the Life of Jesus Christ. In the person of Jesus, God's divine holiness has infected humanity. In these texts, we see the boundaries of our very species-self being compromised and joined to the Divine Other. Even after the ascension Jesus remains forever human, holding together full humanity and full divinity. And rather than attenuating this mixing of human and divine by his physical absence from the world, Jesus has sent the Holy Spirit, indwelling us with God's Self.[10] Christ ascending is not the re-separation of divinity from humanity, as we might expect in the case of some neoplatonic or gnostic heaven;[11] Jesus has brought humanity into "the heavens" and has sent his own Holy Spirit to dwell within humanity.[12] Even in the ascension, God did not purify divinity. God intensified the contamination of humanity even more with the Spirit.

For many steeped in Christian theology, this point may seem mundane or a given. Yet, if we remember the logic of disgust, we can perhaps re-cognize the audacity of such a claim. Contamination works in such a way that the lower, the base, the gross is always more powerful than the pure, the sterile, and the clean. The surgical suite must keep out all bacteria if it is to remain pure. One drop of spit in your drinking water makes the whole cup dirty. This also plays out in our religious and spiritual imagination; as psychologist Richard Beck writes, "monsters are divinity violations. Something 'high' on the divinity dimension is being mixed with something 'low.' A man with a bug-head is taboo as it mixes something sacred (the human person created in the Imago Dei) and brings it into contact with something low and base, in this example an insect."[13] Jesus, the God-man does *just* that, but it works backwards. In bringing the divine into contact with the sinful, it is not God who is at risk, but the sin. Jesus is inverting the power of disgust—contaminating for good.

Following the logic of disgust and contamination, the fallen, broken, sinful nature of the world is such that, typically, it must be kept apart from heaven or the Divine.[14] In fact, the two are only able to make contact in particular, holy places that are kept sacred through careful liturgical and religious practices. Consider the rituals and practices described in the Jewish Scriptures around the temple—or the importance of dressing in one's "Sunday best" for church where no swearing or "potty talk" was

10. John 14:26 and 15:26.
11. See John 15.
12. See Rom 8:9 and 1 Cor 3:16.
13. Beck, *Unclean*, 94.
14. Beck, *Unclean*.

admissible. Strict rules govern who can enter a holy place, when, and in what manner. These thin spaces between the Divine reality and our lowly world are carefully tended. But in Christ we see a radical shift in this logic. At his moment of death, the New Testament writes, the curtain to the holy of holies was torn open, exposing it to the world. The veil between the Divine and human was lifted as the whole of creation was thinned—the boundary between fallen, sinful, humanity and the Holy Divine was pierced. The kingdom of God is at hand. It is here, now—meaning that heaven is not at risk of being polluted. On the complete contrary, it is a sinful world that is at great risk of Christ's contaminating love. We no longer need ritual sacrifice or cleansing because God is near. The Spirit is within us—the dirty, pooping, copulating masses of humanity that God looks on and calls her children!

In other words, St. Paul is making an extremely radical statement. Just as all it took was one person (Adam) to sin for the world to fall, so too does our salvation, not through careful dissection and separation, but through joining and loving—bringing together. The salvation of Christ now follows the logic of contamination.

The Way of Jesus is positively littered with disgust-inducing occurrences, images, and practices. God is joined to humanity and, as we celebrate every Christmas, God is born in blood and pain to a woman—a girl—at the bottom of the social hierarchy.[15] This mixing of the higher, divine, with the lower human ought to be disgusting and shameful, as we noted earlier. We see this in the creation of monsters as the union of "lower" animals with "higher" humans. "Bestial half-humans" are almost definitional monsters in our tales and folklore. The thought of joining what is impure, lower, beneath us, to what is *us* revolts us (well done if you are noticing the roots of some of the more egregious tropes of racism there). But of course, this entire dynamic is subjective. We are not disgusted by the joining of us to what we see as higher, just that which we see is lower. When the peasant girl marries the prince, the nobility is disgusted but the peasantry is elated. When God is joined to humanity, following the logic of disgust, God ought to be disgusted.

---

15. See Gafney, "Wisdom's Table"; Cone, *God of the Oppressed*; Thurman, *Jesus and the Disinherited*.

EUCONTAMINATION

The two events at the center of Christian history are the incarnation and the death and resurrection of Jesus Christ—Christmas and Easter. In the incarnation, God's very self is joined eternally to humanity; the higher conjoining with the lower. In the passion, Jesus drags our humanity down into the very core of corruption, into death itself. And then, rather than being overcome by death, the God-man Jesus defeats death and hell. Instead of the higher being contaminated by the lower, death is defeated when the one who is Life is brought into contact with it. But both of these core moments in Christian history are exactly contrary to what our common disgust-shaped reasoning would push us to believe would happen. In the logic or thinking of disgust, the higher pure should be corrupted by the lower contaminant. In the logic of disgust the contaminant (death) should contaminate the pure (life).

The theological and philosophical point here rests on a question of power and resilience. What is more robust: death or life? Can perfect love cast out fear? Is sin greater than love?

As Christians, we hold dear to the conviction that the Way of Jesus is good news. That love is not just a happy thought and warm feeling. Love—as we will discuss in much more detail later—is a subversive contaminant working its way into the most unlikely places, polluting a fallen, broken world with truth, goodness, and beauty beyond our imagination. As followers of Christ, we need not fear the power of sin, but can audaciously trust in the beauty of love to overcome. We can turn towards those parts of ourselves we most hate and, instead of shame and hiding, we are free to embrace with compassion. We can work towards Goodness in ourselves and our world without fear of corruption. We can pursue Truth wherever she may take us in a radical embrace of trust, wonder, and curiosity. We are freed from an image of who we wish we were, to continue discovering who we may become.

This inversion of disgust and contamination calls for a new word, a new way of understanding the nature and power of Christ. We have suggested the term *eucontamination* as a way to name this inverted phenomenon. Building off Tolkien's concept of a "eucatastrophe"[16] or catastrophe for good—the unlooked-for rescue or relief just when everything was at its most hopeless—and the sacrament of the Eucharist, we chose the Greek prefix, *eu* which means "good." Eucontamination is

---

16. See Tolkien, *Tree and Leaf*, 1–81.

thus a contamination for good, what C. S. Lewis—in the epigraph to this chapter—called "a good infection," and contamination—because this goodness follows the logic of bacteria, infections, and yeast. It works its way into the host like a germ, impacting every part. It is the power of the miniscule and minute. But this infection is not of an illness or pollutant, per se (though it often strikes us as that in the beginning). It is a contaminant for good working within us as individuals and us as corporate, social bodies and congregations.

Eucontamination combines in one concept both the goodness of God and the *logic* of contamination. This is the core of our theological argument: that God's work in the world does not follow the rules that we expect for pure substances. God's work is not fragile; it is not defensive. Rather it is, in the idiom of the Gospels, the powers of sin and death that are fragile and defensive. If we imagine a contaminant as a force attempting to pierce barriers, integrate with undefiled purity, and transform it into its own contaminating likeness, we see then that, in response, the pure adopts a posture of defensiveness and expulsion. It should become clear which side of this equation the Gospel writers represent Jesus as being on. In case it is not clear, let's take a look at John 3:17–21.

This passage starts directly after the famous John 3:16: "For God so loved the world that he gave his only Son, so that everyone who believes in him may not perish but may have eternal life" (NRSVUE) Already we see God taking a posture of love and involvement towards our human existence. But the passage continues:

> Indeed, God did not send the Son into the world to condemn the world but in order that the world might be saved through him. Those who believe in him are not condemned, but those who do not believe are condemned already because they have not believed in the name of the only Son of God. And this is the judgment, that the light has come into the world, and people loved darkness rather than light because their deeds were evil. For all who do evil hate the light and do not come to the light, so that their deeds may not be exposed. But those who do what is true come to the light, so that it may be clearly seen that their deeds have been done in God. (NRSVUE)

Notice how the light is reaching into the darkness—eucontaminating it. Notice that it is the darkness which has to take a defensive posture in this text. Darkness is, after all, only the absence of light and is thus destroyed (contaminated) by any engagement with the light. The power in this equation is all on the side of the light, of Christ, of the Son, of God's very self, of goodness—acting "in truth," of that Love with which God Loved the Cosmos. When the life of God descended into death, it was Life and not death that emerged victorious. Contrary to our expectations, it turns out to be those who cling to purity whose deeds are wicked, who cling to the dark and hate the light—which is the eucontamination of God's very self. In God's economy, in the logic of God's divine Truth, the transformation of God's divine Life and the light of God's Way, the Son is an intrusion into our selves. Jesus is a eucontamination.

When encountering something "other" that threatens to pierce our boundaries, we are faced with the activation of our disgust reactions. And in that, the choice to either welcome or expel the (eu)contaminant.[17] If we welcome it, then we integrate it and let it change us.[18] As Bilbo once warned: "It's a dangerous business, Frodo, going out your door. You step onto the road, and if you don't keep your feet, there's no knowing where you might be swept off to."[19] Often people choose that expulsive disgust reaction. It can be violent and cruel in a way that deliberate and considered actions are less likely to be, and too frequently it is embraced with the sort of consequences we saw in the previous chapter. Jesus did warn us that the world (that world that is "in darkness") hates him—the source of divine eucontamination—as men who love the darkness must hate the light (John 3:20). But "to all who received Him. . . He gave the right to become Children of God" (John 1:12).

EUCONTAMINATIVE THERAPY

While we present this concept primarily as a theological idea, the psychological significance is also important to underscore as it points to an inversion in how many of us approach mental health and wellness at first glance. Freedom, play, and thriving can be found through a process of integration, not through bolstering defenses. Patients often come to

---

17. We use the parenthetical (eu) in (eu)contamination here and in some other places throughout the book to designate a degree of uncertainty regarding the goodness of a given contaminant. Some substances really are poison (contaminants), while others are medicines (eucontaminants), and often we are unable to know which of the two something is in advance.

18. Remember that John 3:21 describes the goodness that the eucontaminant unveils as "worked in God."

19. Tolkien, *Fellowship*, 92.

therapy looking for help to take away a form of suffering like anxiety or depression. One aspect of treatment absolutely entails a degree of symptom reduction and the easing of suffering. However, the hope is to then move beyond a mere absence of pain and towards a more robust flourishing. In other words, psychotherapy transforms our relationship to that which is most threatening instead of doubling down on the guards and protection against it.

In a parallel to fundamentalist, religious discourse on sin, much psychotherapeutic discussion focuses on the level of the symptom, the problem, and how to make it go away. Like with physical pain at a medical doctor, most therapists work to help their patients alleviate their psychological distress. This is not a problem, but an important aspect of treatment. As a mental health counselor, an important goal of my (Paul's) treatment plans often addresses some level of alleviating suffering. When this becomes the end of the story, though, we foreclose the possibility of even greater transformation and freedom. Taking a pain reliever to deal with a headache is not a bad idea, but it would be foolish to assume that your aspirin tablet alleviated the dehydration that caused your headache in the first place. To move past a vision of health that is purely negative—the absence of anxiety, depression, trauma, obsessions, addiction, etc.—towards one of thriving, requires a much more nuanced appreciation of consciousness and reality.

On a very simple level, the work of psychotherapy and psychoanalysis is to make the unconscious, conscious—to help people metabolize what one has been resisting.[20] Many patients come to therapy with some version of a desire to make their symptom/s (anxiety, depression, obsession, addiction, etc. . . . .) go away or be somehow excised from their life. Yet, while there are many helpful skills and techniques that can alleviate some of the intensity and pain from those symptoms, healing is the work of integration, not exorcism. Our symptoms can be thought of as signifiers, signposts to a reality about ourselves that we are not yet able to acknowledge.[21] Treatment involves helping someone reorient their world to account for a reality that has remained unimaginable until now. In other words, the psychotherapist is helping their patients move towards

---

20. See McWilliams, *Psychoanalytic Diagnosis.*

21. See Boothby, *Freud as Philosopher.* This critique of contemporary, Western discourse around symptom-reduction can also be found in Liberation Psychology, which points to the colonial aspects of these approaches to psychology. See Watkins and Shulman, *Toward Psychologies of Liberation.*

the eucontaminant of their symptom, in an audacious hope that it will transform both the patient and the symptom (and often the therapist!).

There are many different ways to conceive of this concept from various psychological approaches and theories. Psychoanalytic theory has long held to the necessity of being able to accept, recognize, and/or integrate the overwhelming, unimaginable, and resisted aspects of our psyche as hallmarks of psychological health. Jung, for example, wrote about the importance of becoming familiar with the shadow self, Freud spoke of making the unconscious conscious, Klein pointed to how we split and project the intolerable aspects of ourselves into another, and Lacan noted the trauma of the unimaginable, unsymbolizable real that irrupts[22] into our imaginary-symbolic realities. Other evidenced-based therapeutic modalities and theories similarly include some level of integration or acceptance in their vision of health. Internal Family Systems (IFS) looks at the parts of ourselves we resist so as to learn how to befriend them. Acceptance and Commitment Therapy (ACT) helps patients make room for unwanted experiences, thoughts, and emotions—accepting instead of resisting. Emotionally Focused Therapy (EFT) walks patients through the steps of accepting, processing, and acknowledging painful experiences and emotions. Interpersonal Neurobiology (IPNB or relational neuroscience) advocates for cultivating the capacity for integration within the various domains of functioning. And finally, Trauma-Focused Cognitive Behavioral Therapy (TF-CBT) fosters the resilience and capacity to process one's traumatic experience through their trauma narrative so as to ease emotional distress. This list is not exhaustive and risks oversimplifying complex and nuanced therapeutic approaches. However, each of them identify that health and thriving involve some form of integration—of telling a more full story of oneself and reality.

When we integrate in therapy an incredible transformation takes place. The binary splitting of in/out, good/bad, me/not me begins to shift as both the contaminant and the host are changed. In trauma, for example, processing and working through one's narrative can bring about not just a simple acceptance of what happened, but a complete reorientation in the person who survived it as well as within the *it* that has been accepted. Freud's language for this process was "*durcharbeiten*," which is often translated into "working through," but in his original use it involved

---

22. To irrupt is to break in to something whereas the more common *eruption* indicates a breaking out. Here we are using irrupt to further underscore the insulated nature of our realities.

more of an implication of metabolization.[23] In working through the very thing we've resisted, we allow it to change into parts of who we are and we allow ourselves to be changed by it. Like the food you eat for lunch, the sandwich must be digested and broken down for it to become nutrition for your body, and your body adjusts as it takes in the sandwich and turns it into energy, muscle, etc. . . . So the simple message of "get over it" or to "just accept" what's happened misses the entire point and is dismissive at best and abusive at worst. Working through is a process, not a moment or choice. It takes time, repetition, commitment, and continued faith in an audacious hope.

Author and psychoanalyst Daniel Gaztambide takes this line of thinking even further in tying a direct connection between psychological health and liberation theology. He writes that "Psychoanalysis, understood in its totality, calls for a critique of the lies of consciousness and society, and a turn toward what is left out, whether we are talking of affects, internal objects, or self-states ghettoized in the mind, or human beings ghettoized in the inner city, marginalized in public policy, and cast out in our communities."[24] It is in growing our capacity to embrace the eucontaminant of the Other, the marginalized, the outcast both within our own psyche as well as in our communities that we are liberated and transformed.

An important aspect for this conversation that Gaztambide brings forward is the significance of social location. He is bringing a direct connection between the disavowed parts of ourselves and the marginalized in society. This means that our relationship to disavowal and disgust must also be considered along the lines of social location and power. Not all contaminants are eucontaminants. Germs do exist in the world. Washing hands before meals is wise. What is important for our reflections here is a question of power and privilege. Jesus's examples of eucontamination involved him as the rabbi, the teacher, the holy man coming into contact with those who were marginalized in relation to him. He, as the *pure* one, moved in love towards those who were further from the societal center than he was without fearing contamination from them. We will unpack this dynamic in far more detail in the coming chapters, but wanted to note here that disgust is not the problem and that eucontamination is not an abandonment of discernment. Social location and cultural context

---

23. Freud, "Remembering, Repeating and Working-Through," 145–56.

24. Gaztambide, "Preferential Option for the Repressed: Psychoanalysis Through the Eyes of Liberation Theology," 709.

are deeply significant factors in moving from an abstract concept to the practical application of our ideas.

WAY, TRUTH, AND LIFE

That's a lot of theory and theology, but what does this add up to? How does (and how doesn't) eucontamination play out in the world when we allow it to inform both our beliefs and our behavior? We will explore those questions over the course of the rest of this book through the claim of Christ to be the "Way, the Truth, and the Life"—three big categories with which Jesus identifies (John 14:6). Throughout his ministry, death, resurrection, and now after his ascension, it is in the eucontaminating person of Jesus Christ that we—all of humanity—have access to the eucontaminating Love of our Creator God. We are, through God's Holy Spirit, able to act as vectors of the eucontaminating Truth, through the eucontaminating Way of Jesus, leading to a eucontaminating Life.

Each of these vectors of eucontamination—Way, Truth, and Life— hold vast richness and depth. They also can each be reduced to a flattened, simplified version that twists them into a tool of control instead of liberation and life. Truth is more than just fact, Life is more than happiness, and the Way is more than "doing the right things." Transformation is fundamental to eucontamination. The thing we fear, or resist, or expel in our disgust is that which, if allowed to become us, will make us into something new. Theologically, God is eucontaminating and cannot be contaminated. At its best, the doctrine of impassibility is an affirmation of the fact of God as the ultimate uncontaminated eucontaminant.

And as those who are being transformed into children of God and beyond,[25] transformation—change from what we are into something we do not yet understand ourselves to be—is central to the Christian life. Theologically, we might call it "sanctification," psychologically we might call it "integration" or "growth" or "health," or we might just call it "developing" or "maturing." Whatever we call it, that transformation requires a catalyst, a eucontaminant. And the old self is very likely going to be resistant. We tend to want to stay who we imagine ourselves to be.

In this book, in order to build out our recommendations for the church, we are going to explore these vectors in the order: Truth, Life, Way. We hope to show how allowing ourselves to be eucontaminated by

---

25. "What we will be has not yet been revealed" (1 John 3:2).

Truth opens us up to recognizing and embracing a eucontaminating Life which in turns allows us to recognize and follow in the eucontaminative Way. Each step is built on the one before. We will devote two chapters to the Truth, two to Life, and two to the Way, and in each case the first chapter (chs. 4, 6, and 8, respectively) will address individual eucontamination while the second (chs. 5, 7, and 9) will speak to corporate or collective eucontamination.

Starting with the Truth, while it is possible to be transformed by information, static data, more accurate ideas, and insights, Jesus is not a list of mere facticities. Rather, he is the Truth whom we can come to know. The Truth invades our illusions and our comfortable delusions about ourselves. The Truth tells us about the world confronting us with Reality in ways that are often deeply uncomfortable—but which draw us further into Life. Jesus's invitation, beyond knowing accurate facts or even affirming the validity of the truth, is to be "on the side of Truth"; a relational posture which requires immense courage, as it means choosing Truth over self-soothing illusion (the darkness). To be on the side of Truth is to live open to eucontamination, vulnerable to transformation, into "we know not what."

We will look at what it means to seek Truth as individuals and as members of a community, and what it can look like for a community to orient itself around Truth, not as a mere set of statements (however accurate those statements may or may not be) but as a living and eucontaminating Person. We will explore prophetic and poetic communication as a vector of eucontaminating Truth and will show how being on the side of Truth works to overcome the false realities our communities too often rely on. We will look at the disgust based methods and structures those collectives use to protect themselves from eucontamination by the Truth to preserve an illusion of themselves as oriented to truth.

In order to explore the shape of a eucontaminated and eucontaminating Life, we are going to have to talk about death and shame. We will show how Life has overcome and is overcoming death and we will dive into how the way to Life lies through the death of our false realities and the imperfection of our identities. Life, Joy, and Flourishing all depend on our vulnerability to eucontamination. While nearly all of us live with the temptation to hole up in our comfortable, unexamined lives, the call to Life demands that we leave our individual and communal identities vulnerable to shame. We will tackle the problem of shame head-on and walk through the necessity of recognizing, integrating, and moving *through* the experience of shame into a eucontaminated Life, where each and every part of our blessed and very good selves are glorified, redeemed, and transformed.

Our society is always telling us a story about who is worthy and who is not, and what parts of ourselves are worthy and which are not. We are pressured to mold ourselves into the shapes that fit the demands of our families, cultures, and churches. But the Life of each individual and the Life of our community is in desperate, hopeless need for eucontamination by Joy from the margins. We will show that the Joy of the oppressed is the eucontaminant that oppressive society hates, is disgusted by, and desperately needs. We will explain why it is that eucontaminating Love from the margins will save society.

A Way is something that is to be followed, and we cannot follow a Way without leaving where we are now. Walking a path or following a road using maps and compasses are not what we mean by following the Way of Jesus. Instead, we are using "Way" to describe something more like a "Way of life" or "Way of being"; the Way is a person after all.

And if Jesus is a Way, then to follow Jesus is to walk into a new self, to change, to become like him, marked and remade and remade and remade with each interaction, each new stop, and each new turn as followers along this Way that is Jesus. We cannot walk along a path and arrive at the end as the people who started out. We will draw out the ways in which God has made us to desire Life and Truth and how listening to, rather than suppressing or denying, those desires can draw us towards the Way of Jesus. And in order to do that, we are going to have to unpack some of the confusion and misinformation the church has created in its fear of desire and its resistance to eucontamination. We will show that following the Way of Jesus is not like following a map or any established road, but is a leap into Mystery, guided only by our love for the One who is Love and trusting in our relationship to him as the Way, Truth, and Life.

In *The Fellowship of the Ring*, the protagonists gather in Rivendell to decide what is to be done with the ring of power. After much debate, it is decided that their only hope lies in taking it to Mount Doom in the land of Mordor where it can be un-made. Having decided what must be done, the council turns to ask who will do it. Frodo the hobbit, whose life had already been changed far beyond anything he wanted by his journey to Rivendell, volunteers: "'I will take the ring,' he said, 'though I do not know the way.'"[26] And that is the thing about following a Way; we do not *know* the way. At best we know *whose* Way it is and we trust them that it will take us into a Truer version of ourselves. Would anyone question that the Frodo at the end of *The Return of the King* is more fully himself than the Frodo we find at the council of Rivendell?

But the thing requires faith, and the thing requires hope, and the thing requires trust. Perhaps the greatest commentary on following, or aligning to, or being transformed by a Way is the *Tao Te Ching*, which famously opens with the aphorism "The Way that can be talked about is not the eternal Way."[27] When we follow Christ in the eucontaminative journey, our capacity for courage, trust, hope, and faith are all going to grow and we are going to find ourselves walking into the becoming of "we know not yet what."

And as we follow the Way of Jesus, we find that our legs gain strength to keep walking, and we find that we are not walking alone. Following the Way of Jesus is something we do in community with one another. Jesus has left us with spiritual practices or exercises—we call them *calisthenics of eucontamination*—to help us develop the courage to embrace contamination, the discernment to know when to risk (eu)contamination and when to establish compassionate or dispassionate boundaries to protect ourselves or our community from harm. Following the Way of Jesus together is a dance and not a march.

In exploring Jesus's eucontamination through these three lenses in chapters 4 through 9, we will describe a practical guide to a eucontaminating faith and life. Our hope is to offer ways forward for the church and for everyone who wants a life less controlled by disgust and the dehumanization that so frequently accompanies it. In the process, we will be diving deeper into both the theory and the theology of disgust, contamination, and eucontamination, and we begin with the Truth as a disgust-evoking eucontaminate.

Additionally, for each of these vectors (Way, Truth, and Life), we will explore how they each eucontaminate us individually and corporately. As we have already shown, disgust operates on both of these levels and senses of self. You are both a singular, *me*, and a corporate, *we*. To ignore either of those aspects of the self is to deny deeply important parts of your humanity. Remember, you are not not-an-individual, but an individual

---

26. Tolkien, *Fellowship*, 354.
27. Ng translation of the *Tao Te Ching*, line 1.

and something more. You are not not-your-social identities, but you are your social identities and something more. For many raised in the West, this idea alone is a eucontaminant, destabilizing tightly held, atomized conceptions of the self.[28] We will attempt to explore each of our three vectors in both of these realms, the individual and the corporate. How does Truth contaminate our personal identities and our social selves? How can Life infect how we are as individuals and as groups? How can we follow the Way in our singular lives and in our communities?

---

28. For more on this, see Lee, *Our Unforming*.

4

The Poetry of Truth

Pilate asked him, "So you are a king?" Jesus answered, "You say that I am a king. For this I was born, and for this I came into the world, to testify to the truth. Everyone who belongs to the truth listens to my voice." Pilate asked him, "What is truth?"

After he had said this, he went out to the Jews again and told them, "I find no case against him."

—John 18:37–38 NRSVUE

Paul and I (Billie) grew up in the late nineties and early oughts, a time marked in the minds of many of us who were also raised in the church by the rise of purity culture, True Love Waits campaigns, Promise Rings, and Kissing Dating Goodbye, so we could hardly keep from addressing the implications of that movement in the coming chapters. At the same time though, that youth group era was also marked by a particular sort of Christian apologetics. I would hazard to say that the decade between 1995 and 2005 may have been the last era of the "Creationism vs. Evolution" and "Why Postmodernism Will Destroy Civilization" focused youth group gatherings. I remember proudly rocking my "Darwin is dead and he ain't comin' back" T-shirt to youth group meetings, paired tastefully with jorts and a backwards, upside down DC Talk visor. It was . . . a strange time to be a teenager.

It seemed back then, that as our youth pastors worked to prepare our faith to survive college, we inevitably ended up in special Sunday school or Wednesday night gatherings, where we were warned against the poison of postmodernism. We were told that it would lead to ethical subjectivism, and from there, to sex, abortions, drugs, homosexuality, and ultimately the decline of Western Civilization.[1] We were taught that the secular academic world no longer believed in *absolute truth* and were given crash courses in Christian philosophy and epistemology,[2] so that we would be ready to give an answer when confronted by secular humanist postmodern professors.

And honestly, I took to the philosophy like a fish to water. I loved it. I was in an airport flying home from a summer trip when I first read Francis Schaffer's *The God Who Is There*, and encountered what I would later hear called "the egocentric dilemma." There are certain ideas which, once in your head, don't seem to be able to be un-thought. They lodge there and will nag at you or irritate you until you find an answer or, at least, some resolution. The egocentric dilemma was one of those thoughts for me. The dilemma amounts to asking, "How can I know that anything but me is real?" It can stick, to quote Morpheus, "like a splinter in your brain."[3]

In this chapter, we will explore the ways that our disgust reactions work to keep us from recognizing and being transformed by the Truth as we instead prefer our own delusions and images. We will look at how the Truth fights back, insisting on us through the prophetic and the poetic. But in order to do that, we are going to have to begin with the basics: let's take a short walk through the history of Western philosophy.

---

1. The apotheosis of these efforts is probably represented by Summit Ministries, a summer course and gap year program that exists to "equip and support rising generations to embrace God's truth and champion a biblical worldview." Summit Ministries, "About."

2. The study of what constitutes knowledge, what can be known, and what it means to know.

3. It may not be a coincidence that *The Matrix* came out around the same time that I first encountered the egocentric dilemma; the Wachowski sisters may have been in league with God to unsettle all of my evangelical equilibrium.

A SHORT HISTORY OF WESTERN PHILOSOPHY

Descartes is generally credited with throwing a monkey wrench into Western epistemology and thereby setting off the chain of questions, answers, and observations that led through modernism to the sorts of postmodernism that our youth group leaders were so intent to protect us from. In his book *Meditations on First Philosophy*, Descartes explored the limits of what it means to know something and of what can be known. In the first Meditation he sets the bar for really knowing something at *indubitability*—the quality of being un-doubt-able—and then demonstrates that just about everything he thinks he knows is based on either his senses or the operation of logic (basically math).[4] He goes on to show that conclusions reached on the basis of sense data are not indubitable because we all know of times when our senses give us inaccurate information or lead us to inaccurate conclusions (think about mirages, hallucinations, or phantom sensations). He points out that when we dream we think we are awake and that we are receiving information from our senses. Descartes also reflects on the existence of people who are delusional, who think themselves to be experiencing reality when they are in fact experiencing only their delusions. Movies like *The Matrix*, *The Thirteenth Floor*,[5] and *Inception*[6] have used similar devices to drive Descartes's point home. He concludes that his reasoning, including his mathematical reasoning, cannot be trusted to be indubitable because he observes that, however unlikely it may be, there is a non-zero chance that some "evil genius" is confusing his mind each time he attempts to repeat a sum as simple as 2 + 2 so that he arrives at 4 when the "real" sum might actually be 3 or 5 or anything else. Descartes is about to give up on the possibility of knowing anything at all when he notices that he cannot doubt that he (or something that is him) exists because he would have to exist in order to doubt his existence. From there, Descartes climbed back out of his "dark hole of uncertainty" about nearly everything by using a version of Anselm's ontological proof for the existence of God.[7] He then reasoned

---

4. This is a wild oversimplification.
5. Rusnak, *Thirteenth Floor*.
6. Nolan, *Inception*.

7. Anselm basically argued that "God" is "that than which nothing greater can exist" and then pointed out that a thing which exists is greater than a thing which does not exist and that therefore the fact of understanding the definition of God requires acceptance of God's existence. This particular argument has a spotty record of acceptance in the philosophical community to say the least.

that if God exists, God wouldn't allow for us to be totally and perpetually wrong about logic and sense experience.[8] We can be happy for Descartes, but few philosophers have found his ladder out of the hole of uncertainty a compelling one.

What Descartes actually managed to create was a chasm between reality *as we experience it* and *whatever it is that is the cause of our experience of reality*. Several philosophers worked on the problem this created; Locke described human development as one of making meaning out of all the data that comes pouring into our senses at nearly every moment; Hume found ways to question even forms of reasoning that Descartes had taken for granted.[9] And Berkeley suggested that, in fact, there is no reality outside of us because we are actually all only thoughts that God is having. And while each of these (and a few others) had (and still have) their followers, nobody was thought to have made the sort of progress on the problem that could amount to anything like a consensus until Immanuel Kant.

For histories of philosophy, Immanuel Kant marks something like the high point of modernism and the beginning of the slide towards postmodernism. Kant set out to synthesize the questions and insights of those who had come before him and ended up concluding that there are two realms of reality: the phenomenal and the noumenal. The phenomenal realm is the world that we create in our own minds on the basis of information we get from our senses (phenomena). When you "see" a red ball, Kant (following Locke on this point) would say that what is happening is that something is entering into your brain and that your mind is interpreting that something (let's call it "data") as redness and roundness and all the other components it uses to create the experience of a red ball. This doesn't actually give us any information about the noumenal realm, whatever it is that is out there where we are getting all this data from. Thus, while the red ball exists *in your head*, we don't really know anything about what is outside of our own minds beyond the fact that whatever it is has the property of sending us data that our minds interpret in reliable and coherent ways. Kant claimed that we all use roughly the same processes to construct our phenomenal realms and that therefore, while we do each live in our own "worlds," those worlds match up well enough

---

8. This is, again, an oversimplification. It is hard to summarize the history of philosophy.

9. Hume will leave you very worried about the legitimacy of the cause-effect relationship.

that we are able to make sense of one another and have roughly the same experiences; when you and I look at a red ball we both experience the same thing.[10]

Kant argued that the phenomenal world is what we can know and therefore ought to study and that we can only know the noumenal world by faith. And since Kant, nearly everyone has thought that sounded perfectly reasonable and then gone on to try to know things about the noumenal world anyway. We just don't seem to be content with the idea that the cause of our entire experience of the world is fundamentally unknowable.[11] Confusing these two worlds (noumenal and phenomenal) is where many arguments around concepts like fact and truth fall apart. Today, and in a lot of those youth group training sessions, the language has evolved and we have focused on various aspects of the problem, but the basic question and problem remain: Our experience of reality is generally an experience of realities that we create on the basis of our sense experiences filtered through the biology and electrical signals of our brains. We are desperate to relate to one another and to connect with a more fundamental Reality—we want to know Truth (Kant's noumenal world), and the imagined realities that we are forever constructing, revising, and deconstructing leave us yearning for (and afraid of) an encounter with the really Real. In this chapter, we will explore that longing, as well as several of the ways that we work to access Truth and what it means to distinguish Truth from facticity, as well as some of the ways that Christians and non-Christians have proposed for us to work towards Truth and to live in and with our imagined realities.

All this brings us to the claim that Jesus is the Truth. What could that mean and how might disgust be helpful in understanding it? To start, Truth is greater than fact. Truth resists understanding and capture because, while fact can only be analyzed *within* our phenomenal worlds, Truth insists from the noumenal world and is therefore both more real and more ephemeral to our minds than facts are. Like chasing your shadow, Truth lies before you always just out of reach, and often now where it did not used to lie.

Now, a full philosophical exploration of the nature of Truth and truth is far beyond the scope of this book. The great debates between

---

10. It has proved distressing to some that, owing to colorblindness, the authors of this book do not, in fact, experience red balls in the same way that most of the readers will.

11. For what it's worth I (Billie) am also not content with this.

modernity, post-modernity, meta-modernity, and post-post-modernity will rage on in far more complex detail than we are able to examine here. However, the very existence of such debates highlights something extremely significant about Truth: it's complicated. In today's hyper-efficient sound bite, tweet-sized information age, we have reduced Truth to fact. Truth becomes binary: fact or fiction. It is or isn't, did or did not happen. Like a computer code that eventually can be broken down to ones and zeros, Truth has been reduced to data. Meanwhile, in the opening verses of this chapter (John 18:37–38), Jesus—who is Truth—makes unnerving and confusing comments about Truth, facts, testifying, and listening. Somehow these are all related and interconnected but separate.

ON BULLSHIT,[12] EGOS, AND IDENTITIES

So how does all this come back to connect with disgust and eucontamination? To begin addressing this question, we have one more ingredient that needs to be added to the discussion: we need to go back to the psychology lesson from chapter 1 and some of the basics around human development. Remember that our conscious, thinking selves are our egos—the image of ourselves that we develop early on in life that sees ourselves from the outside. This means that the ego functions *as-if* it was the entirety of who we are, while only being actually an image, appearance, or avatar. There is so much more to you than you think there is.

What this imaginary ego focuses on is the sense of wholeness and completion—the gestalt of the self.[13] But it is an impression from the outside, the view of the self in a mirror or from another's eyes, so it is also decentered and objective instead of a subjective experience.[14] Lacan calls

---

12. We were tempted to apologize for the indelicacy of this term but on reflection it seems rather out of place to apologize for using the term "bullshit" in a book about contamination and disgust. So instead of an apology we would like to take this opportunity to encourage you to reflect on your experience of encountering the term in an academic and theological context and to think about what that reaction indicates regarding your own experience of sacredness, of disgust, and of contamination.

13. See Boothby, *Freud as Philosopher*.

14. The structure of the self that we have presented so far in this book has relied heavily on the metaphor of sight and images. The ego, or conscious sense of self, comes from the imaginary register and is fundamentally tied to an image of the self from the outside. The use of visual metaphors here can be troubling from an ableism standpoint in seemingly discounting and discrediting the experiences of the visually impaired. As such, it is important to hold them loosely as metaphors and not as concrete reflections of reality. The metaphor of the image, for example, could also be thought of as an

this the imaginary register.[15] It is formed from the semblance of a whole, complete, and unified self but requires the denial, repression, and resistance of the aspects of ourselves that don't fit that whole. Like seeing an image in the clouds, we focus on the shapes that give meaning to what we think we see and allow the extra bits—the gaps and wisps—to fall into the background. In other words, there is always a remainder from the unity we perceive in ourselves.[16] But since that unity is based on an external impression of ourselves, it leads to a focus on the image of ourselves to others. We look to others to maintain a sense of cohesion and uphold our imaginary egos against the real of what has been left out, which constantly presses in to disrupt our world.

Significantly, this places Truth in a complex position. We have a feeling of ourselves that may be true on a subjective experiencing level, but there is also a greater Truth that is always beyond our capacity to name or comprehend. My sense of myself, the "I" that filled out my social media accounts, is imaginary. It is not the whole me. It is—to put it more playfully—the bullshit me.

Now, bullshit is a fascinating concept and requires a bit more exploration than you may first assume. It was well analyzed by Harry Frankfurt in his short book, *On Bullshit*. In that work, Frankfurt distinguishes between lies, truth, and bullshit. Lies are less of a threat to truth than bullshit because a lie still holds regard for truth. The liar believes they know what is true but is purposefully distorting it for whatever reason. The actual state of affairs (the facts) is necessarily relevant to the liar as

---

impression of the self, a gestalt, and not simply a visual semblance. However, using the language of images can be helpful when we place it back into common vernacular and reflect on how the way we talk about something shapes our thinking about it. "Do you see it?" "Can you see what I'm getting at?" are just two simple examples of how we use the visual metaphor to communicate around understanding. Biblically there are also plenty of examples of sight being linked to understanding, insight, and clarity as Jesus gives sight to the blind and brings light into the darkness.

15. Fink, *Lacanian Subject*.

16. It is not lost on us that the subjective view of the self is, in fact, more True than the objective view of the self specifically because the objective view requires distance from the self and is therefore mediated by the ego. In our effort to gain a "God's eye view" of ourselves, we end up baptizing our heavily conditioned view of ourselves. Meanwhile, the truly subjective (and therefore more Truthful) view of the self can never be grasped or fully examined because any attempt at a total observation and analysis of ourselves can take place only by imagining ourselves looking in at ourselves "from without," which turns out only to be the same old objective ego view we were trying to escape. The subjective view of the self can never, therefore, be conceptualized; it can only be experienced, and that only partially.

they must work to precisely misconstrue those facts. The bullshitter, on the other hand, speaks entirely out of the desire to create an impression on the listener. They may say things that are factual and they may not because, significantly, the bullshitter has no concern for truth; it does not constrain them. As Frankfurt writes, "The bullshitter ignores these demands [of truth] altogether. He does not reject the authority of the truth, as the liar does, and oppose himself to it. He pays no attention to it at all. By virtue of this, bullshit is a greater enemy of the truth than lies are."[17] We would add to Frankfurt's model that what he is describing as "truth" is actually more reality as it is understood (Kant's phenomenal)—the shared reality in which we reside and which we all construct. It is the shared, objective world in which our subjective selves exist.

Psychotherapeutic treatment for individuals with more psychotic disorders involves helping them to stabilize their sense of selves enough to exist in a shared reality with others. Therapy focuses on this stabilization, helping them distinguish between internal and external, me and not-me. However, for more coherent self-structures or more organized characters, health is often a movement towards a less stable sense of self. Treatment involves uncovering the unconscious, repressed, denied, disavowed, and dissociated parts of the self because our egos are restrictive and don't contain all that we are. They are an *image* we have of ourselves, not the whole. As such, we need to destabilize these images to integrate a greater fullness of who we are. When teaching on this, I (Paul) often use the analogy of a video game. In order to operate and interact in a virtual fantasy world we require an avatar, a symbol of ourselves as a player. This avatar becomes a way of being in the world and connecting with other players. However, this avatar is decidedly not me. I am a human at home on my computer or Xbox, but am represented in the game and or virtual environment as my character or avatar. The analogy is imperfect, but helps to highlight the connection and difference, necessity and falsehood inherent in a game. So too, my ego is a necessary fabrication that allows me to exist within a shared reality with others. Without it, I have no way of connecting, working, learning, or loving. But it is important to remember that I am not my ego. It is a symbol, a signifier for me, but it is necessarily lacking and incomplete.

As a trans woman, I (Billie) have experienced a particularly magnified version of this. For the first thirty-nine years of my life, I presented

---

17. See Frankfurt, *On Bullshit*, 61.

to the world as a man, despite being, in fact, a woman. Part of that experience involved being in conversation with the expectations the world had for me and finding ways to negotiate my own presence in light of the expectation of my man-ness. For me, that resulted in the creation of an image of myself which was, on the one hand, certainly *not* me (he was a boy and then a man while I was a girl and then a woman) but who was negotiated to be as similar to me as I could manage in order to allow me to express as much of myself as possible. Then, when I came out and began living as my gender, I found myself confronted with a clear conflict between the old (man) symbol of myself in the world and the new, more accurate, symbol of myself as a woman in the world. And I was almost immediately faced with a new set of pressures and expectations I had to negotiate in deciding how I was going to symbolize myself. Would I emphasize my womanhood, my transness, or hold to a continuity with my old (man) symbol? My efforts have been to integrate the total messiness of it all. I am a woman and I am trans and I am the woman who presented as a boy and then a man for thirty-nine years of my life. When people interacted with that (man) symbol of me they were never quite interacting with *me* but they were very much interacting with *me-as-I-presented-a-masculine-symbol*. There was never anyone *behind* the symbol of my old self but me. Yes, I was operating under the false and ultimately impossible constraint of man-ness, but he/it/I was always a symbol of *me*. Integrating my messy self has meant choosing not to distance myself from that old symbol, cut myself off from it, or believe that I can create a non-symbolic, perfectly real and embodied presence in the world. I have to recognize that I am, and have always been, myself and that each day and each moment I am able to bring the symbolic me—the imaginary me—a little more into conformity with more of myself.

When I came out, my church offered to recognize the milestone and the change that it represented in my life with a re-naming ceremony as a liturgy of blessing and affirmation of this new, more accurate symbol of me. I cannot overstate how much of a blessing that ceremony was for me. It meant the world to have my friends, family, and spiritual community come together to recognize this change in who they understand me to be represented in the acknowledgment of a new name which more accurately represents who I am. At the service, the message was based on Rev 2:17: "To everyone who conquers I will give some of the hidden manna, and I will give a white stone, and *on the white stone is written a new name that no one knows except the one who receives it*" (NRSVUE, emphasis ours). This idea that there is a name for us known only to us and to God is something I encountered first in the writing of George MacDonald, who says:

> In this passage about the gift of the white stone, I think we find the essence of religion. . . .
>
> The true name is one which expresses the character, the nature, the being, the meaning of the person who bears it. It is the man's own symbol,—his soul's picture, in a word,—the sign which belongs to him and to no one else. Who can give a man this, his own name? God alone. For no one but God sees what the man is, or even, seeing what he is, could express in a name-word the sum and harmony of what he sees. To whom is this name given? To him that overcometh. When is it given? When he has overcome. . . .
>
> God's name for a man must then be the expression in a mystical word—a word of that language which all who have overcome understand—of his own idea of the man, that being whom he had in his thought when he began to make the child, and whom he kept in his thought through the long process of creation that went to realize the idea. To tell the name is to seal the success—to say, "In thee also I am well pleased."[18]

I am not saying that my legal name now, the name that was recognized in that service *is* "the one which expresses the character, the nature, the being, the meaning of the person who bears it" but it is, as recognized by my friends, family, and spiritual community before God, *closer* to that name.

The process of letting the Truth eucontaminate us, transforming our images of ourselves into something closer to who we really are is painful. It is something that our egos, those images of who we are that we protect and project into the world, tend to resist desperately. Eucontamination by the Truth is rarely easy.

BULLSHIT EGOS

The fact is that our egos, the symbols of ourselves in the world, are bullshit—concerned with the impression we make rather than representing Truth. We are deeply invested in this bullshit as we look to others to affirm the reality of these egos against the gnawing real that keeps disturbing them. We are drawn to this bullshit. It's calming, organizing, and

---

18. MacDonald, *Unspoken Sermons*, 26.

containing. The bullshit-me (Paul) helps me sleep better at night, function with certainty in the world, and even write books about the value of (eu)contamination. Psychoanalyst and theorist Heinz Kohut wrote of the concept of selfobjects—external objects, figures, or experiences that one uses for the construction and maintenance of a stable self-structure.[19] We use objects—others—outside ourselves to help structure and stabilize our sense of self—our imaginary ego. Narcissistic personality disorder is the most flagrant example of this as the narcissist lacks a fully stable sense of self and thus leans excessively on the image they portray to others. It's as if they are compensating for a lack of internal stability and sense a need for others' impression of them to feel stable—usually with an exaggerated sense of grandiosity. However, this never works because that image or impression isn't fully true. None of us are ever enough or fully whoever our friends see. We may try hard to be sincere and act authentically, but as Frankfurt writes, "facts about ourselves are not peculiarly solid and resistant to skeptical dissolution. Our natures are, indeed, elusively insubstantial—notoriously less stable and less inherent than the natures of other things. And insofar as this is the case, sincerity itself is bullshit."[20] So we all carry a degree of imposter syndrome, wondering what would happen if everyone ever really found out who we are, because we aren't who they think we are—we aren't our avatars. The disturbing implication of all this is that when we experience a sense of certainty about ourselves, we are actually most fully caught in the web of our own bullshit, often supported by the affirming gazes of those around us. Truth about ourselves is not on the side of certainty. It is a eucontaminant, daring us to risk facing the complexity of who else we are.

To illustrate this, consider the last time you felt a strong feeling like rage. Typically, there is a catalyzing event—something happens to set you off. With feelings like rage, this catalyst often takes on a lot of meaning and becomes the central focus of our ire. If you were in a space where you were able to regulate yourself or find support in someone nearby, hopefully you were able to begin putting words to your feelings—symbolizing what was happening. This may be a good conversation, some hard yelling, drawing, journaling.... What's important to note in this is that most often, when you are calm again, the truth of what was *really going on*, what was really upsetting you, is far more complex than it seemed. Your road

---

19. See Kohut, *How Does Analysis Cure?*
20. See Frankfurt, *On Bullshit*, 66–67.

rage may have been focused exclusively on the person that cut you off in traffic, as you yelled and cursed at them, but your more regulated mind is able to integrate a much more complex picture of the situation—bringing in other frustrations, disappointments, and hurts that had not yet been able to work through your system. So the truth of your rage is anything but the simple fact of a careless driver cutting you off—that's the bullshit reason you tell yourself. The truth is always far more interconnected and messy, insisting against the bullshit that there is always more to the story, more to what's going on.

This idea of bullshit is incredibly important in bringing another dimension to the usual arguments between fact and fiction, truth and falsehood, in today's epistemic debates. Instead of endless arguing about what is and isn't fake news, we need to begin by recognizing the seductive nature of bullshit. Our conscious desire is deeply tied to bullshit and thus resists Truth. We can't help but add our own bullshit to anything we learn.[21] We fit those facts into our meaning system, our imaginary gestalt for the world. The common joke of the man who goes to a psychiatrist because he believes himself to be dead is a great example of this. The psychiatrist asks him if dead people bleed. The two then look through medical texts and come to the conclusion that in fact no, dead people don't bleed. So the doctor then takes a pin and pokes the man's finger. The man looks at his finger, gasps, and says, "Doc, I was wrong . . . dead men *do* bleed!" Our view of the world, our working meaning-making systems, are imaginary and thus resist knowledge. We will twist any facts or experiences to meet our own image. We buy our own bullshit.

Misinformation or fake news now becomes a great example of this in modern times. James Ball writes of how it is much more concerned with bullshit than falsehood.[22] This is because bullshit feels good and we are actually disgusted by truth that would threaten it. When we buy our own (or someone else's) bullshit it usually comes with a relief and positive emotions, along with the risk that we will then go and sell it to everyone else—spreading the good news of whatever we have just learned.[23]

What is significant in all this though is that Truth does not conquer and colonize through this sort of evangelistic fervor. Jesus is Truth but did not come to the world with hard facts to bash over people's heads.

---

21. See McGowan, *Rules of the Game*.

22. See Ball, *Post-Truth*.

23. For a more humorous example of this, consider almost any of the "5 Stages of Owning . . ." videos on YouTube. Most involve some form of evangelism to others.

Jesus came with a power *under* others not *over* them.[24] The good news of the gospel is an invitation to a relationship with the Way, the Truth, and the Life. If you think you have some difficult truth for someone else to hear, be very careful. I (Paul) have spent too many counseling sessions listening to patients tell me all about what they want to say to so-and-so—things that I so desperately wish they could hear about themselves. We are very quick to find specks in other's eyes and very reluctant to look in our own. Eucontaminating Truth is not for someone else. It's what *you* need to hear, but don't want to. It is what disturbs *your* world, not anyone else's. If you are eager to go tell someone about it, you can be almost certain that you are insulating yourself with your own bullshit. One of the easiest defenses against being impacted by something is to pass it on to someone else.

When beauty and goodness are subtracted from truth, we are left with bullshit. "Hard truth" that is weaponized is not truth, but bullshit. When we don't take our own power into account and instead force painful information onto others, we are more likely to gaslight and abuse than love. Truth and discomfort are not a license to harm. Those who use truth in order to do so are simply dressing up their own bullshit with rhetoric. Remember the power of disgust is in the miniscule, the germ. Truth works like yeast, like a gnawing, nagging question, not like a sledgehammer. If you've got the truth to "set people straight," please shut up and spend more time listening, because in all likelihood you're not going to be helpful.

Social media and online algorithms, however, use the allure and simplicity of rage, along with our penchants for bullshit, to harvest more of our attention.[25] We are more likely to keep watching videos that affirm our existing world (often by sparking outrage at what *they* may be doing to threaten things we like) than to consume content that would encourage us to question ourselves. This is one way that social media has led us to more and more insulated echo-chambers.[26]

---

24. See Boyd, *Myth of a Christian Nation*.

25. Always remember that when you're using a "free" website like most social media sites, you are not the customer, but the product. For more on this, see Wu, *Attention Merchants*.

26. For a more nuanced and complex analysis of the interaction between social media algorithms and polarization, see Tufekci, *Twitter and Tear Gas*.

TRUTH IS DISGUSTING

And now we can return to eucontamination and the nature of disgust. Because our egos are so invested in bullshit and our meaning-making systems are built upon that same imaginary construction, disgust is marshaled to defend this facade. Disgust patrols the boundaries of this imagined false world and helps us reject that which would threaten it. We don't just believe certain ideas because they make the most sense. They make the most sense to us because they fit our imaginary worlds, what we already want and believe to be true. This also means we reject contrary ideas not so much because they are false (though that is often the story we tell ourselves), but because they disgust us, threatening to contaminate our nice, established little worlds. Ideas themselves are contaminants. Return to your own social media account for a moment. What happens inside you when you see a post by someone who voted differently than you? What's your physiological response to those ideas? Can you find your own disgust?[27]

Recall that disgust is not normally a response that we are "supposed" to have. It is most effective when it is preconscious or prereflective. It takes work to slow down and recognize it because our egos have usually come up with a quick explanation to justify our revulsion. "I'm blocking them because they are dangerous." "I'm just not at a good place to see that right now." "I don't need to be bombarded by such filth/idiocy/close-mindedness. . . ." Social psychologist Jonathan Haidt uses the metaphor of a rider and an elephant to talk about this process.[28] Following Descartes, Western culture has conceived of humans as predominantly rational, summarized with the Cartesian phrase "I think, therefore I am."[29]

---

27. This far in, we hope that you are beginning to notice the difference between disgust and fear. Boundaries can be healthy as well as harmful and should be implemented with compassion or dispassion rather than with disgust. Further, it is critical that we learn to recognize and distinguish between what threatens harm and what "threatens" (eu)contamination. We will have much more to say about the different implications that this has for those who are marginalized and for those who occupy positions of privilege in ch. 5.

28. See Haidt, *Righteous Mind*.

29. It has become common for those critiquing the particular form of hyper-rationalism which reduces humans to thinking things to cite Descartes's famous *Cogito ergo sum*, and there is some justification for implicating Descartes in the development of that hyper-rationalism. It is worth noting, however, that, when in the *Meditations* Descartes wrote "I think therefore I am," he was not claiming that humans are merely or fundamentally rational or thinking things. In that quote he was merely making the epistemic claim that it is through the fact of his thinking that he was able to know

Our thinking is considered the primary faculty that makes us human. Yet what the research around disgust highlights is just the opposite. Our reasoning is more rationalization justifying our intuition—that is largely directed by disgust. Haidt writes that our intuition is an elephant and our reasoning the rider. The rider may try to guide the elephant, but in the end it will go where it will. Our hope is to help them work well together. Thinking and reasoning is incredibly important, but wisdom comes from recognizing its shortcomings. As we have argued throughout this book, and will give some practical exercises and recommendations for in chapter 9, we must take our disgust into account before we can have more trust in our reasoning. We must first trust in something greater than our understanding and somatic reactions, without ignoring, denying, or dismissing them. We must hope in a eucontaminant.

The limitations of a mechanistic, analytic way of viewing the world is also highlighted in more recent neuroscience. Psychiatrist and theorist Ian McGilchrist highlights the dominance of left hemisphere brain functioning over the right in modern Western societies.[30] The left hemisphere helps with categorizing and organizing. It deals with the concrete. The right is more holistic, big picture, intuitive, empathic, and creative. The Western emphasis on the left hemisphere leads to an over-reliance on an approach to reality that prioritizes control and mastery over integrating. Western thought encourages dissection over connection, but that is more culture than truth. McGilchrist actually argues that while both hemispheres are important and useful, a healthier and more optimal relationship between the two places the right as the "master." To put all this into Haidt's metaphor, the right hemisphere is the elephant, while the left is the rider. The world is far bigger and more complex than our language and categories can comprehend. We require a more intuitive and creative framework to experience reality than our linguistic taxonomies could handle. Those categories help us make sense of the whole but can never contain it; as Shakespeare wrote, "there are more things in heaven and earth, Horatio, than are dreamt of in your philosophy."[31]

(for Descartes that meant that he was unable to doubt) that he exists. The claim is not "thinking makes me exist," it is "the fact of my thinking makes me unable to doubt my own existence because doubting is itself a form of thinking and therefore even doubting ends up reinforcing my certainty that I exist."

30. See McGilchrist, *Master and His Emissary*.
31. Shakespeare, *Hamlet*, 1.5.167.

Very few would argue that truth isn't important. The arguments and struggle come less from affirming the importance of truth than from being able to recognize truth. "What is truth?" as Pilate asked the one who is Truth, failing to recognize what (who) he was attempting to affirm. So far in this book, we have challenged many of the standard avenues of accessing truth, though hopefully not destroyed them. Having drawbacks to something doesn't mean it's bad, just that it is limited. We are not saying reason is unhelpful—we do need the left hemisphere of our brain. The ridiculousness of any suggestion to the contrary is evident in our very use of reason in this book. Facts and a shared understanding of reality are fundamental aspects of community. What we are saying is that, while important, they are not *enough*. Truth is bigger, grander, more awe-inspiring than any syllogism we could utter. We offer a corrective to an overemphasis, not a replacement. We are arguing for the significance of attaching the playful question "what if there's more?" to the end of every sense of understanding. So it is here that we must begin looking for ways beyond mere reason to encounter Truth.

KNOWING TRUTH

In John 8, Jesus has a lot to say about Truth. Just before his famous line that "the truth will set you free" (v. 32), Jesus says, "If you abide in my word, you are truly my disciples, and you will know the truth" (vv. 31b, 32a). The condition he sets for knowing the truth is that we abide in his word. "Abiding" here is significant because it means a lot more than just memorization, as many Sunday school children were taught. Abiding links us to living and action as well as meditating and steeping. Jesus is asking his followers to internalize, metabolize his teachings so that they will know what is true. This is not the work of flow charts, but of the lover who is able to tell if their beloved is the one texting them or not. There's a familiarity that is born out of experience, relationship, and time rather than discrete factors. If we continue to live in and internalize Christ and his Word, we are shaped in such a way that we can begin to differentiate truth and bullshit. Perhaps a helpful way to highlight this can be found in Turkish—a language we both grew up speaking. Turkish uses two different words that are often translated into the English word "knowing"— *tanımak* and *bilmek*. Bilmek corresponds to a form of knowing that is generally familiar to academic studies. Bilmek is about knowledge, data, facts, objects—the kind of knowing a computer can do. Tanımak on the other hand is far more relational. Tanımak is about persons not things. It is the kind of knowing present in how we know our friends, partners, neighbors, or enemies. It involves a form of intimacy. If we are to know Christ as Truth, we are not simply being invited into a form of knowing about as in *bilmek* but into a relational *tanımak*. Knowing Truth like we know our friends and families.

Developmentally speaking, we learn to experience the world and develop a sense of ourselves in it through relationships. Connections with early caregivers provide the blueprint for our encounter with a world and the development of a mind. Yet when there is an absence of what psychoanalyst Donald Winnicott calls a "good enough" parent figure in the infant's life, they are left without a full capacity to reflect on their internal world, or a stable enough sense of self to facilitate a robust encounter with a rich emotional reality.[32] Instead they are left with facts without meaning. Their N-O parent is replaced with a K-N-O-W parent as an answer to the absence. This KNOWing (bilmek) becomes a vice-grip on concreteness and often an obsession with knowledge as a futile bulwark to weather a complex reality that continues to insist into their world. Instead of grieving the lack (the no-parent) so as to learn to tanımak with Truth, we try to replace them with a knowing (bilmek), a certainty that hides from Truth.[33]

As humans in time, we are constantly being formed. Each moment, every breath, continues to shape who we are. The pursuit of virtuous living is the conscious will to have some agency in the manner—to direct our formation in such a way that we cultivate a character of virtue.[34] In this chapter, we are arguing that followers of Christ are to be formed and transformed by Truth, not malformed by information. The word "information" originally comes from the concept of forming/shaping ideas. However, in our information age, the agency on the part of who is shaping and who is being shaped seems to have reversed. Information has taken over shaping us into collections of data, reducing us to our bullshit egos—facts about us instead of the Truths of who we are—as we have ceded control to big data. Thus, our information has begun a process of malformation. We are less human, less whole, less alive while

---

32. See Winnicott, *Home Is Where We Start From*, 10.

33. For more on the N-O parent vs. the K-N-O-W parent, see Day, "Birthing of a Mind."

34. See Hoard and Suttle, "Lacanian Virtue Ethics?"

seemingly knowing so much more. In the *Phaedrus* dialogue, Socrates is recorded as having said that information and writing will give people "not truth, but only the semblance of truth; they will be hearers of many things and will have learned nothing; they will appear to be omniscient and will generally know nothing; they will be tiresome company having the show of wisdom without the reality"[35]—not a bad description of modern political discourse. Truth, conversely, is less about (though not antagonistic to) information and more about transformation. Truth woos us from the shadows to take agency in how we are forming so as not to be malformed, but reformed in Christ. Truth does not forsake wisdom, beauty, or goodness.

However, as much great scholarship around the limitations of our epistemology has shown, much of what we collectively or individually construe as reality is incomplete.[36] While science, reason, and our five senses have proven exceptionally useful, they are not able to capture Truth. Cognitive scientist Donald Hoffman goes so far as to argue that we have evolved more to perceive what he calls "fitness" than reality, writing that "natural selection favors perceptions that hide the truth and guide useful action."[37] As such, humans over the millennia have cultivated many more paths to knowing and experiencing a reality beyond our natural perceptions and reason, and post-enlightenment modernity is much more the aberration in its restricted view of Truth and reality. It is the inheritors of the enlightenment that have tried to restrict Truth. Most of humanity has long experienced it far more expansively.

THE POETRY OF TRUTH

To that end, poetry could be—and we think ought to be—considered as a fourth term in Frankfurt's bullshit model. Poetry—or art—does not deal with factual statements, but points to a truth that is beyond, different, greater than our given shared reality. Consider the question: what *is the truth of a poem?* There is a story that T. S. Eliot was once asked in an interview if he wouldn't mind explaining the meaning of his poem *The Wasteland*; in response he is said to have leaned back and begun reciting *The Wasteland*. Apocryphal or not, the point of the story should be clear:

---

35. See Plato, *Phaedrus*, 58.
36. See Meek, *Loving to Know*.
37. See Hoffman, *Case Against Reality*, 10.

poetry—art—has a capacity to convey meaning which simply cannot be reduced to rational prose. Art points beyond the facticity of its own medium at Truths that can never quite be expressed as a list of information.[38] As a form of art, poetry ignites an impression and experience in the listener and is thus reminiscent of bullshit. Yet it does so shamelessly, explicitly embracing its own medium and with no pretension at scientific accuracy. It is very clearly not a collection of factual statements, but it is an expression of truth. As theologian John Caputo writes, "to experience a work of art is to enter a world of truth, the truth of a world."[39]

Certainly, poetry and art can be used in the service of propaganda. They are powerful tools that are capable of influencing us in profound ways, including manipulative and controlling ways. When this happens, the poetry is reduced to bullshit—to creating an impression—and loses its place as art. Propaganda begins with a message, art begins with Truth. True art is something one is lost in, not something that directs you to a particular place. Art is on the side of Truth—wild and untamed—propaganda has a specific destination. Said twice more; Art is on the side of Beauty where propaganda is interested in prettiness, or power, or some other aesthetic experience; Art is on the side of Goodness where propaganda attempts to drum up sympathy for some particular morality schema.

All this comes back to say that if we are to pursue Truth, we are going to be pursuing something destabilizing, uncertain, and disturbing. Truth does not leave us comfortable—bullshit does; bullshit is reassuring while Truth is uncanny, numinous, and dangerous. The Truth of who we are is far more than we can imagine and far less comforting than we could hope. Truth nags instead of soothes. It spooks and haunts us, keeping us at night whispering, "what if there's more?"

To return to Jesus and Pilate for a moment, the discussion points to a relationship with truth and reality that seems to escape Pilate. Jesus doesn't answer Pilate in a straightforward way when asked if he's a king. Jesus accepts that he is called a King, but then talks of fact and truth. "You say that I am a king. In fact, the reason I was born and came into the world is to testify to the truth. Everyone on the side of truth listens to me." The fact of Jesus's birth points to a bigger truth—something he has come to testify to. So, facts are one element, like Jesus's literal birth, but truth is of a different nature. Truth is now something that has a "side."

---

38. For a full dive into the meaning making and communicating power of poetry consider reading *Poetic Diction* by Owen Barfield.

39. Caputo, *Hermeneutics*, 91.

It is a direction, an ideal, not an object. Facts are things; Truth is alive. Pilate, however, has no category for what Jesus is saying. His is a world of bullshit, of power games and control. He then demonstrates his allegiance to bullshit against truth and releases a known criminal, condemning the innocent—so much for justice.

When we reduce Truth to data or fact, we, like Pilate, become lost in bullshit because facts will be anchored—made sense of—by something. If we have no relationship to a living Truth beyond our imaginations, we are left with only our existing ideological grid. We are trapped in our own meaning-making systems. Remember the easiest and first one that we deceive is ourselves. A commitment and love of Truth as a north star guide—disruptive eucontamination—is our only hope out of bullshit. That is not to say that facts and details aren't important, but that they are insufficient. The world is so much bigger than data. Truth refuses to be condensed to mere propositions. Truth is alive.

And of course, this makes things complicated for us on so many levels. We in the American church are generally interested in formulas and "laws of religion." We want to be told what to do, and what to believe in order to be a good person, to be a part of our spiritual community. And therein lies the issue—we *want*. Desire precedes knowledge. Until we can learn to laugh with our limitations—at how we are so caught in our own desire—and humbly accept our inability to ever see things clearly, we will continue to take on God's role and create a world in our own image.

5

Prophetic Heresies

This, then, is the work of the churches: to instill a false interpretation of Christ's teaching into men, and to prevent a true interpretation of it for the majority of so-called believers.

—Tolstoy, *The Kingdom of God Is Within You*

Matt Warner was an associate professor of communications at Grace College in Winona Lake, Indiana—my (Paul's) alma mater. The school is a small, Christian liberal arts school denominationally associated with the Charis fellowship (previously the Grace Brethren Fellowship). Matt began his first year at the school after having uprooted his family from Detroit. Together, he and his wife took a 60 percent reduction in income in order for him to work at Grace. Matt was eager to join the community and support the mission of the school. He quickly threw himself into the new job, working to connect with professors outside of his department, attending school events, and upon request, working as a faculty mentor to new students.[1]

---

1. I (Paul) am personally very appreciative of Matt's permission to share his story in this text. Being an alumnus of the school—and specifically of the communication department—I was very disturbed by the story and events.

However, everything changed in October when he learned that a group of local moms were calling for his firing. Evan Kilgore, a former Grace employee, had shared screenshots of Matt's past tweets where he had written things like "I support gay marriage," "My pronouns are he/they," and "When Christendom is conservative it ceases to be transformative." Kilgore told Religion News Service that he had posted these screenshots because "parents might want to be aware of somebody who has influence over their child with these beliefs."[2] The complaints reached the school's board and president's office eventually leading to the school not renewing Matt's contract. In Matt's words, he was branded "a godless marxist who snuck into Grace College to send the kids to hell."[3] The public outcry was enough to end his employment.

What is perhaps not as apparent to anyone outside of American higher education is that Matt was hired as an associate professor, and so should have had a level of security in his position. Professor rankings in most schools go assistant professor, associate professor, and then full professor. Moving from one rank to another is a big deal in academia and comes with a number of significant benefits, including job security via tenure. In many schools, the move from assistant to associate professor happens when someone earns tenure. They are no longer at the entry-level position, but have built trust. Moving up in ranks involves more than just time spent in the job (though it is different at every institution). Typically, it also requires demonstrating excellence in teaching, as well as research, scholarship, and service to the field and institution. Matt had done all that.

Matt said that when he was hired at Grace, he was assured that while Grace did not offer traditional tenure, they did have "tenure lite," and that he should not be concerned about his academic freedom—a fundamental concept to higher education.[4] Moreover, when he was hired, the school was aware of Matt's positions and beliefs. He also signed all of the documents required by faculty of the school, including a lifestyle commitment. He did not break any official rules nor did he violate his contract or the faculty handbook in any way. It was only when his positions that conflicted with an *implicit* expectation for faculty were made public that they became a problem. It wasn't the reality of who Matt is and

---

2. See Post, "Grace College Professor Ousted," para. 7.
3. See Lester and Malm, "112: Dr. Matt Warner Was Canceled."
4. See Finkin and Post, *For the Common Good*.

what he believes, but the image of the school, and the impact his presence and public statements had on it that mattered.[5] Like individual subjects, institutions create images of themselves in the world and then work hard to suppress the truth of who they are from threatening that image.

In this chapter, we want to build on what we said in chapter 4 about the nature of Truth and begin looking at its application to the social and institutional level. This will involve diving into the complexity of our social identities and how they are formed and maintained by our disgust mechanisms, as well their limitations and value. We will also explore more psychoanalytic theory around the way discourse shapes our relational and interpersonal worlds. Guiding us throughout the chapter is the question, "How might Truth act as a (eu)contaminant to the community and why is it so resisted?"

IDENTITY

Identity is where the individual subject and the social order meet. In having an identity, I am now recognized by the social authority (the nebulous *they*) and feel as if I exist—I am recognized. Like developing an imaginary ego, identity offers me an avatar in the world, a way to be experienced and understood by others. As such, identity involves some form of compromise with the given social authority or ruling ideology—it originates externally. When we are speaking of identity we are also working with the categories, limits, and expectations of the language and culture in which we find ourselves. By identifying myself (Paul) as a white, cisgender man, I am fitting into established categories for you, the reader. Those terms describe aspects of myself within the given framework of our day and our culture. They allow me to be part of the social order.[6]

Significantly, there is no way to identify that is not somehow part of the broader symbolic, social order. Even identities that lie outside the typical social norms, simply by being identities, are within the order now. Identifying is a forced choice we all make for the possibility of engaging others in any way. The most basic unit of identity, one's name, allows one to be located within the social matrix.

This social order, though, is not an essential part of you—it isn't who you *really* are. It is the cultural interpretation of you that allows you to

---

5. See Lester and Malm, "112: Dr. Matt Warner Was Canceled."
6. For more on identity and the social order, see McGowan, *Universality*.

think about yourself and allows others to think about you in the context of society. Your identity labels are external to you and link you with others, but that also means that they do not fully map you or map onto you. One's last name in US culture is a great example of this. Billie and I are both "Hoards." I am Paul, she is Billie, but we are both "Hoard." Our first names provide some individual flavor as to what kind of Hoard we each are, but our last name—given to us by our parents—stamps us within the social order. I can be a good Hoard or a bad Hoard—a lazy or successful Hoard—but I am still being judged as to how I conform to whatever a "Hoard" is supposed to be. Growing up, I had an internalized idea of what a Hoard was and I was acutely aware of the distance between myself and it. In my mind, Billie was the epitome of what a Hoard was supposed to be. She was quick-witted, loved trying new foods, enjoyed long conversations, debated philosophy, and appreciated Gilbert and Sullivan. I, on the other hand, felt naive, short-tempered, and picky around food, and could never keep up with the conversation at the dinner table. I always felt that my distance from Billie, the epitome of Hoard, was a mark of my failure to be one—a source of shame I worked hard to hide by always trying to be more like her. As I grew up and had many more conversations with her—and then spent some long years in my own analysis—I realized Billie doesn't feel like she's a true Hoard either! Long conversations into the night with all of our siblings revealed how each and every one of my family members feels their distance from the center, from being a "true Hoard." One part of what it means to be a Hoard must be to feel like one isn't enough of a Hoard.[7] At the same time, because each of us were Hoards, our differences from that "true Hoard" ideal each served to both broaden and further concretize "Hoard-ness" for the rest of us. Collectively *we* constituted the definition of "a Hoard" and yet individually each of us failed to live up to the aggregate definition and felt as though some other member of our family must be more truly Hoard than we were.

This dynamic is not unique to our family. In fact, it's a universal aspect of identity. We all share in the failure of our identities. However you identify, you can never possibly be fully that because that category was made external to you—it was imposed. We are often confused here and can quickly get lost in the idea that our identities *are* us, but closer inspection continues to reveal that none of us actually belong. As psychoanalytic philosopher Todd McGowan writes:

---

7. Yes, I've been through middle school and know what that sentence sounds like.

> Because identity operates in this nebulous realm between an imposed necessity and a conscious choice, we mistakenly believe that it is our essence. The mystery associated with identity—it is neither inherent nor chosen, or both inherent and chosen—leads us to interpret it as who we are rather than just what we are.[8]

So, identity is both what we are and who we are not. It is something imposed on us from the outside so that we can engage with others. This doesn't make it inherently good or bad, evil or liberating. It does mean that identity is never complete. Like with your individual ego (which is made up of your internalized identities) your identities are not the full story of who you are. However, much more so than with your imaginary ego, your identities are also tied to a broader social world. Earlier, I (Paul) identified as a white, cisgender male. What you imagine each of those categories to mean now intimately impacts how you think of me. I am tied to those categories and the other individuals who identify with them.

This is an important point that is worth unpacking. It brings up two different processes involved in identity formation: imagining and marking. Imagining, as we are using it here, involves an internal act of seeing oneself. Marking,[9] on the other hand, comes from the outside and speaks to the impact that the gaze of others has on you. I have always existed within a white, cisgender male body. As such, I have imagined myself that way and have been marked as such everywhere I've gone in the world.[10] Those markings, though, are not neutral. They have tinted every social interaction I have ever had. Later on, we'll talk much more about the impact of social location and privilege on identities and self-image, but

---

8. McGowan, *Universality*, 150.

9. Throughout this book wherever we use the language of "marked" we will be using it in reference to Serano's development in her book *Sexed Up* of Ervin Goffman's work. As she explains: "Human beings are comprised of countless different traits—aspects of our physical bodies, personalities, histories, social roles, experiences, behaviors, interests, desires, tendencies, and so forth. Most of these traits are 'unmarked' in our eyes, meaning that we view them as mundane, unsurprising, and not particularly noteworthy; they seem 'normal' to us and thus are taken for granted. In contrast, other traits are 'marked'—they strike us as 'remarkable' for some reason or other. What makes a trait marked? Well, it depends entirely on the individual, their background, and other situational factors."

10. We say here that Paul is marked as cis because that is what is happening. However it should be noted that most people do not think of cis-ness at all, rather they think in terms of "normal" (unmarked) and "abnormal" (marked). When given cause to reflect on the question, they would default to the assumption that Paul is cis because he does not bear any "marks" of non-cis-ness.

for now I want to stress that they exist and have shaped who I imagine myself to be and how I have been perceived.[11]

These two processes, marking and imagining, exist in constant, mutual interaction and reinforcement. Changing one unilaterally never works. The progressive, white activist who has suddenly become aware of structural racism and so believes they have transcended it, is the one who has now most firmly internalized their own racism unconsciously, and insulated themselves from recognizing it.[12]

Yet many who share similar identities to mine are resistant to this connection between the individual and the group. Whiteness, patriarchy, and capitalism are powerful ideological forces in today's world that work to essentialize and entrench an individualistic view of the self (among other things). Each of those ideologies requires particular individuals who resist seeing their social and communal connections. My desire to be a unique and special individual is inextricably tied (though not fully reducible to) the ideologies of whiteness, patriarchy, and capitalism. This is why in contemporary American culture it can be such a beautiful act of subversive eucontamination to acknowledge our connectivity.[13]

The truth of our relational selves, we argue, goes so far as to be disgusting to Western culture because it poses such a threat to these individualist ideologies and social orders. Here we come to another paradox and dilemma around identity. We are not rejecting identity and saying everyone is just people—a horrific denial of the real impact of the necessary identities we all inhabit in order to engage with each other—neither are we embracing identities so that each of us can find our own freedom in the "right" one. Truth instead walks us through a process of first acknowledging the identities we have been marked with and have used to imagine ourselves, and then embracing the incompleteness of each of those identities. I (Paul) am a white cisgender male. So, yes, I have been marked by whiteness, cis-privilege, patriarchy, and more. However, I am not simply those identities. Freedom for me is found in first acknowledging each of those identities as one among many possible alternatives (denaturalizing or queering them) and then finding the limitations of each

---

11. See Hoard, "Beyond Fragility."

12. For more on identity and whiteness in particular, see Hoard, "Beyond Fragility"; and Hoard and Bland, "'How Am I Responsible?'"

13. For more on ideology and how we are all caught in it, see McGowan, *Universality*; McGowan, *Capitalism and Desire*; and Žižek, *Sublime Object*.

one—my own alienation from each identity—so as to discover common (though not the same) ground with others.

I (Billie) on the other hand am—among other identities—a member of the queer community. You may have observed that many members of LGBTQIA+ and other communities readily identify ourselves as members of our communities and that we seem—as in fact we generally do—to gain benefits like solidarity, support, and a particular sort of situated understanding of various social dynamics as a result of our membership in these identity groups. In chapters 6 and 7, we will spend more time exploring how some of our society's more marked identities (particularly queer and black identities) exist subversively, challenging and working to decenter unmarked identities like whiteness, cis-ness, and straightness. The solidarity among members of these marked identities is multifaceted in purpose and function, but one of its impacts is to visibly challenge the illusion of the unique individual. Merely by showing up in the world as a proud queer woman, I remind cishet people that they are members in cisgender and heterosexual communities of identity—that their social situation exists, and impacts their lives, choices, and horizons.

In chapter 2, we described the horrific impact of an over-emphasis on a particular "Christian" identity that has spread through the white, American church: Christian Nationalism. This is a form of group identity that is built around the rejection and scapegoating of outsiders as contaminants. When a group over-identifies with its particularities, it inevitably becomes oppressive.[14] This is the basis of racism, sexism, and nationalism: an embrace of my particularities over yours (typically around externally visible characteristics). What our current discussion around identity adds to this is an explanation of how all of these movements inherently lead to scapegoating. Because none of us fully belong to our own identities, we all carry a degree of fear that our not-belonging will be exposed. So to protect against the feared rejection of being found out that we don't fully belong, we are often tempted to find someone else with more obvious or noticeable differences and join the mob in rejecting them—hoping to obscure our own contamination of the group identity with our neighbor's "greater" contamination. In this way, particular identities become centered around what they reject more than what they are, specifically because they are all trying to convince themselves and one another that they really belong. This is the essence of the scapegoating mechanism and what McGowan

---

14. See McGowan, *Universality*.

calls "right-wing enjoyment."[15] To create cohesion within the group, we ostracize, excommunicate, or violently suppress an innocent other. Nothing seems to bring people together like hate.[16]

Conversely, when we attempt to tear down all barriers—all particular identities—we end up with no explicit ways of belonging and thus leave nothing but the implicit, unconscious group processes to patrol the borders. The horrors of the "colorblind" approach to racism by white people are a great example of this.[17] Instead of recognizing and wrestling to dismantle systemic and individual racism and oppression, white people were encouraged to act as if they didn't see race. This meant that the existing power dynamics and systemic forms of oppression were left to run rampant and continue harming, while the individual white people could continue to imagine themselves as "good people." Pretending not to see what is there does not make it go away. By focusing on particular, highly visible expressions of racism, they made their own racism invisible to themselves.

This is the group out-working of image management over the eucontaminant of Truth. As long as we look good to a real or imagined outside observer (anti-racist, loving, etc. . . .), then the truth of how we actually behave doesn't matter. Image will always be in tension with Truth.

DISGUSTING IDENTITY

This is where disgust comes into play. Disgust does not just patrol our individual boundaries; it also works on the communal level. Some ideas—like the distance we all feel from our particular identities—can feel destabilizing to a group. As such, like a human body, communities will empower their own social immune systems to eject the contaminant. This is often seen today in the call to protect children from schools and "bad" teaching.

Returning to Matt and his story at Grace, we can now add some more layers to our analysis of what happened. Grace College is a Christian liberal arts school. This already has some degree of contradiction baked into it. The classic liberal arts education is one that encourages

---

15. McGowan, *Enjoyment*, 6.

16. For more on scapegoating and group cohesion, see McGowan, *Enjoyment*; and Girard, *Things Hidden*.

17. See Menakem, *Quaking*.

critical thinking from broad perspectives, utilizing an interdisciplinary approach. It does not, in theory, foster adherence to a particular worldview. Christian education, on the other hand, is often more concerned with protecting and shaping students into a specific type of person.[18] This means that Christian liberal arts schools will necessarily carry a degree of contradiction within them. Are they protecting students from the outside world to make sure they are raised with a "Christian" education, or are they exposing them to the marketplace of ideas and the best form of every argument, trusting the students' own critical thinking to guide their development?

Christian schools are not the only schools that face this tension. Each institution has its own constituents and concerned parents. Every school has an image in the world they are trying to live up to.[19] As such, critical thinking and a liberal arts education is a threat to every institution. This is where tenure originally came from. Academic freedom and protection from reprisal and suppression from administration was recognized early on in the academy as a necessary condition of a liberal education. If professors were to do good scholarship and pursue truth, they had to enjoy a high degree of protection from the impulse of the institution to reject elements it experiences as threatening its image.[20] Truth has always been opposed to the interests of institutions.

One of the more sinister aspects of Matt's story is the way that the image of academic freedom is being maintained by the school, while the truth of the matter is far less open. Post's article quotes Grace employees and faculty talking about their fear and the cultivation of a "low-trust culture" because of how Matt's situation was handled. Here again, the image trumps the real. The predictable result is less trust and more fear about who is next—the very insecurity inherent in any group, because none of us can ever fully belong. When we take matters into our own hands to protect an ideal or image, trust itself is eroded in other areas. Who else will be sacrificed on the altar of the image of the school? When the explicit rules have already been shown to be ineffective guards, what security remains in the community? An over-investment in image leaves everyone vulnerable to becoming the next contaminating scapegoat because none of us ever fully belong.

---

18. See Noll, *Scandal*.
19. See Finkin and Post, *For the Common Good*.
20. For more on academic freedom, see Finkin and Post, *For the Common Good*.

Don't be lulled into thinking this is only a problem of the academy. Truth is a threat to every institution and every group. While not everyone is involved in the academy, social media is another field where these scapegoating dynamics are on full display. Perhaps the most glaring example can be seen in the near-ubiquitous video essays with titles in the form of "X DESTROYS Y." Occasionally these turn out to be thoughtful video essays carefully examining and responding to a well made argument on the other side where the vlogger merely succumbed to the lure of tested and effective click-bait titling in order to promote their work. Occasionally. More often though, content with DESTROYS, DEMOLISHES, etc in the title turn out to be little more than partisan talking points regurgitated in response to a straw-man summary of a cherry picked argument by one of *their* experts.

I (Billie) recently encountered a YouTube vlog from a creator who calls himself Brother Maverick and surrounds himself with crusader and gun imagery communicating a clear affiliation with the contemporary Christian Nationalist movement. The video in question is titled "Gay Pastor Brandan Robertson Gets Absolutely DISMANTLED by Voddie Baucham"[21] and it is helpfully illustrative of the dynamic we are describing here. Despite the title's claim, the video spends less than a minute on any claim of Robertson himself and is primarily ten minutes of the host watching and commenting on a Voddie Baucham sermon which condemns homosexuality with fairly boilerplate non-affirming talking points. Near the halfway mark, Brother Maverick summarizes in a few phrases the argument he tells us Robertson is making and offers one or two counterclaims before returning to the Baucham sermon and ends by again summarizing Baucham's points. There is nothing original about any of the content of this video either in the representation of Robertson, the Baucham sermon, or in the host's summary of "the debate." But the video was nearing half a million views at the time of this writing; so what is it doing?

We would posit that this genre of content exists primarily as a form of catharsis and disgust boundary reinforcement for those who already share a particular partisan identity with the content creator. The formula is, in fact, straightforward: Step 1 (Invite)—invite the viewer to an experience of successful expulsion of some threatening truth claim from "the other side." Step 2 (Trigger)—expose them to enough of that truth claim

---

21. Brother Maverick, "Gay Pastor Brandan Robertson."

to trigger a sympathetic reaction (that sense of danger and the threat of having one's understanding of reality contaminated by a truth claim which threatens its structure). Step 3 (Nausea)—provide sufficient counter arguments or a strong enough counter-narrative to satisfy the audience that Step 4 will feel justified. Step 4 (Purge)—conclude with a declaration that the threatening contaminant is DESTROYED/DEMOLISHED/DISMANTLED by Step 3. The whole process allows the audience the catharsis of enacting the purgation of threatening truth claims in the safety of an environment where they will not have to come into contact with anyone actually defending, embodying, or propounding those truth claims in a way that might cause them to seem stronger than the audience is willing for them to be. The effect of course is to strengthen both the audience's disgust response to the threatening truth-claim and to increase the audience's propensity to engage in the violent expulsion (the purgation) of any vectors of that truth claim. Vaccines "train" our immune system to reject a virus by introducing us to an inert (dead) simulacrum of the virus thereby building up our capacity to rapidly overwhelm and expel any live virus that we might encounter in the future. X DESTROYS Y videos similarly use familiar straw-man or simplified versions of a truth claim to train our mental and spiritual immune system to rapidly react and violently expel any similar live truth claim we might encounter in the future. The consumer is "rewarded" with both an increased degree of partisanship and a decreased critical capacity. Significantly, the consumer has also remained completely passive throughout. Nothing was asked of them in the entire experience. They were taken through the steps as if they were facing a full dose of reality, but instead were carefully insulated by the context of the video, the host's commentary, and knowledge that it would end "happily" for their egos—they knew the "truth" from the beginning.

And this is the key point to highlight: Truth is treated like a stable, known commodity in these situations, not a wild and disturbing haunting. When groups are fooled into protecting a "truth" instead of pursuing Truth, they inevitably end up circling wagons and denying reality. When this certainty about the truth is taken up by believers, disastrous results ensue. Tolstoy wrote the following condemnation of churches as bulwarks protecting against Christ teaching:

> [A] church is a body of men who claim for themselves they are in complete and sole possession of the truth. And these bodies, having in course of time, aided by the support of the temporal authorities, developed into powerful institutions, have been the

> principal obstacles to the diffusion of a true comprehension of the teaching of Christ.
> It could not be otherwise. The chief peculiarity which distinguished Christ's teaching from previous religions consisted in the fact that those who accepted it strove ever more and more to comprehend and realize its teaching. But the Church doctrine asserted its own complete and final comprehension and realization of it.[22]

In other words, the assertion that one group knows the truth, when combined with power, becomes the primary obstacle to the teaching of Christ. Our certainty is the largest obstacle to learning and transformation. The hardest student to teach is the one who believes they already know. How many churches preach a certainty about their beliefs of the gospel instead of yearning for Truth? This shouldn't be surprising. Remember, we are all a bit like Narcissus, in love with our own image. It feels good to hold on to certainty. It feels safe to have our beliefs affirmed. It is comforting to be reminded that *we* know while *they* are lost. We love our own bullshit and work to protect it from the truth that disturbs it—be that personal or collective.

Let us stop here and say that one more time; it is worth repeating. Bullshit feels good and we are disgusted by truth that would threaten it. If this is shocking (and we think it ought to be), notice that it parallels the words of Jesus to Nicodemus regarding his own presence on the earth. In John 3, Nicodemus has come to Jesus under cover of night and is questioning Jesus regarding his identity and his role in the world. It is in Jesus's answer that we find what is probably his most quoted line, "For God so loved the world that he gave his only Son, so that everyone who believes in him may not perish but may have eternal life" (v. 16 NRSVUE), and lest we settle for short impressions that only reinforce our bullshit imagination of reality, let us return to verses 17–21. Jesus explains John 3:16 to Nicodemus:

> Indeed, God did not send the Son into the world to condemn the world but in order that the world might be saved through him. Those who believe in him are not condemned, but those who do not believe are condemned already because they have not believed in the name of the only Son of God. And this is the judgment, that the light has come into the world, and people loved darkness rather than light because their deeds were evil.

---

22. See Tolstoy, *Kingdom of God Is Within You*, 38–39.

> For all who do evil hate the light and do not come to the light, so that their deeds may not be exposed. But those who do what is true come to the light, so that it may be clearly seen that their deeds have been done in God. (NRSVUE)

To "love darkness rather than light" ought to strike us just as bizarre as the idea of using disgust to defend our bullshit from being contaminated by the truth does. But of course they are very nearly the same thing. Jesus is observing to Nicodemus here that humanity is dedicated to the preservation of our bullshit, the bullshit we use to hide our own cruelties, dishonesties, and structural injustices from ourselves. Because "our deeds are wicked," we cover them over to ourselves and to others with bullshit, re-narrating our imagined realities—often with the help of facts and data—with a softening layer of bullshit. So when the Real comes along, when we are exposed to the Light, to the irruption of Truth into our lives, we are confronted with a disgust reaction. This Truth threatens to eucontaminate our imagined realities. If we do not disrupt our visceral disgust reaction, that Truth will be rejected/ejected. It comes down to faith, to trust.

TRUST AND TRUTH

Of course it comes down to trust because Truth is not an abstract set of propositions we can depend on; Truth is more (though not less) than that. Truth is a person: God. And to have faith is to trust in the One who is Truth; as Jesus tells his followers three chapters later in John 6:29: "This is the work of God, that you believe in him whom he has sent" (NRSVUE). When our bullshit lives are confronted with the Truth, we face the choice between acceding to our disgust reaction and trusting the One who is Truth to let that Truth eucontaminate our bullshit realities. And this is terrifying; it requires that we exchange certainty for doubt. Paradoxically clinging to certainty is the rejection of truth, allowing ourselves to be governed by our spiritual gag reflexes. That is what Jesus describes to Nicodemus as "God's judgment." To be left to our little bullshit worlds desperately producing and smearing more bullshit over any cracks with the temerity to let in a little light.

And we know that to be eucontaminated by Truth is not easy. We hold fidelity to the Truth to be a high virtue. But our language and our stories, our whole world, is also heavy with the recognition that the Truth can be severe. Too often we talk about "hard truths" when we are really selling our own bullshit. What passes as hard truth for someone else never seems to be hard for me or my community. It's always hard for them—never in the first person, only in the second or third. The one who takes a posture of being eucontaminated by Truth is not a person who is willing to be scorned by others for telling them what's up. It is a person willing to be impacted by others, open to Truth wherever she may be hiding, pursuing a God who insists from the margins and haunts our comforts. Truth rarely *erupts* out of us and onto others, showering down with power and destruction, but *irrupts* into our own world, destabilizing and disturbing.

In Christianity we speak of prophetic voices or, in Walter Brueggemann's idiom, of *prophetic imagination*.[23] Within the text of Scripture, we encounter both false and true prophets: those whom we might characterize as those who reinforce our bullshit with bullshit confidence (false prophets) and those who eucontaminate our world with Truth. False prophets may say things that we find uncomfortable. They may well demand that we give, serve, or obey *more*; they may strike us as severe or demanding, but at the end of the day their words are not marked by the necessity for any profound transformation of our lives. In contrast to that, the prophetic voices in the Bible and prophetic speech today are marked by suffering. As Brueggemann explains, the prophetic imagination is informed by compassion for and empathy towards the unjust state of the marginalized.[24] The suffering of the oppressed has irrupted successfully into the world of the Prophet and, when she speaks, the greater Truth of her re-structured world insists upon our own bullshit existence. Beyond uncomfortable; prophetic utterance insists on the death of our reality in preparation for its re-structuring around what the Truth conveys. True prophetic language confronts us with the suffering of the other and insists that we break open our insulated reality and accept that suffering into ourselves, first as empathy and compassion, but then in the form of action and a fresh imagination of the world. True prophecy invites us into life through the death of our old comfortable social realities. In Brueggemann's words:

> The cross is the ultimate metaphor of prophetic criticism because it means the end of the old consciousness that brings death on everyone. The crucifixion articulates God's odd freedom, his strange justice, and his peculiar power. It is this *freedom* (read

---

23. Brueggemann, *Prophetic Imagination*.
24. Brueggemann, *Prophetic Imagination*, 85–88.

religion of God's freedom), *justice* (read economics of sharing), and *power* (read politics of justice) which break the power of the old age and bring it to death. Without the cross, prophetic imagination will likely be as strident and as destructive as that which it criticizes. The cross is the assurance that effective prophetic criticism is done not by an outsider but always by one who must embrace the grief, enter into the death, and know the pain of the criticized one.[25]

In John 8, (after the famous line about truth setting people free) Jesus brings some harsh language for those who reject his teaching: "Why do you not understand what I say? It is because you cannot bear to hear my word" (v. 43). This point is important as it raises the question of why they could not bear to hear Truth. The conversation in the chapter is all about identity. Those who can hear the Truth are those that have cultivated a relationship and love for it over and above their imagined identities. These people are less concerned with impressions and images of themselves than they are with pursuing Truth. Jesus is calling us to fall in love with Truth and not trying to control or master it through propositions and data. This means allegiance and trust in something more than our group, risking our own belonging for something far more valuable. Fidelity to Truth will inevitably lead to heresy in one's own group.[26] "Now Jesus himself had pointed out that a prophet has no honor in his own country" (John 4:44).

On the other hand, those who cannot bear to hear Truth are those whose allegiance is first and foremost to their earthly identities—the categories sanctioned by the existing social authority. When we are most concerned with belonging to a group, we will buy any amount of bullshit to be counted in. Consider the ridiculous lengths college students go to join a fraternity. The desire to belong is so strong. Social psychologists have long shown how people will deny blatant reality if they are in a group where everyone else does.[27] Personality factors do not play into this and it's a finding that's been replicated across the globe. People will modify reality to belong and you are no exception. Cults have long preyed on this desire for community, leading to all manner of controlling and horrific behavior. Importantly, one of the biggest risk factors for being lured into a cult is the belief that you are immune. We buy our own bullshit.

25. Brueggemann, *Prophetic Imagination*, 95.
26. See Tolstoy, *Kingdom of God Is Within You*.
27. See Franzen and Mader, "Power of Social Influence."

ON DISCOURSE

Discourse analysis is another place where we find the impact of our own splitness played out in the social realm. The psychoanalytic thinker we have been relying heavily on in this book, Jacques Lacan, had some fascinating thoughts on discourse and how it structures our world and communities for better or ill. According to Lacan, all social relationships are structured through a form of discourse. The very act of communicating is always already within the context of a discourse. While the content of that communication matters, the structure itself also plays a deeply significant role. As Marshal McLuhan famously said, "the medium is the message."[28] How you say something—the form of your communication—is as, if not more, important than the content. Think about how you choose whether to call, text, zoom, write a letter, or meet up with someone in person to tell them something. The context matters—it shapes the very message.

According to Lacan, every act of communication is formed in a discourse and can be analyzed structurally as well for content. His analysis asks about the truth that motivates the speaking agent in the first place (something that is always unconscious to that agent) and what the product of the discourse is. Significantly, he highlights that those two, the truth that motivates and the result of communication, can never connect—all communication involves a failure. You can never say all that you mean but will always say far more and far less than you imagine. Words say too much and never enough. This is in part because the truth that motivates your speech is necessarily unconscious to you. You think you know why you are talking but there is always more to the story. Poetry and myth—wilder forms of communication more inclined to embrace both the limitations and preconscious meaning they convey—are sometimes able to communicate more fully or wholly than didactic prose. Have you ever found yourself wondering what you're saying as you speak or been surprised by what you just said? There's always more going on. We aren't going to get too far into the full theory of the discourses here (though it is well worth it if you have the time) but we do want to highlight one of the discourses that Lacan posited, the university discourse.[29]

The university discourse starts with knowledge that comes from some sacred text or revered master. This would be the writings of

---

28. See McLuhan, *Understanding Media*, 7.

29. For more on the discourses see Verhaeghe, "From Impossibility"; and Leupin, *Lacan Today*.

important theologians and thinkers to a denomination or group, or perhaps even a bit of how we have used Lacanian theory in this text. The university discourse shares more and more knowledge, data, and facts with a desiring other—someone who feels a lack and need for it like a student or parishioner. However, this discourse always keeps two things hidden: the fallibility of the master and the resulting split in the listener. This means that the more knowledge that is shared, the greater the feeling of discontent in the listener because the unacknowledged truth of this discourse is that the master is lacking. The wizard is just a doddling little man with the same lack as everyone else—it can't guarantee its own value. Like drinking coke on a hot day, the student will feel a conscious desire to know more, but that information will never satisfy. While your thirst may be slaked for a moment, your body is still dehydrated and will prompt you to drink more. The product of this discourse is always a further split in the listener because the knowledge being consumed is unable to satisfy.

So the university, or church, will continually produce more knowledge—books, sermons, podcasts, and lectures—that will feel essential, but is actually endless. You could know everything there is to know about something and will still feel incomplete and unprepared. I (Paul) see this in my students every year as they prepare for their counseling internship where they will finally start providing psychotherapy to real people instead of simply reading and learning about it. There is a sharp disconnection between any information I could give them about how to provide therapy better and their own feelings of preparedness. In fact, the more I try to prepare them and teach them, the more insecure they feel. Their imposter syndrome is about something much more human and real than clinical skills, theory, or technique—there's a reason Freud referred to psychoanalysis as one of the impossible professions.

What this discourse helps highlight is that knowledge and certainty is a game. It is the product of obfuscation, of insulating, and is thus more bullshit than Truth. This is not to say that all knowledge is false—remember bullshit may or may not correspond with the given state of things—but that Truth is something more. Information and knowledge is more in service of fantasy and group cohesion than Truth. It more often than not works to insulate us from Truth rather than expose us to it. This again is why Truth is usually found with the heretics, the discarded, the hated. One simple (and inevitably simplistic) heuristic between a true and false prophet is how well they are accepted by their people. A true prophet doesn't help people feel better about themselves—she haunts more than soothes. Insofar as this book has aligned with your own worldview, be careful![30]

And so we can see the language games that are used to silence the messages and messengers that would threaten the official, institutional position. Instead of being recognized as prophets, they are called heretics or apostates because of the very circular reason that they are questioning the core tenets of the institutionalized church. This leaves the institution safe. The act of questioning itself "justifies" the accusation of contamination. Deconstruction became such a polarizing idea for this very reason, but many who deconstructed—ourselves included—would argue we have followed Jesus out of our churches. Pursuing Truth threatened the institution, but not our love for Christ. It was that love that refused to stay settled, silent, and quiet in the face of injustice, racism, and nationalism.

When it is allowed in, when Truth overcomes our bullshit resistance and begins to eucontaminate our minds and our institutions, it confronts us with the failure of our knowledge. Eucontaminating Truth irrupts into our Realities with the hard, antiseptic power of light shining into dim and dark spaces. It will not leave us unaffected, but drives us to change, transform, and grow. Some institutions will find that the eucontamination of Truth destroys them altogether as it exposes the contradictions, suffering, or oppression that form their foundation.

My (Paul) personal journey out of mainstream evangelical Christianity began in college. As I mentioned above, I attended Grace College and majored in communications (after a not uncommon roundabout road through a few other majors). I was looking for a place to answer my questions about God. I came to school believing that my faith was true and that there were good answers to my questions. Unlike Billie, I was not so determined and studious as to keep pushing for answers; instead I was easily lulled into apathetic comfort with chicken wings, Dr. Pepper, and my newfound freedom of adulthood. But the gnawing splinter for me was nationalism. I couldn't believe how many churches displayed American flags outside and inside their buildings. This was during the second gulf war and news of the torture perpetrated by American soldiers was all over the news, along with the other atrocities of that conflict, but very little discussion was to be found on campus. I expected to see Christians, of all people in my mind, being horrified by the news coming out of

---

30. For example, Ezek 37:8–11 deals with the false prophets who preach peace and speak words to soothe instead of truth.

Guantanamo and Abu Ghraib, but I heard nothing.[31] Having been raised in Turkiye—a land that still remembers the horrors of the Crusades—with a heavy dose of Five Iron Frenzy pumped into my head throughout high school, I was ashamed to see the cross of Christ side by side with the flag of the most powerful military in the world—Jesus used as the symbol of empire. Questioning this connection by seeking the God of Love and the crucified Christ has continued to pull me after Jesus but out of and away from many churches.

So it was from my experience of running into a contradiction—how can a church that purports to follow a God who is Love so readily choose to embrace all the trappings of empire?—that took me to a place of questioning and uncertainty. Those questions led to me asking more questions and continued to unravel so much of what I had taken for granted. I couldn't ignore or avoid the contradiction once I'd found it. Like Weezer's sweater, I had to keep pulling while I walked away. Can I still be a follower of the way of Jesus and consider myself a Christian? The uncertainty gnawed directly into my sense of identity. My carefully constructed categories crumbled. I was deconstructing my faith in the face of my doubts. Importantly though, this was not a reactive desertion of everything I once believed. This was a dogged pursuit of what had first wooed me into the church: Jesus. I was reading more, wrestling more, praying more, all while I doubted more. Love led me to deconstruct who I thought I was and what I thought the gospel was.

DECONSTRUCTING TRUTH

We can begin contacting Truth when we are brought to the limitations—the failures—of the given knowledge. Thomas Kuhn wrote about paradigm shifts in science that occur when the accepted knowledge no longer explains the data. Newtonian physics explained the world well enough for most of the world for hundreds of years, until it no longer did. It took an Einstein to shift our understanding of reality and matter to account for what scientists were experiencing, but that shift only came about when Newtonian theory was stretched past the point of failure.[32]

---

31. This is not to say that no one was talking about this in Christian circles. See Gushee, *Still Christian*; Boyd, *Myth of a Christian Nation*; and Claiborne, *Irresistible Revolution*, for examples of leading voices in this discussion, but they were not discussed at all on my campus.

32. See Kuhn, *Scientific Revolutions*.

This is where postmodern deconstruction can run us into dangerous and unhelpful places. Much of the conversation around deconstruction appears to be in the vein of what we have described here in calling out failures, inconsistencies, and contradictions. Yet there is a significant difference between a good faith embrace of an idea that will inevitably lead to its point of failure and the short-cut move to find an inconsistency and reject something. If you are quick to reject an idea, theory, or theology because you have found a problem with it without really studying it, watch out. To abandon an idea, group, or identity at the first sign of cracks is not so much evidence of fidelity to Truth as it is evidence of a fear of doubt—you're still holding on to the fantasy of perfection. If we are unwilling to sit with doubt for some period of time, we are only exchanging one failed certainty for a new certainty (which will itself inevitably fail in time). Like with the DESTROYS videos mentioned previously, you are more likely enacting ignorance than wisdom and choosing bullshit over Truth. Instead, we are advocating for a movement that is not about finding fault and moving on, but pushing in so as to find its full failure. If you haven't exhausted something you've never really known it. If you are afraid of finding a point of failure, you aren't fully trusting Truth. This is where the university discourse fails us. It refuses to encourage the pursuit of the failure of any given dogma, but instead keeps working to problematize the student rather than the established tradition. This does not mean, however, that you should remain in abusive or harmful situations. If you are being hurt, tending to your own well-being is of the utmost importance. As Pastor Trey Ferguson writes in his text *Theologizin' Bigger*:

> There is a wholeness to be discovered along the journey of deconstruction. It is possible to find your truest self as we untangle the many cords of truths, half truths, and untruths that bind us. But it is nearly impossible to know what we look like in solitude. Community is the gift that helps us see ourselves. We will never know authentic community without authentic sharing. The best tools of deconstruction are the narratives that demand that we look at things differently.[33]

Here again we need to pause and highlight what we are *not* saying and warn against a misreading of this chapter. We are *not* recommending that anyone remain in a system, relationship, or organization that has shown itself to be harmful, damaging, or abusive.

---

33. Ferguson, *Theologizin' Bigger*, 105.

In what is a lighter example, I (Paul) have run into this phenomenon often in my own hobby of board games. When trying a new game, there is value in recognizing one's initial reaction to it—and some games I have not found worth continuing to pursue and dive into. However, most games require multiple plays to really appreciate them. It's only by fully immersing yourself in it that you can fully appreciate what the designer is doing. It takes work to access the deeper beauty of the game. This is not an ethical or moral duty to play every game multiple times though. It is an invitation to recognize the level from which you are rejecting or appreciating something. Just because you don't initially appreciate beauty in something doesn't mean that it is not there; it may be that you just can't recognize it yet.[34]

And this is where a misrecognition of Truth and certainty leads groups to become the opposite of themselves—the very things they purport to be against. So many churches have become known for what they oppose and not for who they love.[35] If Truth is about protecting something established, we will lose our souls in its defense. As Tolstoy noted, we will abandon the teachings of Christ. But if we can trust in the goodness of Truth, then we are free to learn, grow in knowledge, develop more theories, and play with ideas—all while pursuing an elusive Truth that keeps luring us from just beyond our understanding. The prophets were branded heretics because they questioned the institutionalized knowledge. May we, like them, forsake the comfort of certainty and power for a reckless pursuit of Truth wherever she may lead us.

---

34. For more on the application of these ideas to the realm of games and play, see Hoard, "On Pleasure."

35. See Hoard and Suttle, "Lacanian Virtue Ethics?"

6

Shame Faced

*If we are comfortable ascribing significance to the **whole truth**—and not just our unexamined stories—we can write new endings to these stories. Our communities can live into the promises we speak over them. We can learn to be trustworthy. Our neighbors can breathe more easily. Sitting with shame might be the only way for us to stand in freedom. We will not find wholeness by weaponizing shame against the vulnerable. We might find liberation by embracing shame as a society. Because there is no love without accountability.*

—Trey Ferguson, *Theologizin' Bigger*

C. S. Lewis's favorite of all the novels he wrote was *Till We Have Faces*. In it he retells the myth of Cupid and Psyche from the perspective of one of Psyche's sisters, Orual of Glome. At the end of the novel Orual, now the queen of Glome, is given the opportunity to make her case to the gods that they are cruel and unjust.[1] But instead of the complaint she had

---

1. In the novel Orual, together with her Greek philosopher mentor the Fox, raise Psyche and love her. In contrast to Psyche, who is the most beautiful and kind child in the land, Orual is profoundly ugly—a fact of which she is ashamed throughout the novel. In Lewis's retelling of the myth, Psyche is sacrificed to "The Brute" despite Orual's efforts to keep her safe, only to find that The Brute is none other than the god Cupid, who falls in love with her, marries her, and takes her to live in his palace. When,

intended to make—we might say instead of the bullshit she had intended to shape—Orual finds that her "accusation" takes the form of an angry and bitter confession:

> That's why I say it makes no difference whether you're fair or foul. That there should be gods at all, there's our misery and bitter wrong. There's no room for you and us in the same world. You're a tree in whose shadow we can't thrive. We want to be our own. I was my own and Psyche was mine and no one else had any right to her. Oh you'll say you took her away into bliss and joy such as I could never have given her, and I ought to have been glad of it for her sake. Why? What should I care for some horrible, new happiness which I hadn't given her and which separated her from me? Do you think I wanted her to be happy in that way? It would have been better if I'd seen the Brute tear her in pieces before my eyes.... Did you ever remember whose the girl was? She was mine. **Mine.** Do you not know what the word means? Mine!

At last the judge spoke.

"Are you answered?" he said.
"Yes," said I.[2]

Orual is confronted with the Truth of who she has been—of who she is. And she is ashamed. And this is the point on which the novel turns. Will Orual accept the Truth of her life or will she return to the bullshit she has been using to insulate herself from it? We cannot grow, we cannot become fully ourselves, until we learn to abandon our bullshit and accept the Truth, shameful though it may be. Or as Lewis puts it in Orual's voice: "I saw well why the gods do not speak to us openly, nor let us answer. Till that word [the confession of Truth] can be dug out of us, why should they hear the babble that we think we mean? How can they meet us face to face till we have faces?"

---

following the original myth, Orual encounters Psyche again, Orual is not able to see or sense Psyche's palace and concludes that Psyche has gone mad. In an effort to dissuade Psyche from her apparent illusion, Orual convinces her to break the one rule she has been given and look at her husband's face while he sleeps. At first Psyche resists but when Orual threatens suicide, Psyche relents and agrees to break the rule. As a consequence, Psyche is exiled from her home and required to complete a series of impossible tasks in order to regain her position while Orual discovers (to her horror) what she has done to her sister.

2. Lewis, *Till We Have Faces*, 291–93.

Lewis's novel is a powerful narration of the way that shame can hide us from really living—cutting us off from joy. In this chapter, we want to explore that shame through the lens of eucontamination and Jesus's audacious claim to be the Life. What does it mean to let life eucontaminate us as we learn to "have faces"?

GUILT AND SHAME

Back in chapter 1, we noted the connection between disgust, contamination, and shame. In order to further explore the notion of Christ as the Life, we want to return to that discussion to say more about each of these through a eucontaminative lens.

Shame is a negative feeling that is linked to one's identity, group belonging, and behavior. It is closely tied to guilt in that both are connected to our sense of right and wrong, but they interact with our sense of self differently. Guilt is primarily concerned with our behavior and how well we have acted in accordance with the moral and ethical codes that we have internalized from our communities. We feel guilty when we don't act the way we think we should. Like physical pain, guilt hurts and in its best form helps us act better. However, like pain, guilt is a double edged sword: it can also be debilitating and pathological. In the now infamous words of the psychologist Albert Ellis, too strong and oppressive a sense of guilt can lead to the experience of "musterbating" and "shoulding" all over oneself.[3] Shame on the other hand hits deeper into our sense of self. While guilt is primarily focused on what I have or have not done, shame connects directly with who I am. In chapter 1 we noted the internal monologue of guilt being closer to "I *did* something bad" while shame tends towards " I *am* something bad."[4]

Shame and guilt also emphasize different parts of the self. Guilt focuses on the individual while shame is all about our communal identity. For exactly this reason, many in the current deconstruction movement or among post-evangelicals have, of necessity, done hard work to protect themselves against shame. Shame has been a favorite tool of evangelical churches for keeping their members inside their boundaries. We

---

3. See Ellis, *Reason and Emotion*.
4. For more on this see DeYoung, *Chronic Shame*.

recognize this reality and want to celebrate everyone who has overcome this coercive, abusive, and manipulative weaponization of shame.[5]

So guilt doesn't necessarily threaten one's sense of belonging unless it bleeds all the way into shame. I may feel like a better or worse member of my family depending on how much guilt is active at any given moment, but when I'm wallowing in a shame spiral, I sense a threat to my belonging in the family. Now, obviously these two concepts intertwine strongly and cannot be so easily distinguished. Like many concepts in psychology, we use separate words to differentiate for the sake of understanding and focus, not necessarily as an accurate reflection of reality.

Both can be devastating. Many recent authors and researchers have highlighted the problems with chronic, toxic shame. Being lost in shame erodes almost every part of one's being and can infect one's life with an oppressive sense of worthlessness and loneliness. Shame is sometimes referred to as a "master emotion" and comes about through ruptured relational moments.[6] It is less about an individual valuation and more the feeling of worthlessness in the eyes of an *other*. DeYoung defines shame as the "experience of one's felt sense of self disintegrating in relation to a dysregulating other."[7] In other words, shame always requires someone else.[8] The disintegration of the felt sense of self is that overwhelming experience that you are *not* who you imagined yourself to be—it unmasks the falsehood of your ego. You have been caught. Remember the important relational aspects of development. Shame hits at the very heart of that development of self. It can truly shape who you are—by pressuring

---

5. While various Christian denominations and organizations publish "statements of faith" which serve to delineate official boundaries to inclusion, many Evangelical groups (denominations, churches, and others) have used shame like an invisible fence. They don't explicitly *say* that you will be excluded from community if you embrace a particular idea or voice a certain set of questions; sometimes they even state that it would be acceptable to do so; but the moment a person starts to get "too close" to those questions, or beliefs, the shame is deployed in tone and in the use of key phrases (e.g., "I'm just not sure about your walk" or "I hope you are open to checking your spirit" or the dreaded "I am gonna be prayin' for ya"). As a result, many post-evangelicals and other deconstructed Christians have come to experience shame as nothing but a toxic and manipulative form of coercion which they have had to work diligently and painfully to overcome. Evangelicals, though, are not alone in their use of shame to patrol boundaries.

6. See Scheff, "Shame in Self."
7. See DeYoung, *Chronic Shame*, 21.
8. At minimum an imagined other.

you to conform to external social expectations or pressuring you to face the false standards you have internalized.

WHEN WE ENCOUNTER SHAME

Many approaches to chronic shame in therapy involve a desire to help patients work to transform their shame into guilt. As therapists, we often try to help people recognize that just because they have done something bad/hurtful/embarrassing does not mean that they are now worthless. Reframing those shame thoughts from I *am* to I *did* can be a very powerful step in freeing oneself from the shackles of chronic and toxic shame.[9] Building off a eucontaminative approach in this text, we are interested in offering a more nuanced approach to shame and its place in our lives. However, at the outset it is so important to highlight that we are offering a corrective and complexification, not a total rejection. If you have found freedom in releasing your shame, that is beautiful and we want to encourage you to not hear what follows as a rejection of your story. If you have found yourself trapped in chronic shame, that can be devastating. We want to encourage you to reach for help because wallowing in a life of shame is not what Jesus meant when he offers life abundant.[10]

That said, shame seems to have become a sort of bogeyman among many therapists and in mental health discourse these days, signifying the big evil that must be stopped. The work of Brené Brown and others has highlighted the value of vulnerability and the importance of erasing shame.[11] However, it is important to wonder if we have perhaps created a straw-man villain out of a human emotion. In this book about the dangers of disgust and an overapplied purity metaphor, it is critically important that you hear us saying that disgust is not a wholly bad emotion—that, in the right context, disgust is vital to keeping us alive. And like disgust, shame exists as one more feeling we have and is a necessary part of the full human experience. We must risk asking, "is it *all bad* or could there be a use for shame?" Why else would it generally be considered a bad thing to be shameless? We believe that shame has an important function

---

9. This is of course a gross oversimplification of therapy. Actual treatment is far more complex and nuanced than this. We are simply trying to note big-picture trajectories.

10. John 10:10.

11. See Brown, *Daring Greatly*; and Thompson, *Soul of Shame*.

in our spiritual and emotional lives, but is an incredibly powerful force and, as such, it often manifests in harmful and oppressive trajectories.

Guilt and shame both have counter feelings that are important to bring into the discussion. Pride is often the opposite of feeling guilt. We take pride in our work. We feel pride when we accomplish something. In the same way, honor pairs as a counterpart of shame. We feel honor from being appreciated by those who are important to us. We can bestow honor on others by how we view them in the same way that we can shame with our eyes. We feel honored when we are seen in a particular manner. As we are doing with purity and contamination, keep pride and honor in your head as you think about guilt and shame. They can't be fully separated as they imply one another—the flip side of each coin.

Shame, remember, is often associated with contamination and disgust. To be stigmatized is to be marked as disgusting or shameful in society. The impact of being the object of disgust—of having been contaminated or being the contaminant—is the experience of shame. We use shame as part of the boundary enforcing mechanism for our individual and group identities. We shame the parts of us that don't fit with our ideal self, saying to ourselves that we are not *that*. We shame members of our group who have been shown to be contaminated. Like the father with the brownies from chapter 1, when we weaponize disgust, we are also spreading shame. This is not to say that there is no place for language around purity or disgust. Perhaps a way to think about it differently may be sitting with the distinction between something being dirty and something being filthy. To be dirty is to imply one is washable and can be made clean. To be filthy, however, tends to imply an ontological status or property of the object. It's just a filthy thing. Excrement, for example, doesn't have a state in which it is not filthy. No amount of cleaning can fix it. Learning to recognize when our purity metaphors have moved from dirt to filth can help us recognize the way shame is operating in the moment.

THE NAIVE OTHER

That said, where do these feelings of guilt and shame come from? Guilt, shame, pride, and honor all speak to the existence of an outside standard, law, or expectation against which we are being measured or judged. We have previously spoken in chapter 5 about this as the social authority and how it is connected to our sense of identity. All sources of social authority (the nebulous *they* who are supposed to know what's right) have the power to bestow honor, pride, guilt, or shame on us. The Lacanian term for this nebulous social authority is the big Other.[12] Little others are the actual individuals you interact with, but the big Other is indefinite. It produces the sense of having or not having been seen. We don't often think about it, but much of our behavior is dictated by this big Other, despite—and this is crucial—the fact that it doesn't actually exist. There is no big Other, only the internal sense of it—the internalized law that comes from having an identity. What this big Other does and does not see structures our world in powerful ways that we rarely notice.

Just down the road from my (Paul's) house is a speed limit sign with a radar gun. As you drive down the road, the radar tracks your speed and flashes it on the sign. If you are going at or below the limit, your speed is just shown, but if you speed the sign flashes and if you exceed the speed limit by too much it will simply flash *too fast*. Significantly, there are rarely any police by this sign to enforce the law, so the radar and sign have no teeth. They can't actually do anything to you. And yet these sorts of signs are incredibly effective at slowing down cars—especially mine. In fact, I will often slow down through the sign and then speed right back up as soon as I'm past. Why is that? What makes me act so differently when my speed is posted by a radar gun and not just displayed on my speedometer? I know how fast I'm going. The sign does not surprise me with either the speed limit or my own velocity. But when my speed is posted, I feel as though the big Other now also sees how fast I'm going. My "plausible deniability" is shattered and I can't pretend to have not known. I feel guilt over speeding when it's made clear to the world (even if no actual human is there to witness it) because my internalized *they* now also knows that I know that I am speeding. Psychology is fascinating.

Think about your own behavior. When do you feel the need to perform the show of doing things right and when do you feel nothing about cutting corners?

Swearing is another great example of this. Growing up in an evangelical home, I was not allowed to say "fuck." "Frick," however, was perfectly fine. It didn't matter if I intended "fuck" and meant all the same emotional emphasis as yelling "fuck" loudly, as long as it didn't sound like I was actually cussing. This only makes sense because the big Other, which would have led me to feeling guilty for swearing, is actually quite

---

12. See Žižek, *How to Read Lacan*.

naive and only judges my outward behaviors, not my intentions. To the big Other, "frick" is completely different from "fuck"—regardless of my intentions for saying it.

Because the big Other doesn't actually exist, we all internalize it differently (though there is a lot of overlap in social groups), and so we may feel guilt or pride for very different things. I see this a lot in board games as each player's relationship to the rule manual for the game highlights their unique relationship to the big Other of the game. It also doesn't need any actual, real others to witness my actions to transfer a sense of guilt. The legalism of what you *actually* did or didn't say/do becomes the important factor here, not your intentions or even the presence of someone else.[13]

What this big Other does and does not see is fascinating when we slow down to analyze it. The big Other doesn't know your intentions, just your behaviors. It can only judge what you do, but not everything you do. Remember that I don't feel guilty speeding unless the radar picks me up, so my conscious speeding at other times is somehow fine. The big Other relies on a very naive perspective. As long as it looks *as if* you are doing the right thing, it does not activate. You need either the appearance of doing the right thing (getting your hands wet in the restroom to look like you actually washed them) or some plausible deniability (I can pretend that I didn't realize how fast I was going) to mitigate the big Other's guilt. What you are actually consciously aware of isn't important, just what you are shown to have noticed.

So the big Other is central to producing guilt, but what about shame? Shame comes less from our outward actions but starts to look at our desires and intentions. Unlike the big Other, shame comes from the perspective of someone much closer to our internal world—our ideal ego, the perfect, imagined version of ourselves that we will never measure up to. Shame is deeply connected to our imposter syndrome and the internal critic—the voice that says we don't belong or aren't good enough. The big Other can be placated by the appearance of doing the right thing, but this ideal ego will never be satisfied. Even if you act perfectly and do everything right, this is the voice that says you only did it so people will like you more and that you're actually really selfish. The perfectionist is someone with a very loud ideal ego (or internal critic) that relentlessly demands more from them.

---

13. See Pfaller, *On the Pleasure Principle*.

The insidious nature of this ideal ego is that it is right. We aren't who we think we are. Throughout this whole book, we have described the nature of being a split subject and the failures of all identities to ever capture who we are. There is always a remainder to your sense of self—always more to you than you think. The fullness of you can never be fully imagined or captured in the picture of yourself. This means that your internal critic will always have some fodder to use, some reality to pull from. This is where psychological defenses come in to protect us from that voice. To protect our sense of self (ego) from the reality of our split-ness and the ego's own incoherence, we rely on many different defensive strategies. We rationalize, minimize, deny, project, react, and a million other defenses as ways to ward off these feelings.[14] Anxiety and depression (along with other mental health symptoms) are often early signs that those defenses are failing or not working well.

The presence of an other (actual person) only heightens the power of this internal critic. Remember the significance of relationships in human development and the working of the mind from chapters 1 and 2. Others in our community can help soothe us through acceptance and empathy or heighten our shame with rejection. When I (Billie) was first working to understand my own trans-ness, I reached out anonymously to several trans people online. Each time their responses included the phrase "you are valid" in the opening (and often the closing) of their replies to my heartfelt, agonized questions about my own transgender status. I wanted or perhaps needed to be recognized as a member of the community by members of my community. Sensing that, having themselves experienced what I was going through, they worked to soothe me as I was internally freaking all the way out over this radical restructuring of my own ideal ego. At the time, I was committed to living my life in the closet as "a trans woman who knows who and what she is but who has chosen to stay closeted for reasons that were very compelling at the time." Even writing these words and remembering back to the intense suffering of that time, I am tempted to break the fourth wall of this book in order to reassure any closeted or recently out queer person reading this that, *yes, you are valid, yes you matter, yes your queerness is real and beautiful*, because the urgency of soothing other members of my community through acceptance remains with me.

14. Ego psychology and cognitive theories in particular focus on these various defenses and how they can be addressed. See McWilliams, *Psychoanalytic Diagnosis*; and Mitchell and Black, *Freud and Beyond*, for more.

When our communal belonging is threatened or lost, our sense of self is also necessarily shaken. It's one thing to soothe myself with positive talk and self-care but much harder to silence the shame when it is coming back at me through the eyes of someone next to me. The shame is either heightened and affirmed or dissipated through our responses to one another. Chronic shame comes from regular experiences of shame from significant others during important portions of our development and can have crippling, long-term impacts on our capacity to love. Anxiety creeps in to prepare us for the shame of rejection and abandonment—for our sense of self to disintegrate. Depression usually follows after the fact—after we've failed to measure up and have lost our sense of self.

THE WOMAN CAUGHT IN ADULTERY

This dynamic is not foreign to the Bible as we see Jesus interact with shame in the story of the woman caught in adultery (John 8:1–11).[15] After setting the scene (Jesus in the temple with "the people" around him as he is teaching), we are told that:

> Jesus went to the Mount of Olives. Early in the morning he came again to the temple. All the people came to him, and he sat down and began to teach them. The scribes and the Pharisees brought a woman who had been caught in adultery, and, making her stand before all of them, they said to him, "Teacher, this woman was caught in the very act of committing adultery. Now in the law Moses commanded us to stone such women. Now what do you say?" They said this to test him, so that they might have some charge to bring against him. Jesus bent down and wrote with his finger on the ground. When they kept on questioning

---

15. In standard contemporary Bibles this account appears at the beginning of John 8 but is notably absent from the oldest manuscripts of John and is written in a style more in line with that of Luke than of John. However, accounts of this story are referenced in manuscripts which predate our oldest manuscript of the Gospel of John including a mention of it as having appeared in the Gospel of the Hebrews. Hart reflects that "it seems that the story was something of a freely floating tradition, perhaps with very deep roots in Christian memory, one that was not originally firmly associated with any particular Gospel text, but that was inserted in various versions of Luke or John because it was too beautiful and too illuminating of Christ's ministry and person to be left out of the church's lectionary cycle (and hence out of scripture)." See Hart, *New Testament*, 187–88. It is worth reflecting on the way in which the account itself might eucontaminate the Gospels as a fragment of "freely floating tradition" which the ancient Christians understood to be both accurate and representative of Jesus Christ but which the original Gospel authors elected to omit.

him, he straightened up and said to them, "Let anyone among you who is without sin be the first to throw a stone at her." And once again he bent down and wrote on the ground. When they heard it, they went away, one by one, beginning with the elders, and Jesus was left alone with the woman standing before him. Jesus straightened up and said to her, *"Woman, where are they? Has no one condemned you?" She said, "No one, sir." And Jesus said, "Neither do I condemn you. Go your way, and from now on do not sin again."* (NRSVUE, emphasis ours)

It is a familiar story to many of us who have spent any time in or around the church. The woman has been "caught in the act" of adultery and is now being reduced to a tool for the purposes of others in order to catch Jesus out. In his own discussion of shame and reflection on this passage, Trey Ferguson, along with many others, wonders where the other participant (presumably a man) in this woman's act of adultery is, how [his] absence ought to shape our reading of this text and how it might have shaped Jesus's reading of the situation.[16] So we have many injustices in play before Jesus even enters the picture: There is the presenting injustice towards the husband this woman was cheating on, there is the evident-as-soon-as-we-think-about-it patriarchal injustice of the woman being subjected to this mob trial while her presumably male partner was spared, and there is the possible injustice against the male partner's wife. Additionally, the narrative highlights the injustice to Jesus of being asked to make a judgment in a seemingly impossible situation (Roman law did not permit execution for adultery while the Law of Moses cited in the story exhorted the execution of *both* partners in adultery). Injustice abounds.

Enter Jesus. In light of what we have been saying about shame and guilt, we think it is notable that Jesus doesn't look *at* anyone for most of this story. When confronted with the accusations against the woman, Jesus looks down and begins writing in the dirt. Possibly, Jesus doesn't want to shame anyone. When pressed by those who are weaponizing shame against the woman, Jesus still doesn't look at her but at them and responds in a way that specifically calls out not her failure to conform to the expectations of their social ideal, but theirs. "Let anyone among you who is without sin be the first to throw a stone at her." This is brilliant. In turning the gaze of shame on the crowd and tossing out that comment, Jesus is also turning their own weaponized shame against them. Now those who brought the woman, and the rest of the gathered crowd,

---

16. Ferguson, *Theologizin' Bigger*, 136.

are looking not at her, or even at Jesus, but *at* one another—at themselves. Which of course means that they are also experiencing the guilt that comes when we realize that our deviation from the ideal/expectation has been noticed, has ceased to be private. Jesus has activated the big Other, engaging their guilt, *and* they are experiencing the shame of the hypocrite—participating in the whole hypocritical spectacle of tangled injustices. The shame and the guilt are too much for them and they leave.

"And Jesus was left alone with the woman standing before him" (v. 9b). Now Jesus turns to the woman, his gaze falls on her. She who, only minutes earlier, was caught up in a hurricane of guilt and shame (pause for a minute here if you haven't yet and imagine the trauma of having a group of religious leaders break in on you in the act of having sex and then drag you in front of a crowd and announce your infidelity to the world). In a few simple phrases, Jesus addresses her guilt. "Woman, where are they? Has no one condemned you?" He invites her to notice the absence of others' judgment of her and she does: "No one, sir." She recognizes that there is no one from the original crowd who is left to condemn her. We will have more to say in chapter 7 about disrupting the gaze of shame, so for now let's focus on the experience of the woman. In the midst of what has to have been one of the worst moments of her life, the rabbi has asked her whether anyone is left to condemn her. Like a good therapist would, he wants her to say—to show that she knows—that their attempt to condemn her has failed. They have not managed to condemn her.

The only gaze that remains is Jesus's.

And Jesus said, "Neither do I condemn you. Go your way, and from now on do not sin again." Jesus, the One who is the Truth, the Life, and the Way, *sees* her. Beyond the bullshit that allowed her to justify whatever sin she has committed, Jesus sees her, and in his gaze there is no shame. The contrast here is important. We saw in the crowd's reaction to Jesus's gaze and to their gazes at one another that Jesus's gaze *can* hold shame. Leveled at those who reduced a woman to a political or ideological *thing* to be used to their own advantage, Jesus's gaze exposes the brokenness—the inadequacy—of their own ideals; it sees their bullshit justice for what it is and it compels them to recognize it. In fact, the shame in Jesus's gaze holds for them the promise of eucontamination. By accepting its judgment that they were not without sin, they were transformed from lynchers and bystanders into more humble and circumspect people. But leveled at a woman whose sins have been shouted at her, a woman traumatized and unjustly singled out for punishment, Jesus's gaze holds a True Seeing of the True Her that she is and can always be becoming. Falling on the woman, Jesus's gaze—which does *not* condemn—transforms her from a stigmatized object of violence and a dehumanized political object into a person worthy of affirmation by God. We say it in a million different ways. He sees the true her; he sees her through eyes that see a person and not a thing; he sees her humanity; he sees her through the eyes of Love and in his doing so she sees herself through those eyes.

GUILT OR SHAME

So guilt relies on the big Other, while shame is heightened by the presence of actual others, but both rely on the reality of our own imposter syndrome—our split-ness. We want to explore this a bit, because if you have been following from the last chapter, you may have noticed that shame is now connected to Truth. Shame is not on the side of our bullshit; it is the result of our bullshit egos. In other words, we feel shame because the image of ourselves, who we think we are, is incomplete. Shame continues to unsettle and disintegrate our sense of self because that sense of self doesn't work—it's not who you are.

The problem with turning our shame into guilt ("My Ego is not bad, I merely did a bad thing") is that guilt doesn't problematize our sense of self. Guilt affirms the world as we see it and who we think we are. It only asks us to act better, to conform better to the big Other. It doesn't critique that big Other. This is especially problematic for those of us with identities that hold more societal privilege and power like the mob who confronted Jesus. Guilt says act better. Shame disintegrates how you see yourself.

One example of this can be found in the mix of shame and guilt that many progressively minded white-bodied individuals (like us) experience when they attempt to engage in antiracist action. We experience what has been called white guilt and white shame when we are faced with our collusion and complicity with systems of white-body supremacy. Now white guilt tends to lead to a manic defense of trying to act better and a fear of the shame of being caught having said or doing something wrong. This can manifest itself in the kind of fragility that DiAngelo described[17] that is actually an enactment of a form of white rage.[18] This

---

17. See DiAngelo, *White Fragility*.
18. See Hoard, "Beyond Fragility"; and Hoard and Bland, "'How Am I Responsible?'"

means that white guilt is usually in service of performative action. White guilt plays whack-a-mole with racist behaviors and, like whack-a-mole, never succeeds in addressing the root cause of those behaviors. It stages a spectacle of antiracist action for the big Other, not for actual subversion or liberation. White shame, on the other hand, problematizes the entire system of white body supremacy and the white gaze through which white people[19] look at themselves and the world. White shame points to the ideal, white self that is the product of whiteness (I should be a good white person) and refuses to let the white-bodied individual ever feel good enough. White shame exposes that it is that *ideal* of whiteness—the white gaze—that is part of the problem and that can't ever be fixed by performative action because that action is always performed *for* that gaze. The problem is bigger than any one person's actions. It has lasted for centuries and will almost certainly continue for generations even with dedicated, collective work.[20] Keeping the focus on individual behaviors by emphasizing guilt alone—and not the ongoing historical, systemic, social struggles that shame points to—helps the broader system continue to function as it has.[21]

The big Other which produces guilt is tied directly to one's internal social authority. This means that while it is individualized for each of us, it is also interconnected. It is tied to our culture and broader social world. So this big Other cannot be untangled from systemic oppression or privilege. Your social location matters. This becomes particularly important as we consider the role of shame in becoming the object of disgust. Our above example highlighted the importance of white shame because white-bodied individuals hold a central social location—they are caught in an imagination of themselves as white. We will unpack this entire process much more fully in the next chapter, but for now we wanted to explore the impact of being the object of disgust as so much of our discussion thus far has centered around holding the disgusted gaze.

---

19. For ease of communication our use of the phrase "white people" here and throughout the book should be read as a reference to Ta-Nahisi Coates's concept of "dreamers" or people who imagine themselves to be white. See Coates, *Between the World and Me*.

20. See Menakem, *Quaking*.

21. We will discuss this in much more detail in the next chapter. For more information on the concept of whiteness in particular, see Jennings, *After Whiteness*; Charles and Rah, *Unsettling Truths*; Hoard, "Beyond Fragility"; Jacobs, "Learning to Love White Shame."

I (Billie) have been told on numerous occasions that I am disgusting. This generally happens because I am queer and because I am fairly public and forthright not only about my queerness, but about how much I love being a queer woman. In chapter 2, we discussed some of the ways in which Christian Nationalism seeks to induce shame in those it categorizes as contaminants to its desired national purity. As a queer woman, and particularly as a queer Christian woman, I am regularly confronted by social pressure to see myself as disgusting in the eyes of my fellow Christians. The straight gaze tries to elicit shame in me on the basis of my queerness. But I had better break that down a little more. Let us bracket my queerness for a moment, and specifically name my trans-ness and my lesbianism as the aspects of myself that society (both Christian and secular) would attempt to use to create shame in me. Because I am transgender, I am, in the opinion of a transphobic world, failing at my gender. I am both performing man-ness badly and am also not qualified to perform woman-ness. As a lesbian, I am perceived as performing woman-ness badly. I am failing miserably at living up to the ideal woman—a social imaginary shaped more by and for the desires of men than it is shaped by or for women. Naturally, I am also failing at living up to the ideal image of a man (as all women are under patriarchy, so I suppose I do have that in common with my cisters). And because I am a *transgender* lesbian, I even manage to fail at living up to certain ideal images of a lesbian.[22] Each of these dynamics creates a tension between me and societal expectations. This tension centers around the question of the degree to which I will adopt the demands of the big Other and succumb to guilt, and whether I will accept the limited and confining images of man, woman, or even lesbian, that try to insist on me through the eyes of the world.

And this is why I say that queerness is a blessing. This is why I glory in my queerness. Not because it is a panacea—queerness in the end is just as capable of generating a shame inducing gaze as all other identities are—but because in this time and place (the US in the mid 2020s), queerness is an identity which exists in opposition to—or better yet in defiant neglect of—particular sexual and gender expectations. When I say that I am queer, I am certainly referencing my transness and my lesbianism, but I am also referencing an understanding of myself as not-defined by those identities, not fully. To be queer is to explicitly acknowledge that our society's sexual and gender gazes—our internalized big Others—are

---

22. See Serano, *Excluded*; and Serano, *Whipping Girl*.

bullshit.[23] Said one more way: to be queer is to tell the demand to see myself as disgusting (deserving of shame) to go get fucked.

So guilt prompts us to behave better in the given sociological system we are in, while shame painfully questions and problematizes that very system. As Trey Ferguson puts it:

> When we understand shame as a friend of the defenseless, we are on the path to wholeness.
>
> Some things we ought to be ashamed of. We ought to be ashamed that many of the people we depend on to keep things running can barely afford to support themselves. We ought to be ashamed of the number of unhoused people who experience homelessness in one of the wealthiest nations in the history of the planet. We ought to be ashamed that children who are learning about themselves and the deeply complicated reality of human sexuality must navigate such a heavy anxiety as a direct result of our inability or lack of desire to walk with them safely through this journey. We ought to be ashamed that we demand better decorum of protesters than we do of our own elected officials.
>
> Shame is an invitation to do better by our neighbors.[24]

EUCONTAMINATING GRIEF

As we move into our shame and face the dissociated, disavowed, rejected parts of our stories, the hope is not that we will be frozen and lost in shame. Shame is the pain that makes us aware of a problem and that awareness is important, but we do not want to stay frozen in shame and collapse. Instead, moving through shame takes us to grief. Without a eucontaminative hope, grief must be avoided and defended against. But having faith in something beyond our imaginations—a eucontaminating love that can transform us in ways we have no words for—opens up the cleansing possibility of grieving. Learning to grieve is an important part of maturing and healing. Grief, like disgust, is rooted in our bodies and often accessed via a more attuned awareness with those bodies. We process grief through our bodies, not just our words. Menakem writes of

---

23. See Tonstad, *Queer Theology*; Halperin, *One Hundred Years*; and Daniels, "Queer Theory."

24. Ferguson, *Theologizin' Bigger*, 137.

the importance of crying, shaking, or even screaming as ways for grief to work through us.[25]

Grief is not pretty. It is not put together and it involves a release of what we had wanted, hoped, and wished for. Learning to grieve is also very countercultural to white Western society. Grief runs fully contrary to the optimistic, comic view of life that has so captured American culture. Psychoanalyst Nancy McWilliams writes that "Americans subscribe to a version of the comic view rather than the tragic vision of human life, the pursuit of happiness rather than the coming to terms with inevitable pain."[26] Limitations and pain are to be overcome and avoided in the comic view.[27] But most therapies walk patients through their pain, help them face their limits, listen to their bodies, and tell a more full story of their trauma. Healing is not found in the comic, but in the eucontaminating acceptance and embrace of the tragic.

This is not to say that mourning and sadness are the only possible experiences. On the contrary, joy and meaning are found when we stop running from sorrow. Joy and life are waiting on the other side of our grief. Sadness does not erase joy—à la *Inside Out*—but allows for a deeper, more robust life. Laughter can be cutting and defensive—used in service of avoiding and hiding—or it can be rich and healing, touching life on the other side of tragedy. Easter Sunday awaits us on the far side of Holy Saturday, but Good Friday must come first.

To make this a little more concrete, I (Billie) want to talk about two of my identities. We all exist as more, but not less, than the intersection of multiple identities. Keeping in mind that our identities are all imperfect—that none of us will ever quite live up to any of our identities—we nevertheless are able to understand a great deal of our experiences in life more fully and accurately when we recognize that our various identities intersect with one another in distinct ways. Those intersections structure our experiences in society (and even with ourselves) in particular ways. As Kimberlé Crenshaw, who first proposed intersectionality as a tool for analyzing social structures, put it, "We tend to talk about race inequality as separate from inequality based on gender, class, sexuality or immigrant status. What's often missing [which intersectionality supplies]

---

25. See Menakem, *My Grandmother's Hands*.
26. See McWilliams, *Psychoanalytic Reflections*, 53.
27. A wholesale elimination of shame would be comic.

is how some people are subject to all of these, and the experience is not just the sum of its parts."[28]

Now I am a lesbian, transgender woman and there is a lot to unpack there (and I will continue to in chapter 7), but here I want to focus on how two distinct identities: my queerness and my whiteness, interact with all that we have been saying about eucontaminative shame and guilt because, while there are distinct differences, I benefit by integrating shame and guilt—allowing them to eucontaminate me—both as a queer person and as a white person.

As a queer person, I experience shame in the form of internalized queerphobia. When I experience myself through the eyes of a queerphobic society (or religious persuasion) I am immediately confronted with the ways that I fail to live up to the ideal sexual and gendered image of a person in that society: I become the object of disgust. At this point, it might seem intuitive to conclude that I would be best served by simply rejecting the shame (and the guilt that occurs when I experience my queer self being seen and judged by a queerphobic big Other); and to some extent that is the intuitive response and it is a better one than accepting the queerphobic judgment as valid. But there is another option. I can choose to recognize the shame, accept it into myself, not as a valid judgment on me, but as a judgment on the queerphobic society which works to exclude, other, marginalize, disenfranchise, and otherwise oppress its queer members. I can allow for that shame to progress into a grief, which then fuels both my empathy and love for my fellow queers, and my appreciation for loyal and loving allies. I can allow that grief to serve its turn, and in its wake I am left with renewed strength and passion to join my fellow queers and our allies in the struggle for queer liberation with a more keenly developed understanding of the nature and activity of our oppression.[29] Sitting with and integrating my shame *in the presence of the Truth that my queerness is a blessing, that God delights in and over me as Their queer daughter* transforms me further into a person equipped to resist queerphobia more effectively and joyfully.

In addition to the joy available to me on the other side of grief and shame, there is another reason that I am well served to integrate and move through the experience of shame rather than simply reject it as my disgust reaction might encourage me to do. If I do not integrate the

28. Steinmetz, "Kimberlé Crenshaw," para 3.
29. See Hoard and Hoard, "Queering."

shame, process it, grieve the fact of living in a queerphobic society and allow that grief to restructure the way I understand the world, I will still be trapped in that world with its queerphobic big Other. In that case, I am far more likely to push my shame off onto other queer people, usually queer people whose identities or presentations are even less socially normative than my own. I will be tempted to become a "pick me" queer or "one of the good ones" who resists, but ultimately makes peace with queerphobic normative society by shifting society's stigma onto other queer folks. Unfortunately, I have seen this tragedy play out in my own transgender community as white trans women who possess conventional femininity and a greater degree of privilege than some of their trans siblings begin to focus on less normative trans people as responsible for the queerphobia that is directed at them. "If they would just try to actually fit in a little better; if they weren't so *weird* (read queer), then cis people wouldn't have such a problem with trans men and women," they say. These transgender people have not integrated their shame and moved through the grief of living in a queerphobic society and are trapped by their own internalized queerphobia in a zero-sum world where *someone* has to be stigmatized. The only way to keep it from being them is to push it off onto someone else. They are still trying to appease their queerphobic big Other.

Meanwhile as a white person, I experience white shame as a sharp and stinging awareness of my own whiteness and of the damage that whiteness as a social, political, economic, and even religious identity has caused in this world. And again and again, we have seen how whiteness reacts against the intrusion of white shame (and for those of us who are Good Progressive White People™ those observations likely compound our own experiences of white shame): we reject it; we rage at whatever or whomever had the audacity to trigger it; we try to ignore it; sometimes we wallow in it. Far too rarely, we work to integrate it. On the occasions when I manage to integrate my white shame, I hold on to it and allow it to become grief in me.[30] I examine the grief and allow it to show me more of how, in my imagined reality, I occupy a position—grounded in my own whiteness—which is created for the express purpose of oppression and the preservation of a particular social, political, economic, and religious hierarchy wherein I am privileged.[31] And it is from the vantage point of that grief that I am sometimes able to catch glimpses of a more just reality: One in which the good of some no longer exists at the expense

---

30. See Hoard, "Beyond Fragility"; and McNeil, "White Rage."
31. See Baldwin, *Fire Next Time*.

of the good of others. It is from the vantage point of that grief that I am able to understand one more facet of how white body supremacy is operating in the world and how I might work against it. Sitting with and integrating my shame *in the presence of the Truth that by imagining myself as white I am complicit in the preservation of white body supremacy* allows me to grow further into a person equipped to resist white body supremacy more effectively and joyfully.[32] Through grief, integrating, and processing shame opens up a path for me to continue moving towards Jesus as Life.

FINDING LIFE IN PAIN

We are all familiar with sorrow and pain. It is here. What Jesus's actions and teaching show us is that life is not found in avoiding and running from that pain, but in facing it and communally grieving. Joy and abundant life will be there if we can risk turning towards our suffering and working together to tell a fuller story of who we are and where we have been.

After her trial at the end of *Till We Have Faces*, Orual is able to watch as (in the past) Psyche completed the tasks assigned to her. Orual sees that Psyche is helped by ants and by her own wits, she see the ways in which her own suffering had been allowed to aide Psyche on her quest, and then Psyche is standing next to her:

> All that had then but flashed out in a glance or a gesture, all that one meant most when one spoke her name, was now wholly present, not to be gathered up from hints nor in shreds, not some of it in one moment and some in another. Goddess? I had never seen a real woman before.
>
> ...
>
> I cast down my eyes.
>
> Two figures, reflections, their feet to Psyche's feet and mine, stood head downward in the water. But whose were they? Two Psyches, the one clothed, the other naked? Yes, both Psyches, both beautiful (if that mattered now) beyond all imagining, yet not exactly the same.
>
> "You also are Psyche."[33]

---

32. See Hoard and Bland, "'How Am I Responsible?'"; and Jacobs, "Learning to Love White Shame."

33. Lewis, *Till We Have Faces*, 306–8.

It is only when we accept the eucontaminating Truth that sometimes only shame is able to show us that we are able to integrate it, walk into and through our grief, and then find that we are becoming the great Beauty that we have always been. In a world so full of oppression and cruelty, it is only on the other side of shame that we are able to hear and see that "You also are Psyche."

There is deep shame and pain and guilt involved in this world we inhabit. But trusting in the eucontaminating power of Christ frees us to move into and not away from that shame, trusting that we are and always have been more than we could possibly imagine. Thank God that we are not who we think we are! Entering into our shame opens up the possibility of joy and life. As Chesterton writes at the end of his book *Orthodoxy*, "there was something that He [Jesus] hid from all men when He went up a mountain to pray. There was something that He covered constantly by abrupt silence or impetuous isolation. There was some one thing that was too great for God to show us when He walked upon our earth; and I have sometimes fancied that it was His mirth."[34]

---

34. See Chesterton, *Orthodoxy*, 299.

7

Recovering Joy

There was something that He [Jesus] hid from all men when He went up a mountain to pray. There was something that He covered constantly by abrupt silence or impetuous isolation. There was some one thing that was too great for God to show us when He walked upon our earth; and I have sometimes fancied that it was His mirth.

—G. K. Chesterton

In the summer of 2024 when Joe Biden dropped out of the presidential race and Kamala Harris became the new Democratic nominee, the first line of attack that the Republicans mustered against her was her laugh.[1] Harris laughing, enjoying herself, was somehow seen by the Republican strategists as a weakness to exploit. Americans, they thought, won't want to see a Black woman laughing. While this thinking may seem strange at first, as we will explore in this chapter, joy is a profound and powerful force. In those who set themselves against it, joy has the power to elicit rage and violent rejection.

---

1. See Huang, "Audacity of Kamala Harris' Laughter." This made enough of a cultural impression to have been included in a Saturday Night Live sketch featuring Harris and Maya Rudolph. See Saturday Night Live, "2024 Pre-Election Cold Open."

The eucontaminating Life that Jesus offers us is not easy. It is often a road of toil and tears; "in this world you will find trouble" as Jesus told his disciples (John 16:33). But the Life that woos us through the Spirit is also one of joy—not always happiness—but of deep joy. The full joy of Christ is one that tears down towers with laughter, and undermines the powerful with mirth. A world of joy is a dangerous threat to empire and oppressive social orders.

Society messes with your head. We do, in fact, "live in a society." None of us exists outside of a context and as much as the American mythos would have us believe that we are all rugged individuals and that with enough willpower and grit you can shape yourself out of unformed clay, the fact of the matter is that none of us can form so much as a concept of ourselves without reference to the societies, cultures, communities, families, and friend groups in which we exist. We shape our understanding of who we are in reference to the messages we are constantly receiving from our communities telling us who we must be, who other people are, and what our identities mean.

To say "I am a Christian" is to call on the centuries of culturally, politically, and economically formed concepts that make up the identity label "Christian." And in the process of declaring that identity, we are simultaneously negotiating the many "Christian" identities which all crowd in on top of one another in that term. If you call yourself a Christian are you saying that you adhere to a particular set of propositional truth claims? Are you claiming membership in a particular religious or social community or tradition? Are you declaring a particular political affiliation? Are you positioning yourself in opposition to some other set of identities (Atheists? Muslims? "false" Christians?)? Are you making a relational claim (I—Billie—once attended a church where the baptismal liturgy involved a declaration that "being a Christian means to me that Jesus is my Forever Friend")? As we discussed in the last chapter, whatever the identity "Christian" means to you at the time you claim it, you are, at some point, going to reach an edge of that identity that doesn't quite fit. You will find that there are truths about you that don't match up to the definition of that Christian identity you hold. As with all identity labels, there are no perfect Christians.[2] There are only failed Christians.

---

2. Let us briefly circumvent certain accusations of heresy here to note that Jesus was not a Christian. To be a Christian (lit. a "little Christ") cannot include being the Christ around whom Christianity is organized. Just as the eye is unable to see itself, Jesus cannot be called a Christian.

Enter: the church.

FALSE CONSCIOUSNESS

If we are not exceptionally careful—and even if we are exceptionally careful—we are going to end up letting various social entities tell us who we are and what it means to be ourselves. This is not something that is always inherently bad or to be resisted. Remember that we develop a sense of self through the dual processes of imagining and marking. We are marked or not marked in various ways by the world around us and the groups we affiliate with. However, what we want to highlight here is that this process of marking is not neutral and equal for everyone; it is impacted deeply by the power dynamics of the culture or group.

On a social scale, one way to think about this is through the concept of *social location* that we touched on in the previous chapter.[3] If you think of society as making up everyone in a large circle, some of us are nearer to the center of that circle and some of us are positioned closer to the edge—marginalized. Now, this is already an oversimplification as intersectional thinking shows that each of us inhabits multiple locations at any given time and the specific context we are in at any moment matters a ton—the high school quarterback may be seen as centrally located at sporting events, but would be a bit more marginalized at a comic con. From a 10,000-foot view though, we can look at broader society to note how some identities are more central and others more marginalized in large part through the lens of what is labeled *normal*. Whiteness in America, for example, is more centralized than other racial demographics in a large part due to the lack of specifier before the word "American." As a white person, my (Paul's) race is rarely mentioned because it is often taken for granted—I fit within the mold of most people's minds of what an *American* is. While specifiers like African or Asian are often used to specify the races of BIPOC individuals with American citizenship, because my identity is seen as the norm, I'm just "American." This dynamic is evident in current nationalist racist rhetoric celebrating "un-hyphenated Americans."[4] Other nationalities in the Western Hemisphere experience this as well. Why is it that the USA is able to somehow claim the term "American" for themselves specifically while others are

---

3. See Hoard and Bland, "'How Am I Responsible?'"
4. See Wilson, "Revealed."

Mexican, Canadian, Brazilian, etc. . . . ? The hegemony of US culture allows it to be the default *American*. So a quick heuristic for one's social location is to what degree you need a specifier because otherwise your identity wouldn't be assumed. In modern US culture, the default identity has largely centered around white, able-bodied, middle class (land owning), straight, Christian, cisgender men. Prior to the election of Obama, this was every president the US had ever had. Think about the use of the phrase "ethnic food." It is rarely used to talk about the cuisine one might find at an Applebees. What makes Thai, Italian, or Mexican food "ethnic" and not steaks, burgers, and microwaved pasta?

One's social location matters. We have talked about this in many different ways through the previous chapters, but one aspect we want to highlight here is that of insulation. If you are more centrally located, you probably won't notice it. The system helps to insulate you from recognizing that it is built for you, because it just runs "normally" to your eyes. We don't notice things till there's a disturbance, a change, or a difference. Many people in the US rarely consider what side of the street to drive on because that's all they ever see. It's not until you almost get hit by a car in London that the thought of driving on the left may ever cross your mind. We don't notice the water we are in. Growing up, you may not have noticed the peculiarities of your family till you started going to friend's houses more. Suddenly your family culture moves from being what all humans do to what your quirky family likes to do. You begin to de-center and de-naturalize your family. It's part of growing up.

This is why those on the margins have a much clearer picture of the group than those in the center. The margins can see what the center has hidden from itself because in order to be accepted, they have learned how to navigate a worldview and way of being other than their own. When you're too far into something, it's impossible to see it clearly. We need others to help us recognize ourselves. Yet, that recognition is rarely pretty and is usually resisted. Because much of the power of the center relies on it being "naturalized" or taken for granted, the recognition that the center's way of doing something is particular—one of many possible ways of being in the world—and not universal—*the* ways humans are supposed to be—is threatening to the social fabric. The center is *meant* to go unnoticed so there are powerful forces that resist when it is called into question. This is the recognition of the Truth of ourselves that we described in chapter 5. The dominant group will resist facing the Truth of itself in favor of the image of how it wants to be seen. We shoot the messengers, kill the prophets, and scapegoat the marginalized instead of listening to what they may have to tell us about ourselves. This is how groups move towards conformity and uniformity even against their own ideals—and the church is no different.[5] Instead of listening to the marginalized, the group demands the margins act like those in the center. "You can be one of us as long as you don't ruffle too many feathers." This is the difference between token acts of diversity—where, for example, BIPOC individuals are often displayed in marketing materials and websites—and acts of actual transformation where a group or institution actually empowers the marginalized among them. The second is much more difficult and disgust-inducing to those closer to the center.

So for the centrally located folks, many organizations and institutions (like church and school) fit well enough with the culture and worldview with which they were raised. However, for those from more marginalized identities, interacting in diverse communities often demands a reframing and loss of yourself to fit the imaginary of the group. This is why membership in a given community (especially church communities) can be conditional upon understanding yourself through the preferred lens of that community. The problem is put brilliantly in Isaac B. Sharp's *The Other Evangelicals* on the struggles of being Black in evangelical churches:

> To be a capital-E Evangelical still meant trying to fit somewhere inside a religious identity originally meant only for white people....
>
> Black Christians who could not shake the conviction that the mainstream evangelical world was somehow their home would **still** be forced to wrestle with their place in a faith tradition that **still** could not shake its insistence on "thinking white thoughts about Black people." As Gilbreath ultimately concluded in **Reconciliation Blues**, being Black and evangelical in the early twenty-first century inevitably required "grappling with what it means to live with this strange DuBoisian dichotomy—a 'double-consciousness' that often requires them to see their faith through a white cultural lens."[6]

In other words, when one inhabits a more marginal social location, belonging in the larger group is contingent on seeing oneself through the lens of the center—not one's own. This *thinking the thoughts of the other*

---

5. See Hoard and Suttle, "Lacanian Virtue Ethics?"
6. Sharp, *Other Evangelicals*, loc. 158–59.

about oneself—being forced to imagine yourself not through your own location, but from the perspective of someone at the center—is very much the "DuBoisian dichotomy" of double consciousness. In order to explore this problem and to situate it in relation to disgust, purity, contamination, and eucontamination, we offer the image of a cycle of identity formation. You exist in a society—in several societies in fact—and it is from society that you get the identity concepts you use to describe yourself. You learned about whiteness and straightness or queerness, and Christianity, and post-evangelicalism, and "being an enneagram 7," and being a Swifty, all from the societies you exist within. And at the same time, all of those identity categories are taxonomies of real, individual people. Queerness can only exist because some people are queer. Christian-ness is only a thing because some people are Christians. The whole dynamic is self-referential and recursive and, at the same time, it changes over time as people work out implications, assert differences from existing identity categories and either shift the categories to accommodate them or develop new categories. We are in a sort of "causal feedback loop" with our own cultures, societies, and identity groups wherein they derive their meaning from who we are while, at the same time, we construct our understanding of ourselves out of the categories they supply us with. We have talked about this process through the language of marking and imagining. We are marked (or unmarked) by those around us in various ways and that informs how we imagine ourselves, which then influences how we are marked (as we talked about in chapter 5).

These categories though, and the cultures that produce and modify them, can be thought of in terms of entities with "desires." As Matt Croasmun describes in *The Emergence of Sin: The Cosmic Tyrant in Romans* using racist/racism as his example:

> This multilevel description demonstrates that any adequate analysis of racism in the United States will have to account both for "upward" and "downward" causation—that is, it will be best described in the language of emergence. Race as a category seems to be constituted and maintained through multiple feedback loops of supervenience [upward causation] and downward causation. The consequences of racism, in turn propagate in all directions: "upward" from racist individuals to social institutions; "downward" from those institutions to racialized actors; and even to the unconscious neurological activity within their

brains, whence come psychological impulses not unrelated to racialized ideology (racism).[7]

Racism here serves as Croasmun's example of a social force or pressure which both is created by the fact of individuals holding to it (being racists) but then turns around and exerts pressure on individuals to conform to its precepts (to act or think in racist ways). And racism is far from the only force that acts in this way. In fact, each of our identities—whether they are good, neutral, or bad—is constituted and acts on us in this way. If there were nothing at hand to help us escape from this cycle then our lives would become increasingly bound up as the constraints of identity expectation wound themselves tighter and tighter around us. In fact, our lives would become a sort of living death as we were progressively alienated from our own particularities and molded into zombie clone molds.[8]

QUEER JOY

It may seem odd, but at this seemingly depressing point, we want to turn towards joy as a response and embrace of the Life that Jesus embodied. The dominant group's imaginary view of the world is threatened when the joy that is supposed to be reserved for the center explodes from the margins instead. The entire social system is created so that the margins will envy the center's joy and not the other way around. The joy of the margins is meant to be foreclosed by the system and is an "impossible enjoyment"[9] in that it destabilizes the system and is not *supposed* to be possible. This is a joy that disrupts identity and social locations.

---

7. Croasmun, *Emergence of Sin*, 52.

8. Complementing Croasmun's abstract theory based approach, Tamice Spencer-Helms, writing from the intersection of blackness and queerness in their book *Faith Unleavened*, describes whiteness first as "an ideology that normalizes the practices, beliefs, perspectives, and culture of white people so that they are the unspoken standard by which everything else is measured," clarifies that "Whiteness isn't an ethnicity. It is the subtext of everything whether theology, or ethics, or history, or economics. It is a logic and a hermeneutic," and finally relates their own experience of whiteness as a force or leaven which "alters our ability to recognize the fruit of Christ in people with whom we don't agree. It is that toxic infiltration that enables people to see Jesus in war, borders, segregation, greed, land theft, and violence, but not in me. Whiteness obscured the truth about me" (122).

9. See McGowan, *Enjoyment*, 19.

Queer joy is powerful and subversive. This is a secret that the queer community understands deep in our bones. We know it because our joy elicits rage from non-affirming people; those who have not taken the journey of queering their identities, whether they are cisgender, heterosexual, allosexual, asexual, gay, lesbian, bi, pan, or transgender. The contemporary queer pride movement began as a protest and a riot, but even in those first Stonewall nights in New York, it drifted into a celebration. There is something heady—almost intoxicating—about looking around you at hundreds of other people who, like you, have been told by society that their sexual or gender differences make them inferior, perverse, *other*, and then collectively choosing to embrace and celebrate those differences. Harkening back to chapter 6, to celebrate LGBTQIA+ pride is to know the shame of being queer in a cis-allo-heteronormative society, to understand it, process it, and recognize that it is society's queerphobia that is actually shameful—and then to turn and say to that society "no." "No, you are wrong; no, who and what I am is a blessing; no, I am not a mistake, *I am not disgusting*." To be queer, no less than to be straight, is to be created and to exist in the image of God. The moment that queer people look around at one another and see our strength, see one another's glory, the spell of cis-allo-heteronormativity is broken. I (Billie) can only begin to imagine the rush on that June night when street queens[10] and furtive queers looked around and recognized their own beauty, belovedness, and power; recognized that not only were we a community, we were a community who was standing up for itself.

While we were working on this chapter, evangelical and conservative social media erupted in a furor over the opening celebration to the 2024 Summer Olympics. The core source of angst was over a performance wherein a troupe of drag queens and other queer presenting people danced and at one point posed in a way that struck many American and Christian conservatives as a reference to Leonardo da Vinci's famous painting of the Last Supper. This proved sufficient fodder for a culture war battle in which France was accused of mocking Christianity. Non-affirming, and especially politically conservative Christians, are not particularly adept at distinguishing between a drag queen and a trans woman, so it was not surprising to me (Billie) when, in the wake

---

10. "Street Queens" was a contemporary catch-all term for people that today we would call queer sex workers; twinks, trans women, and drag queens. "Street Queens" were the lower/lowest class of queer society, unable or unwilling to blend in with respectable folk and banished to the utmost margins.

of the event, I observed an uptick in anti-trans rhetoric from "the usual suspects." I was, however, caught a little off-guard by the piling on of a number of public Christian figures who have been more moderate in their approach to queer people.[11] What I found really disturbing was that the dominant pushback from the more progressive "side" of this debate focused on (accurately) debunking the misinformation that the tableau was ever intended as a portrayal of the Lord's Supper. The progressive side of Christian Twitter jumped to point out that the performance was actually a reference to a painting of the Greek gods as a recognition of the Greek origins of the Olympic Games. While there is nothing at all wrong with correcting misinformation and setting the record straight,[12] what dismayed me was that the response seemed to take for granted the proposition that *if* the tableau had actually been da Vinci's *The Last Supper* then it really would have been an insult to Christianity. The idea that it would genuinely be insulting to Christianity for queer people to reenact an event from the Gospels necessarily assumes the incompatibility of queerness and Christianity. Further, it assumes the inferiority of queerness to Christianity; the idea that queerness would *contaminate* a Christian image is core to the idea that the participation of overtly queer performers in the scene would be an insult. Why this assumption?

Personally, I (still Billie) was and am quite taken by the idea of queer and drag performers reenacting scenes from the Gospels. Here in my home of Baltimore there is a local church which, for several years, put on a nativity in which the entire cast was queer and trans. And the idea that this would somehow mock Christianity was never on the minds of anyone involved. The message of the Nativity to queer and trans folx was that we, too, are included in the body of Christ. The message to straight people is an invitation to notice ways in which the story of (in that case) the incarnation is itself a little bit queer, a little non-normative.

It is hard to overstate the importance of this point. Systems of oppression are deeply threatened by the joy of the oppressed. That joy is "supposed" to be impossible—reserved only for those at the center. And yet at Pride parades and Juneteenth celebrations it bursts forth anyway as an impossible enjoyment that subverts and disturbs the system. It throws the entire system into question. This is why racist and queerphobic (among other) responses so often center on forms of enjoyment they

---

11. See Pidcock, "Offense Taken."
12. See what we did there?

see. The racist complains about dancing, music, and food because they all point to a freedom the racist can't experience. He is too locked in his own world of domination, and their joy declares aloud his own unfreedom. The joy of Pride parades boldly proclaims the restricted unfreedom of the queerphobic person. It elicits envy and disgust because that joy threatens the dominant social identity. Like the Grinch with all the stolen Christmas toys and decorations, the white (or centered) imagination can't fathom the joy that persists despite the oppression.[13]

SOCIAL SHAME

To this day, the very idea of queer pride infuriates a particular class of people for whom the very idea of queerness as something to be celebrated—to be proud of—is anathema. "Queer Pride" acts with a power which echoes the power of the civil rights slogan "black is beautiful." It is a simple truth, which subverts and begins to deconstruct the foundations of straight hegemony and oppression. Both of these phrases lodge in the gears of oppression and put pressure on the system. To say that Black is beautiful is to draw the attention of whiteness both to the ways in which it denies that statement and to its own unstated insistence, not that "white is also beautiful" but that "white alone is beautiful." In our own day we have seen this dynamic play out in the culture war battlefield over "lives that matter." The declaration that "Black Lives Matter" will only occur in a world which acts as if Black lives do not matter. By declaring that Black Lives Matter, we are saying to a white body supremacist society that it has not treated Black lives as though they matter.

When I throw a fist up under a rainbow banner and declare my queer pride, I am telling cis and straight people that my queerness is worthy of dignity; that *I* am worthy of dignity. And for them to hear that they have to recognize that the identities they inhabit tell them, and have always been telling them, that I am not worthy of that dignity, that only *they* are. The retort "*All* Lives Matter" in response to Black Lives Matter is, in effect, to say "Shut up! Stop making me aware of the ways in which society has said that Black lives don't matter. Stop making me recognize that whiteness oppresses Black people, that our system isn't already just." Ironically "All Lives Matter!" when spoken as a retort—and when is it ever spoken in any other way—is actually the assertion that the status

---

13. See Seuss, *How the Grinch*.

quo should remain and that Black lives should not have to matter. "Pride is a sin" or "What about straight pride?" when offered as a retort—and, again, those phrases are only really ever offered as a retort—is really an insistence that queer people ought to be ashamed of ourselves.

Whiteness, like straightness, maleness, and able-bodied-ness, prefers to exert its power without having that power identified. Hegemonic identities want to have their cake and to eat it too. They want to exercise power over the *other* while simultaneously seeing themselves as egalitarian, colorblind, indifferent to those differences. Not content to oppress marginalized identities, hegemonic identities need to pretend that no oppression is taking place. They have to. To identify the oppressive nature of whiteness, cisness, straightness, able-body supremacy, and patriarchy (to name a few) is to make them problematic, to diminish them. In a word, calling out the fact of oppression threatens to shame and eucontaminate oppressive identities with the truth. Those identities are deeply threatened because they are illusory—dependent on the facade of symbolic identity. This is where concepts like white rage and white fragility come into play.[14] They are the defensive responses to having one's symbolic identity threatened because it is illusory.

And so here we return to our discussion around shame from the last chapter. The joy of the marginalized calls out the shame in the oppressor in a way that points both towards freedom and life. In the last chapter, we touched on the individual nature of shame and how that can manifest in each of us. Toxic shame can be devastating and crushing, but not all shame is toxic. Healthy shame can problematize the unseen structures and systems in which we have lived and benefited, but been too insulated by our power to recognize. The shame of the oppressor can liberate the oppressor from a hierarchical world that they feel a compulsion to defend. White shame can call out those of us who have been marked as white to reimagine a world where our identity no longer requires the subjugation and marginalization of others. As I will describe later, on in this chapter, the shame I (Paul) felt at my own reaction to Billie coming out to me as a trans woman helped me begin to queer my own identity and find joy and freedom in being me—not defensively making sure I was never seen as queer.

Suzy Hansen, in her book *Notes on a Foreign Country*, talks about the naivete of Americans from her experience as an American journalist

---

14. See Hoard, "Beyond Fragility."

living in Istanbul, Turkiye.[15] It is a naivete that at first may come across as innocent or childlike—Americans really do tend to believe that they come from "the greatest nation on earth" and that the American influence on the world has been a boon for humanity. But as she unpacks her experiences abroad she speaks to the malignant and defensive nature of that naivete. Americans aren't naive but defended against reality. Our childish belief in white hats and black hats in the world is actually a cause of deep suffering. The world is messy, America's history is far from pure, and the refusal to see that continues to perpetuate harm. She quotes Curzio Malaparte in his novel *The Skin* on the American occupation of Italy after WWII that "it is a shameful thing to win a war."[16] Hansen goes on to add that Americans rarely feel that shame. Until we can begin to let ourselves experience the shame of what we have done in the name of a greater good or some other motto, we will continue to hide our heads in the sand from reality and history—trapped in a story we refuse to understand. Stepping towards shame by acknowledging what has been, what is in our past, is an important first step.

But remember power dynamics and social location. The shame to be faced is the shame of the center, the shame of the powerful, the shame of Caesar and Pilate. The center will try to pour shame on the marginalized—those on the periphery of societal power. To build off of what I (Billie) wrote in chapter 5, "being ashamed of *ourselves* as queer people is precisely what we must not do—what we cannot afford to do." In the face of an institution, whether it is a church, a church tradition, or queerphobic society as a whole which tells us to be ashamed of our queerness (or other marginalized label), it is critical for marginalized people to recognize the shame; to integrate into ourselves the fact that we live in a world that wants us to be ashamed of who we are so that they do not have to be ashamed of how they mistreat us, how they harm us, how they have killed us. We have to allow that shame to transform into a grief which will—which must—eucontaminate us, changing the structure of our world so that we know that injustice is in the water we drink and in the air we breathe. We must take into ourselves the shame that a queerphobic world tries to lay upon us because when and as we process it, integrate it—but *do not believe or accept it as true*—our worlds can be reformed and made fit to fight for justice. This, as we understand it, is a

---

15. See Hansen, *Notes*.
16. Malaparte, *Skin*, 343.

key insight in James Baldwin's letter to his nephew James about living as a Black man in a white supremacist society that appears as the first chapter of his book *The Fire Next Time*.[17] Baldwin writes:

> The details and symbols of your life have been deliberately constructed to make you believe what white people say about you. Please try to remember that what they believe, as well as what they do and cause you to endure, does not testify to your inferiority but to their inhumanity and fear. Please try to be clear, dear James, through the storm which rages about your youthful head today, about the reality which lies behind the words *acceptance* and *integration*. There is no reason for you to try to become like white people and there is no basis whatever for their impertinent assumption that *they* must accept *you*. The really terrible thing, old buddy, is that *you* must accept *them*. And I mean that very seriously. You must accept them and accept them with love. For these innocent people have no other hope. They are, in effect, still trapped in a history which they do not understand; and until they understand it, they cannot be released from it.[18]

To live in this world as a queer or otherwise marginalized person is to always be told that acceptance awaits around the corner if we would only integrate and become a little more normal, a little less flamboyant (different from the norm/center), if we would just tone it down a little. What Baldwin testifies to in this letter is the fact that liberation simply does not exist on this side of seeking acceptance. Acceptance and integration into normative society may be sweet on our tongues but will always be un-digestible—bitter in the stomach. So long as we accept the premise that, for example, our queerness is something that a heteronormative society is generous to accommodate on its own terms, that society will continue to oppress itself, both its queer and non-queer members. Cisgender, straight, allosexual people will only be free when their society no longer oppresses those who are not like them; white people will only be free when our society ceases to oppress people of color; the able-bodied will only be free when we live in a world built for all. And this is why marginalized, impossible joy is so desperately needed. Queer joy refuses, at every turn, to accommodate itself to queerphobia. We are here—here

---

17. Kimberlé Crenshaw's analysis of oppression as intersectional highlights both the ways in which different marginalizations impact communities in distinct ways *and* the way in which oppressions overlap and draw upon similar tactics. See Crenshaw, *On Intersectionality*.

18. Baldwin, *Fire Next Time*, 8–9.

in your schools, in your churches, in your parks, at your supermarkets, and in every place you call a place; we are queer—blessedly, beautifully, fabulously, and flamboyantly queer; and it is your job to get used to it. And queer joy holds a hand out to you and offers you a chance to be released from a history of oppression in which you are trapped and which you do not understand.[19]

Queer joy is powerful because it exists in the face of a world to whom it makes no sense. Expressions of queer joy are inscrutable to a world determined to believe that queer people are shameful, that queer love is to be hidden or erased, that queer existence ought to be a source of misery. Queer joy shines a spotlight on this particular pile of bullshit with which they have caked their imagined realities—queer joy is therefore defiant down to its DNA. This is the first level on which queer joy acts as a eucontaminant for society. But the transformation that queer joy enacts works on another level as well.

Queer joy exposes to queerphobic people the limitations of their own worlds and their own unfreedom. When a young trans girl expresses gender euphoria over an opportunity to wear a dress or when she is accepted by her classmates, *yes*, it tells the world that she has refused to accept inferiority as a girl, as a child, as a person; but it also demonstrates to them the profound joy that could be had if only they were free to explore, play, and delight in gender. The belly laugh of an asexual teen hanging out with their dear friends tells the world that its allonormative expectations have robbed so many of the goodness of friendship unburdened by sexual expectations. Queer joy does not only tell society that its disgust has been rejected, it draws society's attention to how much it has lost in listening to and cultivating that disgust. The love of brides for one another is profoundly disturbing to a world that centers men. The love that husbands on their wedding day demonstrate to one another holds the possibility of eucontamination for a patriarchy which tells men that their value and validity lies in the pursuit and domination of women. When I (Billie) chose to have my renaming ceremony performed in my church surrounded by friends, family, and my church community, when that transgender renaming ceremony included a communion service presided over by an Anglican priest friend of mine, the entire event carried with it the eucontaminative potential to show the non-affirming church

---

19. We focus on queer joy in this section anecdotally so to be speaking from our own experiences. This is not to say that other forms of joy are not liberative, only that we want to stay closer to our experiences.

just how beautiful it can be when a community celebrates its own in the presence of Christ.

When Billie first came out to me (Paul), I was unprepared. I was working as a counselor and professor at the time. I taught on issues of diversity, and imagined myself an open and affirming person, but I wasn't prepared for what her coming out could do to me. I had always known myself as the younger brother. I imagined myself as the second son. Billie was the one who showed me what it meant to be a boy and then a man. She modeled fatherhood to me. I watched her get married and learned from the way she loved her wife. So on that sunny afternoon when she told me over the phone that she was a woman, I wasn't prepared. My first thought after regaining my mind, thanking her for telling me, and asking for some clarifications was, "you can't be trans, 'cause what does that mean about me? I learned to be a man from you!" And there it was for me to see. I had already made her disclosure be about *me* and a fear of what her identity might mean about *my* identity. My internalized patriarchy and queerphobia was now blatantly obvious for me to see and I felt the shame bubble up. Over the following weeks, months, and years I've been unpacking how I learned so much of what it means to be a man from a woman—and what a gift it has been. Witnessing Billie's transformation and joy in herself has invited me to question and queer myself—facing the shame of my once fragile, cishet identity. I had grown up in a culture that had left me terrified of being labeled "gay" or having my masculinity questioned. Queering myself in this way was a dangerous and powerful eucontaminant for my own liberation. I still identify as a straight, cisgender man, but those are labels that serve as best-fit descriptors of my experience—not fragile identities I have to prove to the world for fear of losing some recognition that doesn't actually exist.[20]

As for me (Billie), I have seen the eucontaminative power and potential of this queer joy play out time and again, online and "IRL." For several years now I have made a practice of posting a picture of myself and a few lyrics from a hymn (different each week and usually one that we sang during the service) on social media with the hashtag #transinchurch; a simple declaration that I am here, that I am glad to be in church, and that I, too, am a member of the body of Christ. Sometimes these posts go unnoticed, but frequently they catch the attention of some still transphobic Christian who immediately performs outrage at me in

---

20. We have written more extensively on the process of Billie coming out to Paul in a previous essay. See Hoard and Hoard, "Queering."

the form of slurs and denials of the possibility of my Christianity. For these people my own celebration of being in church, a member of the body of Christ, is an insult to Jesus, a contaminant in the public image of the church. Rather than celebrating with a sister in Christ, much less honoring one whom the world sees as dishonorable,[21] they mock, rage, and lecture. As James Baldwin put it, "They are, in effect, still trapped in a history which they do not understand; and until they understand it, they cannot be released from it."[22]

LOVE YOUR ENEMIES

In Rom 12:14–21, St. Paul gives the church in Rome direction regarding those who are persecuting them on the basis of their Christianity. He tells them:

> Bless those who persecute you; bless and do not curse them. Rejoice with those who rejoice; weep with those who weep. Live in harmony with one another; do not be arrogant, but associate with the lowly; do not claim to be wiser than you are. Do not repay anyone evil for evil, but take thought for what is noble in the sight of all. If it is possible, so far as it depends on you, live peaceably with all. Beloved, never avenge yourselves, but leave room for the wrath of God, or it is written, "Vengeance is mine; I will repay, says the Lord." Instead, "if your enemies are hungry, feed them; if they are thirsty, give them something to drink, for by doing this you will heap burning coals on their heads." Do not be overcome by evil, but overcome evil with good. (NRSVUE)

This passage has historically been more than a little challenging for Christians. For those who are not from historic peace churches,[23] parts of this passage ("never avenge yourselves" and "if your enemies are hungry, feed them; if they are thirsty give them something to drink") are hard to square with even a just war theory approach to violence, while those within historic peace churches are apt to find the idea that God will enact vengeance or that the purpose of kindness is to "heap burning coals" on the head of anyone, whatever the context, rather alarming.

---

21. 1 Cor 12:22–23.

22. Baldwin, *Fire Next Time*, 20.

23. Church of the Brethren, Quakers, and Mennonites, although this phrase can and should be easily expanded to include all Christian denominations and sects which are explicitly theologically committed to non-violence.

In light of what we have been observing about eucontamination, disgust, and our collective human reticence to allow the Truth to rearrange our imagined realities, St. Paul's comments here make a lot of sense. To play it out in the context of queer joy, the expression of queer joy as an enactment of a better world[24] involves living as people who are in better relationships with one another across differences. Or as Franz Fanon writes in *The Wretched of the World*, "The colonized subject . . . discovers that his life, his breathing and his heartbeats are the same as the colonist's. He discovers that the skin of the colonist is not worth more than the 'native's'. In other words, his world receives a fundamental jolt."[25] When I live *out* of my own queer joy, I am motivated to enact kindness across the board. Deep joy (queer or otherwise) is motivated to rejoice with those who rejoice, to mourn with those who mourn, and to work for the fulfillment of everyone's material needs, including those of our "enemies." And at the same time, as we have seen above, when a queerphobic person, or the queerphobia within each of us, is exposed to queer joy, we are confronted with good shame—an experience for which "to have burning coals heaped on one's head" and "to experience the vengeance of God who created and sustains the Real, who *is* the Truth" are apt analogies.

There is a particularly powerful passage in C. S. Lewis's book *The Great Divorce* where we see this dynamic played out exquisitely. The book is an imagined "field trip" to the outskirts of heaven where the narrator gets to see spirits given the opportunity to choose whether or not to journey towards heaven (referred to as "the mountain"). Again and again the spirits end up turning away from Joy until Lewis encounters a spirit with a little lizard on his shoulder making his way towards the mountain (heaven). The lizard, however, is chattering in the spirit's ear and eventually convinces the spirit to turn back just as an angel shows up and invites the ghost to keep journeying toward the mountain. The ghost clearly wants to but explains that he is ashamed of the lizard whose "stuff won't do here" and has therefore given up on journeying to the mountain.

Even when, in our most honest moments, we can accept that our prejudices and understanding our ourselves are preventing us from moving towards a more just and flourishing world, we can find it hard to abandon them; like the lizard, they "insist on coming along" and we find ourselves caught between our desire for Joy and our desire for comfort.

24. This same impulse and power is also notably present in decolonial and afro-futurist literature.

25. Fanon, *Wretched of the Earth*, 10.

"Would you like me to make him quiet?" said the flaming Spirit—an angel, as I now understood.

"Of course I would," said the Ghost.

"Then I will kill him," said the Angel, taking a step forward.

. . .

"Get back! You're burning me. How can I tell you to kill it? You'd kill *me* if you did."[26]

And this is the crux. The loss of our imagined realities and self-image is something that we fear and experience as a death. The great and terrible truth at the heart of the gospel is that Jesus Christ has made joy—everlasting joy—available to us, but that he accomplished that through his own death and resurrection and that therefore the road to joy—to life—lies through death. Again and again, on this side of the literal grave and (we pray) in eternity, the way to joy passes through death. The ghost continues somewhat frantically to try to make a decision as the angel waits for permission.

"I know it will kill me."

"It won't. But supposing it did?"[27]

And here we are at the moment within the moment of decision. Unable in the end to keep the truth from breaking into our little realities, we are confronted with the choice between the death that leads to life and slow lingering life that leads only to "almost innocent" dreams and a fading death. This is where joy from the margins comes into its greatest power. If we on the margins have done what we can to love our oppressors without for a moment denying the joy of who and what God has made us to be, then when they are in that moment, they will have (together with every other stirring of longing and desire and whisper of a better world that the Holy Spirit has managed to smuggle into their little worlds) a stronger, more compelling case for joy and a more stark and honest understanding of the dreariness, the banality, of injustice to draw on. This time the ghost relents and gives the angel permission.

I (Billie) will never forget the moment I chose to stop pretending to be what I never was and to come out to the world as trans, as a lesbian—more than half convinced that it would cost me everything, and how after the dysphoria, the depression, the dissociation, the anger, the terror, and the panic, I ended whimpering, "God help me. God help me," only to find

---

26. Lewis, *Great Divorce*, 107–9.

27. Lewis, *Great Divorce*, 109.

the door to life and joy swinging open in my face. In *The Great Divorce*, the angel "kills" the lizard and the ghost reels in pain and shock only to find the killed lizard miraculously transforming into a majestic and glorious stallion. In choosing the joy that lies on the other side of death we often find life and the resurrection and glorification of the very things we thought we were giving up.

Going further, it is here that we begin to see the real power of Christian enemy-love. We can only love our enemies from a place of deep (albeit sometimes *very* deep) personal joy. When Jesus told us to love our enemies as well as our neighbors[28] and to love our neighbors as ourselves,[29] a love of the self in all of its particular and varied identities (the necessary condition and cause of joy) is the assumed prerequisite. Thus enemy love is very fundamentally the enactment of power, not against the truth of our "enemy" but against all within our enemies' imagined reality which stands between them and life and joy.

It is also the necessary step to not re-enact the very same form of oppression and marginalization that we have experienced. When we harbor a disdain for enemies, we maintain and affirm their identities as enemies. They become the focus around which our identity is formed. We are not *them*—the same language that was used to ostracize us. Instead Christ is calling us to love—not pretend there is no threat or there was no harm. Loving our enemies means recognizing that when we continue to keep them as enemies, we are playing the same game they are and working against the kingdom of God. True emancipation lies in the hope of transformation for enemies. It "provides an opening for the adversary to join the struggle and absolutely refuses to place the adversary in the position of an enemy."[30] In other words, when you love your enemies a funny thing happens—you stop having enemies. You stop seeing the world in the grand struggle of us and them. Instead, you have people. Some are adversarial and you will struggle against them, but never so as to other, ostracize, marginalize, or oppress them. Struggle is real, pain is real, but joy is also real. The command to love our enemies helps undermine the very system that manufactures enemies. It is an impossible command to our dysfunctional social systems. It is a command that sees the world upside down saying that the blessed are not the rich and powerful, but the meek and poor in spirit. It is an upside-down world where God is

28. Matt 5:44.
29. Mark 12:30–31.
30. McGowan, *Enjoyment*, 20.

found among the tortured and executed; where leadership is service and strength is weakness.

God's upside-down community rejoices when persecuted, finding that when they are ostracized, they are standing with Christ who was ostracized. It grows through death and spreads through weakness. The kingdom of God is the contaminant. If we allow our institutions, communities, and churches to be eucontaminated by life, we will not be playing the same game as the world. We will be following the upside-down logic of St. Paul, who says that only by losing our life can we find it. Only by facing our shame, can we move to grief; only by finding our belonging in the non-belonging of Christ, can we ever be home. Regardless of your political views, a person's joy (not just mere happiness) should never be a source of scorn, but life. If you aren't able to "rejoice with those who rejoice" and "weep with those who weep" (Rom 12:15), it may be time to reflect on what's become so important and fragile that it has cut you off from the life that Jesus brings.

8

Yuck Walks and Desire
The Way of Jesus

Take delight in the Lord, and he will give you the desires of your heart.

—Psalm 37:4

As we turn now to our chapters on the Way, it's important to remember where we've been. Disgust is an oft-ignored, but foundationally important aspect of humanity. Disgust regulates our sense of self on an individual and communal level. Our hope in this book is to point towards the good news of Christ's eucontamination by following his teaching about Truth, Life, and now the Way. Truth was shown to be far from straightforward, as we are inextricably caught in our own bullshit. Life is paradoxically found in moving through our shame and into our grief, not running from them. Likewise, the Way of Jesus is not the path of least resistance. In the parable of the seed and the different soils,[1] Jesus talks about the seeds that are sown in thorny soil which spring up but are then choked out by the "cares, riches, and pleasures of this world." He recognizes that his Way is often difficult to follow; it is opposed by the cares and riches and pleasures of this world. There seems to be something in us that longs to be left alone, not to have to buck against the pressures and expectations of the world too much. The Way of Jesus is fundamentally antagonistic

---

1. Matt 13; Mark 4; Luke 8.

to the systems and cultures of the world. If we are to follow the Way, we must be willing to continually fall into our failure and humanity, trusting in the eucontaminating power of love to undermine our expectations, subvert our desires, and transform our world.

Truth offers us hermeneutic or interpretive tools to better discern ourselves and the work of God in the world. Life offers us a hope towards which we press on. The Way now takes us to practices and liturgies upon which we fall when we are lost; actions and steps that we faithfully follow which shape our hearts and our desires. But therein lies the crux: how can we tell what is the Way of Jesus and what is some other aspect of this world or our own psychological process tricking us? We've gone to great lengths to underscore how easily we fool ourselves first. How can we follow a Way if we are so adept at self deception? The answer, we believe, is freedom. As we will unpack in this chapter, St. Paul writes in Gal 5:1, "for freedom Christ has set us free." This freedom though, is all wrapped around our desire and requires that we recognize the myriad of ways we become trapped in the "yoke of slavery." Learning to follow the Way of Jesus is about learning to be free, a hard task. In our world today, there are those who peddle an attractive but false "libertarian freedom," which amounts in the end to nothing more than enslavement to the whims and dictates of our bullshit egos: the false self-images we hold to and project to the world. As David Bentley Hart writes, "freedom is never then the mere 'negative liberty' of indeterminate openness to everything [libertarian freedom]; if rational liberty consisted in simple indeterminacy of the will, then no fruitful distinction could be made between personal agency and pure impersonal impulse or pure chance."[2] On the other side are those who promise flourishing (joy, abundant life) at the cost of our freedom, telling us that the Way requires obedience to their leadership and submission to their bullshit images of reality wherein all are forced to conform and perform to strict religious paradigms of "the common good."[3] This is going to require a little more theorizing before we arrive at the freedom St. Paul is describing but we hope you will stick with us through the chapter as we explore the complexity of desire.

2. See Hart, *That All Shall Be Saved*, 172.

3. Speaking very broadly, the false promise of libertarian freedom that amounts to nothing but enslavement to the ego can be understood as the goal of the neo-liberal project while the fetishization of a forced "common good" flourishing is the ideal of the contemporary post-liberal Christian Nationalist project. Both amount to ultimate un-freedom and death.

PRECONSCIOUS INSIGHTS

Much of the discussion thus far has focused on our conscious world—what we think and consider about ourselves. When we begin to bring in the unconscious aspects of ourselves, the story grows far more complicated. As we have been saying, there's always more to the story and to you than you think. We have mentioned the unconscious before but we wanted to dive a bit deeper into it here. What do we mean by that term and what on earth does it have to do with disgust and the Way of Jesus?

To begin with, let's note the difference between the conscious and the unconscious. When I (Paul) teach on this topic, I like to use the terms "thinkable" and "unthinkable" for them. The conscious parts of your mind include everything you are able to think. Those things you imagine about yourself and the way the world works. Importantly, this will always require an awareness of your knowing/thinking/believing. If I am aware that I believe something, then I am conscious of it. But there are many things that I seem to believe but don't realize I believe—the stuff of therapy and outside observation. When you notice a gap between what you thought you would do and what you did, it speaks to a desire or force outside of your awareness that is also very much a part of you. These processes that happen outside of our awareness point to two other parts of our minds: the preconscious and the unconscious. Simply put, the preconscious is thinkable, but not yet thought. It fits within your existing worldview, but may not have been anything you had thought before. The unconscious, though, is not just outside of your awareness but is actually unthinkable. You are unable to think it. The unconscious points to an aspect of you that resists words and symbolization. Importantly, it's not that you are just putting it out of your mind, it is unable to enter your mind on its own.

Significantly, your preconscious and conscious world are all caught up in your bullshit—as we described in chapter 4. When you hear something that *scans* or already *makes sense*, you've probably just interacted with what was your preconscious—thinkable but not yet thought. Additionally, much of what may strike you as new understandings about yourself and the world are actually preconscious insights. McGowan, for example, argues that what Nietzsche called the will to power—the fundamental driving force behind all human actions and ambitions—isn't actually foundational or unconscious. "The status of this lust is not unconscious but preconscious. . . . We might not be aware of it, but with sufficient prompting, we can bring it into consciousness. It may lead to an unflattering self-conception, but it will not force our consciousness to confront something foreign to it."[4] Imagine that you have been trying and trying to fit a puzzle piece into a puzzle and, as much as you have rotated and shifted things around, you just can't seem to make it fit. Then you notice that there is a similarly colored section of the puzzle up in the top-left. You try the piece there and . . . boom, it fits. That is a bit like what happens with a preconscious breakthrough to the conscious. In contrast to that, now imagine that you are trying to complete a jigsaw puzzle and the next piece turns out to be either a live trout or the entire Byzantine empire (somehow you aren't quite sure which). It just . . . doesn't work in the context of the whole paradigm.

These preconscious insights can be really helpful and life changing—recognizing the impact of a lust for power on behavior is not bad—but they don't structurally alter who and how you are in the world.[5] They aren't traumatic.[6] Preconscious insights instead tend to feel good, like you've discovered something, and lead to exciting *aha* moments. However, after a short while, everything returns to how it was. Instead of a splinter in the brain, like Billie's egocentric dilemma that won't stop gnawing away at her, these insights are like a good back-crack that releases some tension and pressure. In many ways, our fear is that this book will only lead to preconscious realizations and be used to insulate your bullshit instead of opening up to something far more disturbing, but life giving.

What all this comes back to is the failure of self-help books (like this one). No matter how much you may meditate, read, study, introspect, and ponder, there's only so much about yourself and your world that you will be able to recognize. All of those (often very helpful and worthwhile) tools and information about developing ourselves are inherently limited because they all necessarily exist within our given social and symbolic worlds. They are all thinkable. The way of Jesus, though, points to failures, problems, and limitations of what's thinkable and keeps pestering us with "What if there's more?" The Way isn't about what you know, but about

---

4. See McGowan, "Lust for Power," 211.

5. McGowan uses the phrase "lust for power" as his translation and interpretation of what is more commonly termed "will to power" for particular reasons which relate to the way he talks about desire that we will discuss later in the chapter.

6. There are many different theories around trauma that can make our use of this term confusing. We are building off the Lacanian use of trauma that is connected to an irruption of the real. See Žižek, *How to Read Lacan*.

who you are, and what you *desire*. It (he) is, after all, a Way and not a destination.⁷ That is not to say that union with Christ isn't our goal; rather it is to say that union with Christ means "walking" in the Way of Jesus. Specifically because the Way is a person, we will never reach the end of the journey into knowing him; instead we are drawn ever "further up and further in"⁸ into the Person who is the Way, the Truth, and the Life.

In the "Concluding Scientific Postscript" to his translation of the New Testament, David Bentley Hart explains that he elected not to translate the term *logos* (λόγος), saying that,

> In certain special instances it is quite impossible for a translator to reduce to a single word in English or in any other tongue (though one standard Chinese version of the Bible renders *logos* in the prologue of John's Gospel as 道 (*tao*), which is about as near as any translation could come to capturing the scope and depth of the word's religious, philosophical, and metaphoric associations in those verses, while also carrying the additional meaning of "speech" or "discourse").⁹

This convergence of Jesus's claim to be the Way in John 14:6 with John's description of him as the *logos* (most frequently translated as "word") in John 1:1, and Hart's recommendation of 道 (*tao*) as a legitimate (possibly the only legitimate) translation of the term resonates strongly with what we have been saying and will say in this chapter. In *Tao Te Ching*¹⁰ (generally translated as "The Classic of the Way and Its Power"), the classic axial age text on the nature of 道 (*tao*), the text opens with the assertion that "the Way that can be talked about is not the eternal Way."¹¹ A Way is not something that we ever get our heads totally around; that would be a destination. Rather a Way is something that is followed or is not followed. One might say (trying to synthesize the depth and complexity of both 道 and λόγος) that the Way who is Jesus is the organizing principle of flourishing. C. S. Lewis used the word "joy"¹² to describe our heart's longing to walk along and order our lives and hearts towards the Way. *Joy* was his popular English translation for the German word *sehnsucht*, the heart's

---

7. We are going to say this a lot over the course of this chapter and the next.
8. Lewis, *Last Battle*, 151.
9. Hart, *New Testament*, 549–50.
10. The more modern transliteration ought to be *Dao DeJing* but we have elected to use the older transliteration for the sake of consistency and to avoid confusion.
11. Ng translation of *Tao Te Ching*.
12. See Lewis, *Surprised by Joy*.

longing for we-know-not-what, homesickness for a place we have never been. Like the smell of baking bread, or hearing strains of a song we can't quite place but know that we love, it is the part of us that responds with attraction to the prospect of living in a loving relationship with the Way.

Maybe this understanding of Jesus as the Way and Joy as our longing for him which draws us to conform to the Way will be easier to grasp if we abandon the habit of thinking of ourselves as points traveling and changing along a timeline and begin thinking of ourselves as stories that we are telling across time. Thinking of ourselves as points moving along a timeline, changing as we go, cuts us off from our paths and can lead to fear of the future. Of course what we are experiencing is always ourselves *now*, but each and every *now* for us is built on all that came before and every *now* is pregnant with infinite possibilities for what might be. As we live, we are growing like trees or vines through time; we aren't every moment cutting ourselves off from the history on which our present is built. When we think of ourselves as stories that we are writing at every moment, it can help us to think more clearly about what being followers of the Way looks like. We can choose to shape our stories around what we learn and experience of Jesus and who he is. Vitally, one of the beautiful things about stories is that a good author can always cause a re-evaluation (we might even say the redemption) of all that has come before with what she adds to the narrative. What seems for some time to be the story of a villain can, under the influence of the right author, turn into a story of a lost and alienated hero on the path to joy and connection. If we are stories, then, as we are eucontaminated by Truth and Life in the present, our past—never cut off but always a part of who we are—can be re-interpreted as we incorporate and allow ourselves to be eucontaminated towards the Way of Jesus.

Sehnsucht then—joy—can be understood as an attraction that we who are writing our stories feel towards the Way. Not a force that originates *within* us, this joy is the gravity of love that calls to us to shape our stories towards truth, goodness, and beauty, towards God. "*Pondus meum, amor meus,*" said St. Augustine in the *Confessions*, "my love is my gravity." In the last lines of his *Divine Comedy*, Dante despairs of expressing in words his experience of God and concludes with:

> Here powers failed my high imagination:
>   But by now my desire and will were turned,
>   Like a balanced wheel rotated evenly,

By the Love that moves the sun and the other stars[13]

"The Love that moves the sun and the other stars" is the gravity that is the love of God and which gives birth to the joy that calls out to our unconscious, guiding us towards the Way who is Jesus.

DESIRE

This desire for flourishing: the desire for something more, something beyond, is critical in any attempt to follow the Way of Jesus. In the global West, we have an established tendency to think of humans as primarily emotionless thinking machines. We have taught ourselves to be suspicious of our desires. And in white evangelical churches, it isn't uncommon to hear warnings that "the heart is wicked above all things" as an admonition against ever listening to or being guided by our desires. But this idea that humans are, or should be, mere reason machines is deeply mistaken. Instead of humans as thinking beings we are first and foremost desiring beings.[14] Lacanians are also not alone in this assertion. James K. A. Smith, for example, argues that we are primarily shaped not by thoughts but by our loves and that desire and habits are central to our formation.[15]

Desire is not what it often presents itself as at first blush and if we are going to incorporate our desires as signposts along the Way of Jesus, we need to learn discernment. On a simplistic level we often think that desire is all about what we want and thus reducible to a feeling and thought. I (Paul) am currently hungry as I write this and feeling my desire for lunch. In this case desire is all about the food I intend to eat. But this misses a significant point: the object of my desire (what I think I want) and the cause of my desire (why I'm wanting in the first place) are not the same thing. Consciously, my mind is on food (perhaps an egg sandwich today) so I think that it's the sandwich that is causing me to want it. Agency from this perspective is on the side of the sandwich and I'm just a passive player in this game. The sandwich has lured and wooed me into preparing and eating it.[16] We often think that our object

---

13. Translated by Robin Kirkpatrick. Dante, *Divine Comedy*, canto 33, line 45.

14. See Fink, *Lacanian Subject*; McGowan, *Enjoying What We Don't Have*; Žižek, *Sublime Object*; Copjec, *Read My Desire*.

15. See Smith, *You Are What You Love*; and Hoard and Suttle, "Lacanian Virtue Ethics?"

16. In her book *Sexed Up* Julia Serano, theorizing about street harassment and

of desire holds the power to create desire within us, but this is actually the work of fantasy at play. Our desire actually comes from our own lack. In the example of the sandwich, it's my hunger that causes me to start searching for an object to satisfy it. The process starts with an emptiness (in my stomach). The sandwich is just the thing that fits within my mind's frame as a possible answer to this lack. The fantasy of my satiated hunger lands on the sandwich as the thing I want—if not now feel I *need*. In this way, the fantasy—fueled by my lack—is what imbues objects with their imagined power to satisfy. In other words, fantasy gives structure to my conscious desire but is not the *cause* of it.

But, as you may have just noted, this desire is still conscious: what I am aware of wanting. There may be far more complexity to what I think I want on a preconscious level, but both my preconscious and conscious circle around the object of my desire. Unconsciously, a very different mechanism is at play because the conscious and unconscious are not just different but in tension with one another. Consciously, fantasy structures desire around an object of desire. Unconsciously though, desire is more structured around the obstacle to that object.[17] It is actually aimed at creating more desire and so is resistant to attaining what you think you want—more about the obstacle than the object.

To return to the speed radar by my house for a moment, there's a funny thing that happens when we are given a limit or obstacle. Some part of me (Paul) definitely wants to be a good, safe driver and follow the rules—and not get speeding tickets. But another part of me doesn't just want to get where I'm going faster, it enjoys breaking a limit, pushing into or past a barrier. The very fact that I have been given a limit to my speed creates a desire for me to surpass it and I feel guilty when I don't listen to this desire. This all means that if I follow the rules and drive slowly, I feel a sense of deflation at having been put in my place by a dumb sign and my own lack of agency. If I drive fast and ignore the sign, I feel guilty for having broken the rules. There's no way through the knot without feeling guilt. Damned if you do and damned if you don't. Desire is thus related to limits/obstacles and fuels a motivation to break them. We are continually

---

unwanted attention, makes a compelling case that those with marked characteristics are experienced as *inviting* the desire or attention of those who experience them. People locate the desires which originate within themselves (hunger, loneliness, arousal, etc. . .) in the marked person their desires have latched on to. See Serano, *Sexed Up*.

17. See McGowan, *Psychoanalytic Film Theory*.

drawn to what we don't or can't have because the obstacle itself is what makes us want.

In my (Paul's) clinical work, I find this point incredibly powerful. The question, "What do you want?" is actually deeply unsettling when we begin to explore the incredible complexity, shame, and confusion wrapped up in it. What we want is always more and less than what we are getting. What we want is paradoxically impossible and at odds with itself. What we want is always just outside of our reach and we can never fully know what it even is.

To further complicate the situation, we look to others (big and small others) to tell us what to do, what to pursue. Society (the big Other) is what helps shape our fantasies for the objects that we consciously pursue. I learned I was supposed to pursue good grades, hard work, and a large income. Capitalism is so ubiquitous in part due to its ability to commercialize this aspect of humanity and continually offers up new products and services that will disappoint, but that we all fantasize that we want. It's a perfect, unending loop of lack, fantasy, and disappointment that will always have another object ready to be imbued with the fantasy of a satisfaction that can't exist.[18]

The children's show *Bluey* hits on this topic in a number of episodes, but one episode in particular, "Shadowlands," brings it to the fore. In the episode three children are playing together, but the lead character, Bluey, grows frustrated that her friend, Coco, keeps making games easier for herself so they aren't fun for anyone. As the episode continues, they play a new game of trying to traverse the park without stepping in the sun. They run into various obstacles that lead to innovations, creative responses, and excitement because they refuse to alter the game to make it easier. At the end, Coco realizes that it was the struggle and the difficulty that actually created the fun of the game. She thought she just wanted to win the game and reach the end, but having that goal and struggling through obstacles to achieving it actually opened up the possibility of fun.[19] As the acclaimed philosopher of games and play Bernard Suits wrote, "playing a game is the voluntary attempt to overcome unnecessary obstacles."[20] In other words, play requires obstacles.[21]

---

18. See McGowan, *Capitalism and Desire*.
19. Brumm, *Bluey*.
20. See Suits, *Grasshopper*, 43.
21. See Žižek, *Sublime Object*.

The impossibility of satisfaction and the inherent failure of all objects to ever satisfy is due to the nature of language, consciousness, and subjectivity.[22] Remember all communication is a failure. We can never fully articulate—to ourselves or others—the fullness of our desire. We are always saying more and less than what we think we mean. The truth that motivates our speech can never connect to the product of that speech. When we feel a need (like babies being tired, wet, or hungry), we are forced by language to turn that need into a demand by expressing it symbolically (using signifiers/words). These signifiers are finicky though, because they have been externally imposed on us (no one person came up with English) and they never fully map on to what we mean. If I say the word "chair" we may both have a close-enough idea in our heads to communicate intelligibly, but are not thinking of the same exact thing. Poetry and art play with this very gap between language and intention to draw out inexhaustible meaning and beauty. Poetry, unlike academic essays, utilizes the very failure and limitation of language to *accurately* and definitively say what we mean. Language never fully maps onto reality.

So, when a baby calls out to their caregiver, they are always signifying some form of neediness or lack to be met (like a feeling of hunger, tiredness, or discomfort). But what is demanded in the enunciation (cry or act of speaking) is always more and less than what can be communicated in the words or sounds used. This means that when the caregiver responds to the baby's demand, they can never fully meet it. They may meet the need for food, but something is always left—there's always an excess. This excess is desire. Desire is what remains after need is subtracted from a demand. Or as Bailly puts it, "Desire is the by-product of language in the Other, and is the result of the impossibility that demand can fully articulate the need."[23]

---

22. Back in chapter 1 we mentioned the mirror stage and the advent of consciousness as the time when the ego and a sense of the self emerges through a misrecognition of oneself in the mirror (or some reflection). This image of the self is always external and captures a sense of you, but always leaves something out. Another important thing happens at this time as well. In this mirror stage, the subject enters into the symbolic world of language. This is not necessarily a particular spoken language like English or French, but the symbolic realm of communication—cries, coos, pointing, smiles, etc. This imposition of language leaves a psychic cut and sense of lack that can never be met—the sacrifice of what is called the lost or privileged object. In other words, developmentally, when we begin to communicate with others, we also experience the loss of something that never was but we spend the rest of our lives trying to find.

23. See Bailly, *Lacan*, 111.

Importantly, here every demand—arising out of any need—is also a demand for love. And love, by its very nature, is both inexpressible in language and the most significant of all psychological needs.[24] Without love, babies fail to thrive. But love cannot be experienced if it is demanded. It is only encountered through an excess, by going beyond. Buying my wife flowers because she asked for them doesn't carry the same level of care as picking them up on my own. If I (Paul) only meet the needs of my children, I am not showing them love (ironically even though love could be considered a need), I am actually only doing the bare minimum to not lose my kids. I demonstrate love by working to meet not just their needs, but by going beyond to try to meet the non-essential aspects of their demands—their desires. Love is not in meeting a need, but found in the excess encoded within the demand.[25]

The 2006 film *The Breakup* showed a failure of this well in a scene where Jennifer Aniston and Vince Vaughn's characters get into a fight. Aniston's character at one point says, "I don't just want you to do the dishes [the seeming catalyst of the fight]. I want you to *want* to do the dishes."[26] Him doing the dishes can only be a demonstration of love if she hasn't asked for it. The need for the house to be clean is not the full story. Her demand[27] for him to help was also for him to show love by responding to the excess—hearing the wish for love encoded in the demand for help. Even though he is willing to do the dishes, it is no longer a sign of love because he's now only responding to the explicit need, not the extra. In this way it is both about the dishes (the need) and also about love (going beyond).

This is why a robot can never show love. It will only do what it is programmed to do. If you could make someone do everything you think you wanted, you wouldn't feel loved because love requires responding to the excess, the unconscious (and not just the conscious or preconscious) part, of our speech. Love is never found in just meeting needs. Even if that robot were programmed to recognize your wants and delights and to occasionally surprise you with an excess, it would still fail to show love specifically because that "extra" would be obligatory, "programmed in." Rather than coming from a place of desire for you and your flourishing,

24. Bailly, *Lacan*.
25. See Bailly, *Lacan*.
26. Reed, *Break-Up*.
27. The use of the word "demand" here is to show consistency with the Lacanian language we have been using, not a reflection of the quality of her request in the scene.

the "extra" would be nothing more than the robot doing what it had to do thanks to its programming.

Love is found in the desire (not need) for another. This means that love requires two lacking beings because lack is prerequisite for desire. If I feel a desire for your love, then I am experiencing a lack that your love is intended to fill. For you to be able to show love though, you must also have a desire for me—indicating your own place of lack. Let that sit for a moment. We can love only because we lack. To love and to be loved is to be occupied with filling and being filled by the beloved. Children grow to recognize a lack in the other (primary caregivers) through their experience of the care from those others. In a healthier home, they find themselves occasionally, almost accidentally, meeting a desire of their parents. When the parent laughs in delight at the cuteness, cleverness, or simple real person-ness of the child or becomes a little sad when the child doesn't want to spend time with them, they communicate that desire. So the child then keeps searching for what it is that their caregivers lack. What does the other want?

Now we have previously spoken about the big Other—nebulous *they* of the rest of society. Its first manifestation is in the bodies of the specific others who care for the child. So this lack in the caregivers is transferred into the big Other which is able to be manifest in different groups and bodies throughout our lives. Human development tracks this progression from primary caregivers, to families, to peers, to partners, social groups, etc. . . . The consistent question throughout it all, though, is what does the Other want?

Following this logic, Lacan argues that "desire is the desire of the Other."[28] This cryptic phrase is usually understood to hold two different meanings. First, that we desire what the Other desires—like Girardian mimetic desire, we learn what to care about by what others and society shows us is important.[29] Second, that we desire to be the desire of the Other—we try to become the object of other people's desire and to be recognized by them. In other words, what you think you want is not fully your own. You have internalized it from your relationships and the social world in which you live. This means that there's an inauthenticity and externality to our desire—to our very selves.

---

28. See Lacan, *Four Fundamental*, 235.
29. See Girard, *Things Hidden*.

As third-culture kids, we spent the majority of our childhood years outside the US. This meant that returning to the States periodically was always fascinating because we were not swept along in the same movement as everyone else from fad to fad, but experienced snap-shots each summer we returned and were inundated with the latest craze. I (Paul) distinctly remember how my confusion about pogs transitioned over one summer until I was obsessed with filling out my own Apollo 13 collection from Hardee's kids' meals—or being completely bewildered at the sight of my high school friends raving about Beanie Babies. Each of these fads were new occasions of the youth learning what to desire from society around them. This is why they have come and gone with very few still holding on to their collections of pogs (though I still have a few good slammers if anyone wants to play).

Bringing all this back together, we desire because of a fundamental lack within each of us that comes from the failure of language. Love arises as our response to this lack—a search for fulfillment via the Other. This relationship with the Other, though, also shapes our desires and imparts desire into us. Our desire is complex and multifaceted in that it has both objects of desire as well as an aim of desire that work antagonistically to one another. Consciously we try to possess things and work towards attaining them. Unconsciously we pursue obstacles, driven by a fundamental lack and a satisfaction that is only found in failure. In other words, Burger King lied. You can never fully "have it your way" because what we want is always multifaceted and contradictory.

Therapy with people of faith demonstrates this often in the tortured search for a "calling" and "what God wants from me." Our image of the Divine takes on the projections of our early caregivers (often a father-figure) and we try to figure out what God (dad) wants from us. Our desire is thus decentered from us as we keep searching for God's lack and how we can try to meet it. But our theology and imaginations of a God who doesn't lack (like god as the supreme Odin All-father) leaves us incapable of being loved. Love requires lack. The wounds and failures from our parents are then transferred through our projections to this ultimate supreme being "God"—the biggest big Other. In contrast to this, the way of Jesus leads to a cross and the death of this supreme being.[30] We are instead gifted the Spirit along with the mystery and impossibility of a desiring God—one who lacks. From "before" the beginning God

---

30. For more on the theology of a God who lacks, see Caputo, *Folly of God*; Lewis, *Weight of Glory*; and Rollins, *Idolatry of God*.

is a Trinity; Eastern Orthodox theology speaks beautifully of God as a perichoretic[31] dance wherein the three Persons are perpetually loving towards one another.[32] When we say that God is Love we mean that God is more (but not less) than a desire for the other two Persons of God's self. And then out of that abundant desire and its eternal dance of longing and fulfillment, God chose to create more persons with whom God also desires friendship (love). God is not indifferent to our love; to say that God loves us is to say that God desires our love in return, just as to say that we love God is to say that we want to be beloved of God. In this way, lack is not a problem to be overcome but a generative connection to the Creator.

We can no longer blame that big Other for what we do or don't do, saying "this is what God wants." It's always been our own projections into the heavens. We are faced instead with our impossible desires and lack. This is why Meister Eckhart famously claimed that he prays to God daily to rid him of God.[33]

When I (Billie) was in therapy trying to decide whether or not to come out and live as who I am, I made a point of praying regularly, hoping with each prayer that God would "convict" me with what I ought to do: come out or stay in the closet. Each time, the response I got to my prayers was a sense, not of what God wanted or commanded me to do, but of God's profound love for me and of God's promise to remain with me no matter what *I* chose. At the time, I almost resented the lack of direction. But after the fact, once I had chosen to live openly and authentically, I saw that my prayers had been motivated by a desire to shift the burden of the decision—and of any negative consequences that accompanied it—off of myself and onto God. More than a loving relationship with a Living God, I wanted a big Other whose ordinances I could conform to who would absorb the guilt and internalized transphobia I was feeling.

PLEASURE AND ENJOYMENT

Now remember that the reasons we tell ourselves that we do things always come second to the feeling. We feel a desire and then rationalize a reason for it, but the desire precedes the logic. The rationale for

---

31. Perichoresis references the relationship that the Trinity has to itself in which each member is forever relating to, and being related to, by each other member.

32. See Waitz and Tisdale, *Lacanian Psychoanalysis*.

33. Eckhart, *Meister Eckhart*, 200.

our desire will be made to fit into our sense of self—our ego—but the cause of that desire is usually something totally different. This is because the barrier that we most enjoy pushing into is our own.[34] And here is where the split between our egos and the real of us—our conscious and unconscious selves—comes to the fore. Consciously, we desire comfort and pleasure—experiences and things that would soothe and affirm our sense of self. Unconsciously, though, we enjoy disturbing and shattering that imaginary world—experiencing the obstacle to that very comfort. So pleasure is that positive feeling on the side of comfort and ego, while enjoyment—as we are using it—is on the side of disturbance.

Pleasure and enjoyment, then, are different motivating forces within each of us. One way to think of their difference is that pleasure makes you feel good while enjoyment makes you feel alive. This is extremely counterintuitive so bear with us as we unpack it. Pleasure makes sense. We pursue pleasure and appreciate it when we get it.[35] Most of my (Paul) therapy patients have sought help because of some contradiction between the pleasure they thought they were pursuing in life (jobs, relationships, hobbies, success) and what they actually did and experienced (act out, abuse substances, depression, anxiety). The common refrain of psychotherapy clients is eerily similar to St. Paul's famous lines in Romans 7: "For I do not do the good I want to do, but the evil I do not want to do—this I keep on doing" (v. 19).[36] So as humans, we don't always do the things that we think we want. Something more than pleasure motivates us.

In his later work, Freud revised his original theory to talk about something that exists "beyond the pleasure principle" that could help explain our contradiction.[37] Freud posited a conflict that exists between the life drive (eros) and the death drive (thanatos).[38] Having witnessed the horrors of World War 1, Freud noted that people seem to have a counter desire to pleasure and life that motivates and pulls them along—something that is more aggressive and active. Lacan later reinterpreted Freud's drives, playing with his language to say that the life and death Freud

---

34. Here we are using the English word "enjoyment" instead of the French, *jouissance*. Lacanian scholars debate which is more appropriate for English audiences.

35. Freud's initial metapsychology was based around the pleasure principle—that humans are driven to seek pleasure and avoid pain. But that's not the end of the story. See Freud, *Beyond*.

36. Rom 7:19 NIV.

37. See Hoard and Suttle, "Lacanian Virtue Ethics?"

38. See Freud, *Beyond*.

identified was not that of the organism, but of the ego. The pleasure principle, or life drive, motivates the preservation of our image, while the death drive works to dismantle that ego—the two remain in conflict. So on the one hand, we desire comfort, stability, and affirmation—pleasure—while on the other, we desire disruption, novelty, and disturbance—enjoyment.

Now this enjoyment can never be a conscious aim, because then it would be something that fits within our ego and image of ourselves. Instead, it is always something that comes about seemingly outside of our control or as a by-product from pursuing something else. A Way is only worthwhile if we have some sense of purpose or orientation towards which we travel. The real treasure may well be "the friends we made along the way," but it was the expectation of finding treasure at the end of the journey that made those friendships possible. Fun is our favorite example here. One of the quickest ways to ensure that no one has fun is to set "having fun" as your goal. However, if you play a game and make winning or accomplishing something your goal, fun is often the dominant experience along the way. If you know you're after it, it's not what you'll get.

Moreover, enjoyment and pleasure exist in a symbiotic relationship. Enjoyment is found in the build-up and movement towards what we want, whereas pleasure comes from reaching it. Enjoyment is in the pursuit, pleasure in attaining. Pleasure then functions like a release or relief; it's the denouement after the climax of the story or the sigh after a great meal. Enjoyment on the other hand is bound up with all the tension, excitement, anxiety, and energy inherent in the chase. Consider where you most feel alive: in the build-up or the release? We often think that we want the release, but the build-up, the enjoyment is where life is found. The pleasure at the end of the struggle is like a tax you have to pay to your conscious self in order to keep experiencing the enjoyment of pursuing.[39] It's the rationale for the whole thing, but is really just rationalizing. This is clearly witnessed after every super bowl. There are some moments of celebration by the victors and questioning what it feels like to win, but the reporters will always inevitably turn to the question, "what about next year?" or "what's next for you?" The enjoyment has already been spent from this season. We quickly start looking to the next because that's where our enjoyment and desire now resides. Hiking and board games are more fun examples of this mechanism at work. We go on hikes in theory to reach a particular place, like the summit of a mountain or

---

39. See McGowan, "Lust for Power."

great lookout. We play games presumably to win. Yet in both cases, the vast majority of the actual activity is spent striving towards that goal and on closer inspection is the real motivation. We hike instead of driving even though driving would be easier and quicker because the climb itself is the goal—we desire the obstacle. We learn the rules and play through the whole game because while we trick ourselves into wanting to win, we are really motivated to struggle towards victory. Win conditions just help orient that struggle and justify the effort. We are most alive when we struggle towards, not when we achieve, or in other words, "humans need something to pursue (enjoyment) much more than we need something to possess (pleasure)."[40]

Being oriented purely towards pleasure would actually be a form of death.[41] Remember what we have said before about comfort zones. When you stay well within one too long, it will begin to shrink. Your world collapses into itself and grows smaller and smaller if you never stretch or push past the comfort and pursue something beyond what you think you want. Think of every character building exercise—they all require a trust in something more important, more valuable than your own comfort or pleasure.

If we are to follow the Way of Christ, it will require that we move towards those things that push beyond our comfort zones, that threaten our egos. We must recognize the difference between Life and happiness; Truth and bullshit; Flourishing and comfort. The Way requires discernment. It will require us to take responsibility for our own desires and stop blaming a big Other god for what we have actually wanted ourselves.

Not everything which threatens the ego is good and not everything that produces comfort is bad. Again, what we are offering here is a corrective and a complexification, not a rejection. Wisdom is so important to hold on to. Trauma, abuse, and oppression are all far too real. The body may be strengthened by micro tears in the muscles from exercise, but it still requires rest afterwards in order to grow; whereas strained muscles from overwork lead to long term damage. We need to keep both quantity and quality in mind. Vaccines may have a strain of the virus in them to

---

40. See Hoard and Suttle, "Lacanian Virtue Ethics?," para. 12.

41. It is worth noting here that many conceptions of heaven through this lens are actually visions of hell. The static ideal of a place of pure hedonistic pleasure completely misses the joy inherent in desire, movement, and enjoyment. For this reason, Lewis's heaven is a movement towards, not an arrival. Or, from a more modern example, viewers of the show *The Good Place* (NBC, 2016–2020) may recognize that getting everything you want is actually a form of hell and torture.

help the body know how to fight in the future, but they are not the full virus at top strength. In the same way, we are encouraging you to see value in pushing yourself outside of the places that are comfortable and to recognize that Christ is often found in the places we don't want to go. We are not saying that you should throw wisdom and caution to the wind and place yourself in danger. These tensions are complex and not something that anyone can answer for you, but each of us must wrestle with ourselves—we can no longer blame a big Other god.

DISGUSTING DESIRES AND FREEDOM IN CHRIST

So what is the way forward? How do we make sense of the multiplicity of our desires and the contradictory, interacting directions they push us towards? One of the first steps is trusting in Christ's eucontaminating power in order to start telling a fuller story of ourselves. We must face our disgust and recognize what it is protecting. We are not who we think we are.

In Gal 5, St. Paul writes that it is "for freedom Christ has set us free" (v. 1, NRSVUE). So we are free and the Way of Jesus emphasizes that freedom. The big Other god that gave us all those rules died. But what a terrible burden this suddenly is—especially to those of us in the US today. What is it that we are free to do? How can I possibly know what I actually want? We just outlined the impossible, contradictory nature of desire. Now, the neo-liberal, libertarian, and frankly capitalist, conception of freedom—the cultural and ideological waters of America today—extols a form of freedom that actually controls us. We are free to consume, but must follow the imperative of consumption[42] as our discussion on desire just highlighted. So which desires are truly ours? What are we free to pursue and when is it actually our desire and not just the big Other's desire?[43]

St. Paul continues, then, with a very different vision of freedom than we are used to. He lists the "fruit of the Spirit" (vv. 22, 23) in this chapter as a guideline for us to consider what following the Way in freedom may mean. If you are living in freedom and following the Way, this is what your life will yield: "love, joy, peace, patience, kindness, goodness, faithfulness, gentleness, and self-control" (vv. 22, 23). That is not to say that these are a new set of goals which we fail if we don't achieve. Instead,

---

42. See McGowan, *Capitalism and Desire*.
43. See Žižek, *Sublime Object*; and McGowan, *Capitalism and Desire*.

these are the products of a life of freedom in Christ. You know you are free when these are your footprints.

This may sound odd. Many raised in the church have long and painful histories of this list being used as a yardstick of behavior that has induced shame, hiding, and rejection when someone couldn't measure up. Others may read this list as restrictive and oppressive, having only seen what power combined with ideology has done to the terms on the list. So it's important to unpack the list but also the rest of the chapter in Galatians to see where freedom may lie and what St. Paul is actually pointing towards.

The chapter is complex and we don't have space to unpack the whole of it (though it is fun that St. Paul makes a penis joke in v. 12). He starts with his assertion of freedom and then gets into the debate of his day in the church—circumcision. St. Paul argues against those who say that the Old Testament law is still required to be kept by gentile (non-Jewish) Christians. He then invokes a leaven (yeast) metaphor (v. 9) and uses contamination logic to make his point about the importance of understanding freedom. We are so easily confused by it. We don't know our own desires. Without diligence, the structures of our world will seduce us back to a form of slavery and we will sacrifice our freedom in Christ—like leaven working through a loaf of bread.

Instead, St. Paul orients our understanding of freedom around the commandment "you shall love your neighbor as yourself" (v. 14) and says that we are to serve one another through love. He contrasts this with a concept of "flesh," differentiating the "desires of the flesh" from the "desires of the Spirit" (v. 17). St. Paul pits these two against each other. The desires are contradictory—like how we've analyzed desire above—but this antagonism has a result. St. Paul writes that they are in tension, "to prevent you from doing what you want" (v. 17). He is highlighting how these two desires end up alienating us from our own desires. We are caught up instead in the desires of someone else—an Other. This is crucial. When we are stuck in the never ending war between our contradictory desires, what ends up being lost is ourselves—our own agency and authenticity. We are caught in the desire of the big Other (and all the literal others around us). We can't know what we want.

St. Paul then writes that in being led by the Spirit, we are no longer "subject to the law" (v. 18), taking away the taboos, limits, and obstacles that would actually have created our desires in the first place. This is radical. In Romans 7, he wrote that "while we were living in the flesh, our sinful passions, *aroused by the law*, were at work in our members to bear fruit for death" (v. 5, emphasis ours). In other words, the law itself is what created the desire for its own transgression—as Lacan taught us. St. Paul is thus saying that if we are following the Spirit, we no longer need to follow the law—removing the taboo and thus the desire to transgress it. Those desires that were cultivated from the very presence of the law are thus not our own—they never were. Those desires belong to the Other—we are free from them. He then lists examples of the works of the flesh and then the fruit of the Spirit—the products of following different desires. What we find fascinating about this list is the role that others play in both lists. The works of the flesh involve others, but in the service of one's own comfort. They utilize the other for one's own pleasure—reducing them to an object. The fruits of the Spirit, on the other hand, also directly confront the other, but from a posture of love and service, not pleasure. The fruits of the Spirit are much more concerned with enjoyment and the well-being of the other (fostering intimacy) than affirming one's own self-image. St. Paul is saying that we are freed from our own ego. We don't need to pursue pleasure and the comforts that the Other sells because the law that cultivated those desires originally no longer binds us. That's not the God of Jesus. Moreover, we are freed from having to harness our desires and follow strict rules of self-renunciation. Instead, we are free—truly free.

McGowan writes that "the free subject ceases to concern itself with the question of the desire of the Other and pursues its own satisfaction regardless of its relationship to the Other. It neither tries to follow the desire of the Other nor deviates from this desire."[44] The fruits of the Spirit are the product of this freedom. We can be free to love, to be patient, and to show kindness and gentleness because we are no longer enslaved to an ego that is fighting to maintain its imaginary hegemony over us. We don't need to bow to the demands of a society telling us to pursue pleasure at all costs. We are freed from a tyrannical oppressor in the sky who could never love. We are free to discover our own desires.

These fruits may sound childish and naive to those of us who have been inundated with neutered versions of them, when they are actually anything but. Living in such a way as to *produce* patience and gentleness requires a confrontation with disgust and a death of one's image of self—particularly for those of us who have been marked as white and

---

44. See McGowan, *Capitalism and Desire*, 47.

male in our society and most especially by evangelical expectations of masculinity.[45] I (Paul) cannot be wallowing in my own bullshit and working to be *seen* as strong, confident, and powerful if my life is cultivating gentleness and self-control. Remember, they are not goals but outpourings. The fruits of the Spirit flower on their own when we live following the Way of Jesus. We don't pursue them directly—like fun in games. If you consciously try to make yourself more patient, you're sure to experience impatience.[46] In fact, it is in making them into goals that we end up being back under the law and cultivate not the fruit, but the desire to transgress them.

C. S. Lewis described this process in his essay *First and Second Things*:

> Apparently the world is made that way. If Esau really got the pottage in return for his birthright, then Esau was a lucky exception. You can't get second things by putting them first; you can get second things only by putting first things first. From which it would follow that the question, What things are first? is of concern not only to philosophers but to everyone.[47]

While in this book, we chose to start by discussing the Truth and the Life as necessary theory and background, it is only in seeking to follow the Way of Jesus, which is the way of real and not imposed freedom, as a "first thing" that we begin to develop the "second things" in the form of the fruit of the spirit.

Here the limitations of an Aristotelian virtue ethic come into play. Classical virtue ethics argues that we can cultivate desires and character through habit and practice. There is definite wisdom in this tradition with a number of leading Christian voices tying this approach to Christian discipline. But what our discussion of the unconscious and desire shows is that if we are not careful in where we aim, we will inadvertently cultivate the desire to transgress our virtues instead of internalizing them.[48] The Way of Christ invites us into humility and failure. In recognizing the ultimate inadequacy of our egos—bullshit self-images—to ever fully embody the virtues, we are able to let that failure point towards a more real us. "In the end, what the practice of virtue ethics elicits is an encounter

---

45. See Du Mez, *Jesus and John Wayne*.
46. See Hoard and Suttle, "Lacanian Virtue Ethics?"
47. Lewis, *God in the Dock*, 280.
48. See Willard, *Divine Conspiracy*.

with both our unconscious desire (which is typically horrifying) and our enjoyment. So while the pain of facing our unconscious desire hurts, it also vitalizes us, as we become more able to encounter the real."[49] The Way of Christ is through the death of self and the crutch of a big Other in the sky, an embrace of that failure, and an encounter with what the world sees as folly (Rom 1:25).

In John 15, Jesus tells his disciples that the world "hates you" (v. 18) because his disciples no longer belong to the world. This, we believe, is what St. Paul is saying with regards to the Spirit. We are free from the dictates of the big Other. We are free to pursue our desire, not the desire imposed by a patriarchal, capitalist, racist society. Instead, we are becoming truly free. And this freedom requires a confrontation with disgust through love. This freedom is the Way.

YUCK WALKS AND DOG POOP

As we move towards the end of this chapter, we wanted to highlight some practical approaches to eucontamination that we have witnessed, practiced, or seen. These practices involve a recognition of disgust, the presence of a healthy context, and the courage to move towards the contaminant with a posture of love. In going through these steps, we engage the disgust mechanisms within us—stirring the risk of contamination. Disgust can be a helpful alert that something is stirring on an unconscious level, that the real is pushing into our bullshit world. We often try to hide disgust from ourselves—rebranding it as fear and keeping it preconscious—so the purposeful move toward disgust helps us recognize it when it surfaces. Then, from this position of excited disgust, in the context of love—not dominance or pressure—we choose to stay in the position of threat, risking contamination, instead of acting out our disgust. It is in this position of activated disgust and intimacy that a transformation of ourselves and it (the object of disgust) is able to begin.

These steps aren't magic. There is no fool-proof method. Eucontamination is wild and untamable—we work with it rather than control it. In this way, we hope to cultivate a character of trust and love so as to recognize and then lower our protective disgust responses.

We recently received a letter from a woman named Deb who had encountered our work around disgust and its effects. Deb told us that her

---

49. See Hoard and Suttle, "Lacanian Virtue Ethics?"

daughter Alina is autistic and experiences pronounced sensitivities regarding sensation. Deb related having talked about disgust, its operation, and the role and nature it plays in our lives with her daughter and that Alina suggested that they go on what Deb has termed "yuck walks." After a rain they took off their shoes and went walking around outside paying particular attention to the sensations of mud and wet ground and to any other stimuli which started to arouse a disgust response. They greeted their disgust responses by recognizing them for what they were, processing them and appreciating what their bodies were telling them regarding the safety and advisability of their situation. In this context those sensations which would otherwise have triggered extreme discomfort instead resulted in curiosity and even a form of delight.

We noted that several key elements were present in the experience of a disgust walk: First the exercise was undertaken with mindfulness and preparation. Deb and Alina set out prepared to experience disgust but equipped with a sense of curiosity and interest. Thus when the disgust reactions arose, they were able to notice, examine, and appreciate them rather than simply react. Second, the walks were taken together. Critically, intimacy decreases or limits our disgust reactions. Experiences which would arouse disgusted alarm, disturbance, or even deep violation in us when intimacy, trust, and connection are absent, will routinely have lowered or even reversed impacts on us when intimacy is present. Both of us are parents of multiple children and have accordingly done our due diligence in changing countless diapers. While certainly not a pleasant activity, it is far less disgust-inducing to change our own children's dirty diapers than it is to react with the same substance in other contexts. We are also both responsible dog owners who live in cities and are regularly called on to pick up after our dogs. And again, while far from delightful, the experience with the little bags is less onerous when cleaning up after our own pets than it would be cleaning up after someone else's dog. In both instances we are interacting with a substance which, while we certainly wouldn't want it to be integrated into "us," is at least familiar due to the affection we have for its source.

And when intimacy really gets amped up, disgust can be so thoroughly mitigated as to be reversed. If you have an opportunity and the right sort of mind, you might find it engaging to replicate the paper cup experiment. Distribute freshly opened paper cups to a number of friends and acquaintances (it is helpful if they see you break the seal on the cups) and ask them to spit into the sterile cup. Then ask them to drink their spit. You will find that most people are disgusted by the idea even though that same spit was in their mouths mere moments ago. We even have different words for the substance depending on whether it is still part of "us" (saliva) or has stopped being "us" (spit). Now contrast this experiment and your own reaction to it, with the reaction that most allosexual people have to the idea of kissing someone they love. Anticipating and engaging in kissing someone we love mitigates to the point of reversal, the negative reaction we have to "swapping spit."

I (Billie) am a member of a writers group composed of dear friends who, for years, met weekly and shared our work with each other. Over the years, we have all learned to recognize certain themes and refrains that we each return to in offering suggestions and feedback. Mine, as it turns out, is "do it on purpose." After hearing or reading a friend's work, I will often summarize or highlight my own reaction to it and ask them whether that was the understanding, feeling, or impression they hoped to leave me with. "It isn't that there is any problem with my thinking the queen is a villain for the first half of the story, so long as that is what you were hoping to accomplish with those adjectives; you can totally do that and it has a powerful effect, just make sure you are doing it on purpose."

When it comes to our physical, psychological, and spiritual disgust reactions, the key is that we *do it on purpose*. Along the Way of Jesus, there is a place for disgust, and there is a place for embracing our own eucontamination. What matters is that we engage one another and the world in love so that when disgust shows up and we listen to its alarm, the actions we take, the positions we adopt, and the life choices we make are all on purpose.

9

Of Flames and Ashes

Tradition is not the worship of ashes, but the preservation of fire.
—GUSTAV MAHLER

FOLLOWING THE WAY IS not something that is done in isolation. There is a well-known anecdote in Quaker circles that our aunt shared with me (Paul). A member of the Friends had stopped attending meetings. One day, an elder visited this Friend and together they sat at a fire. The elder said nothing but then moved one of the logs away from the rest. Soon, that log stopped burning and began to smolder. After a time the elder pushed the log back together with the rest of the logs and it reignited. The elder then left and the Friend soon began attending meetings again.

    I have always loved this story and the image of the silent elder tending to the Friend. When we are separated and isolated, it is difficult to continue burning. Following the Way of Jesus is a task of the community, not just the individual. Our dad has often lamented the way that the English translation of the word "you" in the Bible has been so easily understood to be singular in an American context. However, a more accurate translation may have been to incorporate the word "y'all" more as the authors of the Bible were more often than not addressing the collective, not the individual. The Bride of Christ is the corporate body of followers, not individuals. It is so difficult to remember this in our hyper-individualistic world that leaves us isolated and alone.

Christian love for God and others is the central teaching of the gospel and the greatest commandment—pushing directly against a Western penchant for isolation. The beauty of this kind of love lies in its ability to maintain the contradiction we have been describing throughout this whole text. Christian love maintains the separation of the beloved and the lover while simultaneously uniting them. It holds the paradox and refuses to err on either side. Love refuses to let me be lost in you—for I must stay me to love you—but it also crosses that very barrier in bringing us together. And it is in that mingling of ourselves that disgust is most fully negated. The foundation of Christian community is this impossible, powerful love first demonstrated by Christ who became one with humanity. This means that to be a community that follows the Way of Jesus is to be a people who love.

WHAT IS LOVE?

C. S. Lewis's classic book on Love, *The Four Loves*, has a wealth of insight to offer on the complexity and beauty of love, but his most beautiful and succinct summary of the paradox of love's capacity to encompass both union with and distinction from the beloved appears in the second volume of his *Cosmic Trilogy*, *Perelandra*, where two angels paint a picture of reality for the protagonist, saying:

> He [God] has immeasurable use for each thing that is made, that His love and splendor may flow forth like a strong river which has need of a great watercourse and fills alike the deep pools and the little crannies, that are filled equally and remain unequal; and when it has filled them brim full it flows over and makes new channels. We also have need beyond measure of all that he has made. Love me, my brothers, for I am infinitely necessary to you and for your delight I was made. Blessed be He!
> He has no need at all of anything that is made. An eldil [angel] is not more needful to Him than a grain of the Dust: a peopled world no more needful than a world that is empty: but all needless alike and what all add to Him is nothing. We also have no need of anything that is made. Love me, my brothers, for I am infinitely superfluous, and your love shall be like His, born

neither of your need nor of my deserving, but a plain bounty. Blessed be He![1]

The call of Love is a call to delight in the beloved; to want union with the beloved. We can only be ourselves and are most fully our own selves in relation to the beloved, as Martin Buber has put it in *I and Thou*: "I become through my relation to the *Thou*; as I become *I*, I say *Thou*."[2] Thus our need for one another is both absolute and a blessing: in union with the beloved we become most fully ourselves. Love of the other nearly always begins as a desire for the them whether we are speaking of Love for God or of love for our neighbor; but if it does not stay there, it grows into what Lewis calls a *Gift-love* desiring the good of the other. The *I-Thou* relation of Love is established and in the moments and spaces where we are most concerned with Gift-love of the beloved, we become most fully our own unique selves. "Cast your bread upon the waters:" says the author of Ecclesiastes, "for thou shalt find it after many days."[3] Love bridges the gap between Need and Gift.

Lewis recognizes the necessity of both Need-love and Gift-love. In *The Four Loves* he observes that

> God will have it so. He addresses our Need-love: "Come to me all ye that travail and are heavy-laden," or, in the Old Testament, "Open your mouth wide and I will fill it."
>
> Thus one Need-love, the greatest of all, either coincides with or at least makes a main ingredient in man's highest, healthiest, and most realistic spiritual condition. A very strange corollary follows. Man approaches God most nearly when he is in one sense least like God. For what can be more unlike than fullness and need, sovereignty and humility, righteousness and penitence, limitless power and a cry for help? This paradox staggered me when I first ran into it; it also wrecked all my previous attempts to write about love.[4]

So too in our communities and churches; the Way of Love draws us to experience division, separation, and exclusion as intolerable. We must begin by recognizing our need for one another—a need that our bullshit constructs work very hard to keep us from recognizing. In our bullshit worlds, abled bodied Christians use concepts like "accommodation"

1. Lewis, *Perelandra*, 217.
2. Buber, *I and Thou*, 11.
3. Eccl 11:1 KJV.
4. Lewis, *Four Loves*, 4.

or "accessibility" to think about the physically and mentally disabled members of our body; cisgender, heterosexual, and allosexual Christians talk about "toleration" of our LGBTQIA+ sisters, siblings, and brothers; White Christians talk about "integration" of and "colorblindness" towards our black and brown siblings. And those tepid concepts are sometimes enough to facilitate Real encounters of the other: encounters which under the grace of God may crack open our bullshit realities just enough to let in the Truth of our Need for those *Thous*. Because of course we do need them. No one of us can become ourselves until we recognize our interdependence with all other Members of the body of Christ.

And once we begin to recognize that need, once Encounter begins to dissolve into Need-love for one another, those original, tepid, concepts begin to look first farcical and then horrible. How could we have ever imagined that we were condescending to make space at our tables for these members of our very body?!? What hubris we had! The gall to imagine that *we* were doing *them* a favor when we invested in "accommodating" them, we were investing in our own flourishing; we were restoring severed limbs to the body we all inhabit.

And then, once this Need-love has set in and eucontaminated our worlds, only then will we have grown enough to experience Gift-love for one another. Once we are grounded and blessed in our need for all of our sisters, siblings, and brothers, we start to recognize the overwhelming joy of serving one another out of delight in who they are and a desire for their good. Once each of them is well on their way to joining us as *I-Thou*, we find ourselves longing to bless those with whom we are united.

And then, in Lewis's words, if this process continues:

> [God] communicates to [us] a share of His own Gift-love. This is different from the Gift-loves He has built into [our] nature. These never quite seek simply the good of the loved object for the object's own sake. They are biased in favour of those goods they can themselves bestow, or those goods which they would like best themselves, or those which fit in with a pre-conceived picture of the life they want the object to lead. But Divine Gift-love—Love Himself working in [us]—is wholly disinterested and desires what is simply best for the beloved.[5]

---

5. Lewis, *Four Loves*, 128.

When we have begun to desire and work for the well-being of each other, that is a real indication that we are following in the eucontaminating Way of Jesus.

LOVING THE SPLIT

Because of course, the New Testament authors make a big deal about love. Jesus points to love as the greatest commandment. St. Paul writes that love is the fulfillment of the law (Gal 5:14; Rom 13:8–10) so it is worth exploring in a discussion of the Way of Jesus.

Love is a word that carries a lot in the English language. It is an omnibus concept that we use for all sorts of things, making it difficult to understand what is meant when we read it in the Bible. We may love cheeseburgers, our romantic partners, friends, and kids, but beyond a vague sense of positivity and appreciation, there's not a lot of overlap between those experiences. In this expansive use, love runs the risk of losing its precision and thus its sharp edge. If we love everything, do we really love anything? Is it a thing we feel towards or for something/someone else? Is it a thing we do to or for another? How is love different from appreciation, liking, attraction, desire, or connection?

Throughout the book we have relied upon a particular understanding of the human subject as divided. What it means to be a conscious being is to have a separation between thinking and being, as Lacan would say. Because of the cut that we experience by being able to think and communicate in language, we are distanced from ourselves. In other words, there is always an *other* to each of us. We are never fully and truly ourselves. There is always more. Viewed negatively, this might lead to a sense of alienation from ourselves, a sense of being adrift without anything or anyone to hold on to; viewed from another angle though, the fact that we are never fully and truly ourselves means that we are eternally becoming—that we are infinite. This has a lot of important implications that we've discussed in the past few chapters. But it's here that we want to start unpacking what that means for love.

Disgust is the emotion that helps us navigate these splits in ourselves. It clarifies and distinguishes me from not-me in the face of uncertainty. This, remember, is a really important function. In the world of mental health we talk about enmeshed relationships or psychotic breaks at the extreme end of a lack of distinction where someone isn't able to exist in a shared reality with others—confused between what's inside and what's outside, what's a thought and what's a sound, what's a feeling they have and what others are feeling. For most people, disgust is what arises when their sense of themselves is violated. Like the irritation of having a sticky substance on your fingers, we react in charged ways when that distinction between us and the world is not clearly marked. It's disturbing.

The philosopher Sartre famously declared that "hell is other people." This was not so much a statement of misanthropy as it was a conclusion based on the dilemma of being experienced by others. When someone perceives you, they are constructing a particular version of *you* in their heads, and that version of you is going to be different, both from the real you that you can never fully and truly be, and from the you that you imagine yourself to be. And at the same time, by perceiving them, you are creating a version of them that is different from the Real them and from the version of them that they imagine themselves to be. The result for Sartre was a world in which we are always on some level at war with everyone we encounter, a war for our very selves to determine whose understanding of ourselves will win out. Hell is other people.

And yet, that exact scenario can be constructed quite differently when we bring love into the picture. While the cynic might be inclined to say that love causes us to see one "through rose colored glasses," we might also say that it is only when experiencing one another in love that we catch a glimpse of the beloved as infinite. If you have ever had the realization that you could spend eternity learning to know a loved one more and better and that there would still be more of them to know and have been overwhelmed with delight at the realization, then you know what we are talking about here. So when we are perceived by someone who loves us, when we are beloved, we encounter someone who sees us more (if still not ever perfectly) truly and fully than we are ever quite able to imagine ourselves. It is the lover who sees the infinite shining through the cracks in the bullshit facades we have built between ourselves and ourselves, and thus as lovers and beloveds we are able to experience ourselves.

Importantly, while we are split, that split is also not real. We are contradictions, existing on both sides of the split, not just the one we identify with—again there is always more. So while disgust helps us feel as if we are separate, it is defending the illusion of a distinction and not the reality of it. We are haunted by an urge towards connection, intimacy, and relating while we fight against it. We are drawn toward that which we also put up walls against. My (Paul's) children demonstrate this when they are emotionally charged. Many times I've been in their rooms when they are upset and feel stuck between their anger at me (Daddy go away!) and their fear of being left (no! Don't leave me alone!). They vacillate between the two impossible, contradictory desires: for space and for fusion. That's what it means to be human. Peekaboo is another classic example of this. Kids want you to disappear so you can reappear so that you disappear again.

Classic analytic theory plays with this. Freud and Jung use the gendered metaphors of fathers and mothers to talk about these opposing forces.[6] The paternal function separates us from others, giving us an identity and name in the world, while the maternal function joins us to others. They are perhaps more clearly seen in their obscene forms from scary movies. The paternal threat comes from the symbols of authority, protection and control that are twisted into sources of fear, perhaps most strikingly portrayed by the character of Jack Torrance from *The Shining*. He transforms from the loving father to a homicidal maniac.[7] Conversely, the maternal function becomes twisted in the form of the devouring mother who consumes her victims as they are dissolved into her. The aliens from the movie *Nope* are an example of this as they exert an overwhelming fear of being consumed and dominated.[8]

Contradiction, in other words, goes all the way down, or as McGowan writes, "every being, even those that appear substantial, exists through contradiction."[9] So love must somehow contend with this contradiction. Love, if it is to be anything more than a mere sentiment, must somehow speak to both sides of our divided selves—calling us to something more.

Much of the way that love is talked about in the contemporary West is actually an attempt to neuter love and constrain it into an affirmation of our bullshit. We speak of love for things that make us happy, comfortable, and cozy. My "love" for a cheeseburger is not really love. I enjoy cheeseburgers. They spark feelings of contentment and pleasure, but that connection is anything but love. I don't *love* them because the relationship is one-sided. They are a tool for me. I am drawn to them for what they do for me. There is no affirmation of the cheeseburger in the relationship. I consume cheeseburgers—they exist for me. In this same way, many of our relationships, if we look at them honestly, exist in the same structure. We

---

6. See Creed, *Monstrous-Feminine*; and Žižek, *Looking Awry*.
7. Kubrick, *Shining*.
8. Peele, *Nope*.
9. See McGowan, *Emancipation*, 135.

look to other people to help us feel better, because they are fun, because of what *they* do for *us*. This is not love. This is inherently self-focused. It is a form of relating that is all about supporting ourselves and who we think that we are. These relationships are better described as the relationships of *selfobjects*—affirming our self esteem and self concept.[10] Love, on the other hand, is necessarily unique. The other can't be substituted because they aren't just a function but an individual. *Selfobjects*, whether they are actual objects or persons whom we have reduced to tools for our own satisfaction and self-affirmation, are limited and finite. In contrast, persons are infinite; each person we encounter is, and will always be, more than we can experience.

When I (Paul) was in college, I remember living out this form of relating. My goal each weekend was to maximize the amount of fun that I could have. To that end, as the weekend approached, I'd think through which friends were available and how much fun I imagined I could have with each one. I then ranked them in terms of maximizing fun and would go down my list looking for the most fun. I was, in other words, a jerk. My relationships were entirely about me and my fun. Note that there was no concern for others. My friends in this logic were all interchangeable facilitators of my enjoyment, not unique, infinite image bearers of God. I reduced everyone around me to objects for my own fun. If asked, I would have said that I loved my friends because I didn't even have the capacity to recognize how self-centered my world was and this was the best I knew of. It took years of therapy, maturing, and patience for me to begin even being able to hope for a form of relating deeper than this.

Beyond the selfishness of it all, that form of relating was also incredibly lonely. I was reducing others to objects, but also fearing that I was being reduced in the same way. My value to them, as far as I could see, was reducible to how much fun I could help them have—it was always contingent. I needed to keep up the charade of being cool, funny, or charming in order to have friends because I was reduced to being a function at the same time that I was reducing them to the same. Buber writes that in I-it (as opposed to I-thou) relationships the result is that they eventually devolve to it-it relationships. I can only be an *I* in relation to a you that is recognized as a subject (*thou*) and not just an object, otherwise we are

---

10. See Kohut, *How Does Analysis Cure?*

both reduced. It was, to put it harshly, a minor microcosm of hell. When we look at others as objects we become objects ourselves.[11]

Conversely, other forms of love take the inversion of this. While some of us are more prone to reducing others to objects in order to prop up a false sense of ourselves, others reduce themselves to objects for the sake of the other. This is the position that is often seen in what is sometimes called codependence. When your form of love is only focused on the other and neglects the importance of your desires as well, it isn't love. This is a more insidious misstep in love as it takes on the appearance of self-sacrifice, but it does so in a way that completely overlooks the care of the self. When someone struggles to articulate their desires, or stretches themselves so far as to hurt for the sake of someone else who does not necessarily need it, we are in the terrain of this inversion.

There is a gendered component to these two misapplications of love. In a patriarchal society, those marked male are socialized to objectify others in order to try to make themselves seem complete.[12] This is perhaps most caricatured in the narcissistic frat guy who uses others for his own status and sense of worth. Those marked female, on the other hand, are more often socialized to devalue their own desires and interests for the sake of caring for others (children, family, partners). When one's desires aren't taken into consideration or valued, it is often felt easier to disconnect from them or turn them into demands and needs to be heard.

But love constantly resists this. Love doesn't help us feel better about who we are or reduce ourselves to an object for someone else; instead it actually destabilizes and disturbs our sense of self (however we've developed) through its valuation of the other and self. "Love . . ." as McGowan writes, is "the way that otherness disturbs identity."[13] This means that love is revolutionary, subversive, and dangerous. Loving is in and of itself a resistance to empire, oppression, and dehumanization. When you love someone, neither you nor they will end up the same.

---

11. See Buber, *I and Thou*, 4–6.

12. In saying that those marked "male" and "female" are socialized in particular ways, we are not suggesting that trans, non-binary, and intersex individuals are socially caused to be men or women; rather we are saying that, in patriarchal societies, society attempts or pressures a particular mode of engagement onto those it marks. This pressure lacks significant nuance and can therefore result in substantial harm to gender non-conforming people who receive complex and mixed messages over the course of their lives. For more on the social impact of marking, see Serano, *Sexed Up*.

13. See McGowan, *Emancipation*, 102.

This subversion is true communally as well. Remember that identity is often wrapped up in our own sense of non-belonging. Each of us is far more attuned to our threats of non-belonging and rejection than we are aware of our proximity to the center of any group. This means that belonging is too often founded not in a bond with others but in a shared rejection. Nothing unites like a common enemy. This malignant form of unity, though, always requires a scapegoat and leaves everyone at risk of being the next sacrifice for the group. In contrast, the Way of Jesus is predicated on our shared non-belonging. Jesus doesn't side with the powerful but insists that all are inside. Instead, Jesus—the one who is God—located himself on the margins. Through Christ we belong in our very non-belonging. Like in individual love, when we learn to love as a community, we forsake the myth of total satisfaction or belonging.[14] We fall into the disturbance of our identity and radically embrace the other. When we love as a community we can transform the very nature of belonging.[15]

ASHES AND FLAMES

We opened this chapter with a line from Gustav Mahler: "tradition is not the worship of ashes, but the preservation of fire."[16] I (Paul) have been drawn to this for many reasons and I think it beautifully captures the struggle we have been attempting to articulate in this chapter. Flame and ash point to two parts of an active chemical process. Ash is what remains after the fire. It is the monument or memorial of a fire that once was. The flame, on the other hand, is the evidence of an active, ongoing, combustion. Flame is happening; ashes are remains. Love is often associated with fire. It burns, it keeps us warm, and it lights up a room. But it is also dangerous and consuming. If left unattended, it can cause devastation. In my home state of Washington each year, the smoke from wildfires settles on the city, polluting the air and highlighting the devastation in the wilderness. Fire is dangerous. Ashes, though, are pretty safe. The ash is what's left. It won't burn you. It can't get out of control. You can touch ashes, collect them, and store them. But you won't have fire. You will have mistaken the memorial, the ebenezer, for the real. It is so tempting to

---

14. See McGowan, *Enjoyment*.
15. See McGowan, *Universality*.
16. See Lebrecht, *Mahler Remembered*.

worship the ashes and the familiar instead of tending to something alive and dangerous. Like the lion, Aslan, from *The Chronicles of Narnia*, Love isn't safe or tame. When you risk loving others, there's no telling where that flame will spread.

But loving is not an excuse for folly (though it may seem foolish). Flames are to be tended lest they burn or rage out of control. Flames require fuel to burn—effort and care. Love is not merely following passion. Sometimes flames need to be fanned because left to themselves they will burn out. Love must be cultivated. If you don't pour care and effort into your love it won't last. We easily confuse love with warm feelings and the honeymoon infatuation with genuine care. Love is what remains after the excitement wears off. Reducing it to sentiment leaves you using others to make yourself feel better and, at the same time, neglecting the sentiment for too long can allow the fire to become ash. Tending the flame also means watching for when it begins to harm—when it threatens to hurt others. In chapter 7, we noted the insulating effect of power. Too often those with social or institutional power have let a flame burn through a community—typically those more marginalized—using "tough love" as a justification or excuse. When your "love" demands sacrifice from others, it's more about you and less about love. This false-love is often only maintained as a category with recourse to bullshit stories that explain away the clear and documented harms that it causes. While we are all called to do the difficult, even painful work of exposing our illusions to the light of Truth, the moment we notice ourselves reaching for something to explain away objective and observable harm caused by some purported "tough love," we are in dangerous waters and likely embracing a false-love.

Similarly, love will not look the same today as it did yesterday. It can't be captured, tamed, or packaged into a five-point plan for success. Those are ashes. They can tell a story and we can learn something from them, but they aren't the flame. Tradition, as Chesterton argued, is giving the dead a say in influencing the present.[17] That is not submitting entirely to tradition, neither is it ignoring it, but being in conversation with it. The ashes of where the flame once was can be helpful to study, but are awful to worship. We follow a living God, listening to a Holy Spirit, not creating idols of what once was. If we choose to risk loving, we will be following the flame of the Spirit who acts as a hearth around which community gathers, who refuses to engage in disgust-fueled rejection of

---

17. See Chesterton, *Orthodoxy*, ch. 4, 82–83.

the marginalized. Let us follow to where she is leading today instead of growing moss around the monument to where our ancestors first felt her.

CORPORATE EUCONTAMINATION

Let's now turn to the question of how we can corporately practice cultivating a community of love. Learning to love in this way requires that we face our disgust reactions and the resistances we have built up to seeing one another as full subjects and image-bearers of God. To do this, we take two crucial disgust-diffusing ingredients that we talked about in the last chapter: mindfulness and intimacy, and look at how traditional and historic Christian practices and sacraments can, under the right circumstances, act as what we have called "calisthenics of eucontamination"[18] for the community and not just the individual. These practices are calisthenics in that doing them well and regularly builds up our mental and physical capacity to manage and more intentionally direct our disgust responses in the same way that ordinary physical calisthenics help build our physical capacity to achieve physical goals. They are calisthenics *of eucontamination* because these practices (and the mentality that accompanies them) help to reorient our disgust reactions away from persons and help us to appreciate the crucial role that contamination-for-good plays in developing a healthy spiritual and psychological world for ourselves.

Each of these practices holds great potential. This means that they are as capable of being weaponized and used to control as they are to point us communally to Christ. Be careful about how something is being used. If you have been harmed by these practices, please listen to that story and honor what you've been through instead of forcing yourself back into a practice that may be more damaging than helpful. However, if you've found these practices dead, rote, and devoid of life, then we want to invite you into a playful reflection of what else may be within them. How might a eucontaminative lens help you re-engage with these ancient Christian sacraments?

While these practices have become ordinary to many in the Christian tradition due to repetition, they are really anything but. Each of these calisthenics of eucontamination are powerful and, therefore, profoundly dangerous to our established sense of self and comfort. To risk being

---

18. See chapter 3 of this book.

eucontaminated by love is to be vulnerable to all that comes with it and, returning again to *The Four Loves*, we are well advised to remember that:

> To love at all is to be vulnerable. Love anything, and your heart will certainly be wrung and possibly be broken. If you want to make sure of keeping it intact, you must give your heart to no one, not even to an animal. Wrap it carefully round with hobbies and little luxuries; avoid all entanglements; lock it up safe in the casket or coffin of your selfishness. But in that casket—safe, dark, motionless, airless—it will change. It will not be broken; it will become unbreakable, impenetrable, irredeemable. The alternative to tragedy, or at least the risk of tragedy, is damnation. The only place outside Heaven where you can be perfectly safe from all the dangers and perturbations of love is Hell.[19]

The practices we are endorsing here are also not of our own creation. In looking at what following the Way of Jesus looks like in community, we are falling back on the tradition of the church over the centuries and focusing on the sacraments. For the sake of space, we are going to narrow our engagement with the sacraments as eucontamination calisthenics to the three which are generally accepted by both Protestants and Catholics:[20] communion, marriage, and baptism.

COMMUNION

Since both of us have our roots in the Anabaptist tradition, we will be exploring communion in its threefold expression: foot washing, the love feast, and the Eucharist. The act of washing one another's feet, as ordained in John 13:1–20, is disgusting—even on its surface. Feet occupy a strange liminal space in contemporary Western society, somewhere between private and embarrassing. They are sometimes sexualized, but more frequently are just viewed as smelly and dirty. We cover them much of the time, but outside of formal settings, bare feet are not a scandal. In first-century Judea, where sandals were more common than shoes or boots and the streets were far from sanitary, feet were far more than simply

---

19. Lewis, *Four Loves*, 121.

20. While we are limiting the scope of our exploration here to those sacraments which are generally accepted by *both* Protestants and Catholics, we suspect that confirmation, reconciliation, anointing the sick, and holy orders are also pregnant with eucontaminative potential and we eagerly hope to read of a Catholic and/or Orthodox theologian who takes up the task of exploring them through this lens.

"yucky" and it was the job of a hospitable host to ensure that guests' feet were washed. In either context, other people's feet aren't something we expect or hope to engage with publicly. Furthermore, washing any part of another person is intimate. We wash our children and categorize the act as nurturing and caring, and we wash our elders and categorize it as respectful, if a little embarrassingly infantilizing.[21] Peers do not, as a general rule, wash any part of one another.

And yet, Jesus said that we are to wash one another's feet.[22] The acts both of washing someone else's feet or of having our feet washed by another are intimate already and can become more so when we engage them with Jesus's servant leadership in mind. To allow someone else to wash your feet is to allow them to assume the position of a servant leader in relation to yourself; to wash another's feet is to assume the position of a servant who—in an act which, by Jesus's example, eucontaminates and deconstructs our whole concept of authority, leadership, and power—stoops to cleanse the dirtiest non-private part of another. When we enter into this practice both focusing on intimacy—our one-ness in Christ with one another—and mindfully—ready to greet and process any disgust reactions that might arise—we are able to experience, appreciate, use, and diffuse our tendencies towards disgust.

Following the foot washing, we collectively move on to the love feast. Eating with one another is a critical and traditional component of peace-making. When we eat, we are, in some ways, most vulnerable to being contaminated. We are literally taking substances into our bodies which will become part of our body. To do that in the presence of the "other" is both deeply vulnerable and, thanks to millennia of social conditioning, deeply intimate. Most often we seek to eat with those we love, and those we like. Friends and families take meals together. When we take the love feast sitting, not in small, socially comfortable cliques determined by social status and comfort but, as St. Paul commands in 1 Cor 11:17–33, collectively and without favoritism or reference to social privilege, when we pay attention to, recognize, and process any discomfort, we

---

21. It has been well and accurately observed that Western culture as a whole has an unhealthy relationship to aging.

22. It needs to be noted that, while foot washing is an important and powerful eucontaminating calisthenic, it—like many other activities—is open to abuse. You do not need to let anyone wash your feet, nor should you ever feel pressure to wash someone else's feet if you are not comfortable doing so. Power dynamics matter deeply, and forcing someone to participate in any religious ceremony with which they are uncomfortable constitutes spiritual abuse.

are making (or reinforcing) our peace with one another and are stressing, deconstructing, and enlarging our internal definitions of who is allowed to constitute "us."[23]

To engage the love feast as a spiritual calisthenic of eucontamination, the focus we need is on eating it as equals; we should notice the discomfort of nascent disgust as it arises, and then allow that disgust or discomfort reaction to come into communication with the presence of God and of the holy other in our shared space of vulnerability, connection, and nourishment.

Moving from the love feast proper into the celebration of the Eucharist, the vital thing is to attend to the deeply disgusting nature of what we are doing. We don't believe it was an accident that when Jesus set up this practice, he selected one of the most universally disgust inducing human taboos as its central practice: the cannibalism taboo. "Take, eat. This is my body, . . . this is my blood of the covenant, which is poured out" (Matt 26:26–28 NRSVUE). By way of repetition we have far too successfully managed to ignore the disgusting nature of this sacrament. When we are taking communion, yes, we acknowledge that (depending on our theology) we are eating and drinking the body and blood of another person, but we spiritualize it, we focus on the God-ness of Jesus rather than on his humanity. We find ways to not *really* think of it as eating a person's flesh and drinking that same man's blood. We drown our disgust in reverence and ritual. We need to stop it.

To encounter the Eucharist as a spiritual calisthenic, we recommend embracing the grossness of it; focus on the cannibalistic and violating nature of the act. And then, or at the same time, bring to mind all that it means to have the boundary between your physical self and God's physical self blurred. To take the Eucharist is to enact the unification of yourself and God. That wine and communion wafer will be taken in, digested, and their molecules will become . . . you. You have been made up, in part, of all the Eucharists you have ever taken part in.

Richard Beck notes in his book *Unclean* that we experience horror and disgust when something we think of as "lower" is joined to something we think of as "higher"; that is how monsters are made. In Beck's words,

> Given that sociomoral disgust is implicated in the creation of monsters (e.g., stigmatized groups like the Jews in Nazi

---

23. We have put together an outline for how to engage in love feasts with special attention to disgust and the eucontaminative potential of eating together in appendix 1.

Germany) it should come as no surprise that monsters are *divinity violations*. Something "high" on the divinity dimension is being mixed with something "low." A man with a bug-head is taboo as it mixes something sacred (the human person created in the *Imago Dei*) and brings it into contact with something low and base, in this example an insect. By contrast, in Western traditions wings are symbols of the heavenly and the angelic. Thus, when wings are seen in depictions of angels we find the human/wing hybrid elevating rather than monstrous. In the propaganda art of Nazi Germany the Jew was hybridized with rodents. This rat/human hybrid allowed the Nazis to create a monster out of the Jew and, as a consequence, create widespread sociomoral disgust within the German population.

In short, the monster is often a symbol of degradation and contamination.[24]

Think of *The Island of Dr. Moreau* by H. G. Wells, or of werewolves and minotaurs and harpies: all monsters formed by the conjoining of the "lower" (animals) with the "higher" (humanity). In contrast, when the higher is joined to the lower, we experience that differently: think of demigods and angels and of how we experience the incarnation as a blessing. When we take communion we are enacting a unification or blending of the second sort; that is the thought to hold on to in tandem with a heightened awareness of the cannibalism taboo. In the act of communion, we bring together a mindful awareness of the "naturally" disgusting nature of the act in tandem with the intimacy that it represents—the love of God "poured out" for us. Jesus told us to eat his flesh and drink his blood as we simultaneously remember his death for us—the ultimate expression of God's profound love for us.

Pushing further into the disgust logic of the Eucharist, meditate for a minute on what it means from God's perspective. From the Divine point of view, when we take the Eucharist, what is "lower" (created humanity) is being united with what is higher. While we are invited to understand this as being raised up—following Christ through his death into the eternal Life of his resurrection, what the Orthodox call theosis—from the perspective of the "higher," this ought to be nightmare fuel, the stuff of monsters and disgust. And yet; in Their infinite love for us, God is not disgusted by our ritual unification with them. God's love results in invitation, welcome, and unification—a shared Life—where disgust would allow only for violent rejection. All of that might sound like condescension,

24. Beck, *Unclean*, 93–94.

and certainly there is a robust Christian tradition encouraging us to embrace humility and to understand ourselves as utterly dependent on God's grace, but in fact there is nothing of tolerance or condescension in it at all. When we operate out of Love, the whole higher/lower distinction dissolves and disgust is destroyed, killed, and reborn as its own opposite: the longing for unity. God will not *tolerate* union and shared life with Their creation for even a single moment because *tolerance* is far too weak to bridge the gap. God desires, embraces, died for, and delights in, union and a shared Life with Creation. We are not tolerated by the Divine, we are celebrated. Love is the only force in existence which could possibly bridge the infinite Gap between creation and Creator, but Love will have nothing of gaps at all; what Love wants is unity with the Beloved. When Love acts, the gap is not bridged but erased. The father in the parable of the prodigal son does not condescend to or tolerate his son; the Father runs to him, embraces him, kisses him, and throws a party. Lovers delight in their union.

MARRIAGE

The second eucontamination calisthenic ought to be disgusting. At least so long as we are thinking about disgust only and not about love as well. In the Bible, we first encounter marriage as we understand it in the second chapter of Genesis. Starting in verse 18 we find:

> And the Lord God said, "It is not good for the human to be alone, I shall make him a sustainer beside him." And the Lord God fashioned from the soil each beast of the field and each fowl of the heavens and brought each to the human to see what he would call it, and whatever the human called a living creature, that was its name. And the human called names to all of the cattle and to the fowl of the heavens and to all the beasts of the field, but for the human no sustainer beside him was found. And the Lord God cast a deep slumber on the human, and he slept, and He took one of his ribs and closed over the flesh where it had been, and the Lord God built the rib He had taken from the human into a woman and He brought her to the human. And the human said:
> "This one at last, bone of my bones
>   and flesh of my flesh,
> "This one shall be called Woman,
>   For from man was this one taken."

> Therefore does a man leave his father and his mother and cling to his wife and they become one flesh. And the two of them were naked, the human and his woman, and they were not ashamed.²⁵

And of course Jesus cites the conclusion of this passage in Matt 19:4–6 as part of his answer to a question about divorce.

> He answered, "Have you not read that the one who made them at the beginning 'made them male and female,' and said, 'For this reason a man shall leave his father and mother and be joined to his wife, and the two shall become one flesh'? So they are no longer two but one flesh. Therefore what God has joined together, let no one separate." (NRSVUE)

The whole business is the blending into "one flesh" of what was distinct, and disgust doesn't like that. As we have said, disgust is concerned with maintaining distance between *me* and *not me*, so the idea that, in marriage the distinction between the two is dissolved is really a defeat of all that disgust works to preserve.

And yet we are rarely disgusted by the sacrament of marriage; most often we find it heartwarming. We like weddings—they are celebrations! This mystical union of two becoming one is a regular experience (who has never once encountered married people?), which is so powerful that St. Paul borrowed it as a metaphor in Eph 5:28–32 to describe the union of Christ with the church. "When you think of the two-who-are-oneness of a married couple," St. Paul says, "Christ is two-who-are-one like that with the church." And again, by rights, our disgust alarms ought to be blaring; and again, they often aren't. We typically find the symbolism comforting and intimate.²⁶ We experience it that way because, at least in the idealized way that we tend to imagine it, marriage is bathed in intimacy. Lovers delight in their union.

An important note here is our use of that word, "idealized." In writing this, we are very aware of the many horrors that can be wrought in a marriage. By naming the possible eucontaminating beauty of marriage as it is described in the Bible, we are not naively stating that all marriages at all times are good. Marriage in Western society has historically been used to control women and maintain patriarchal power. Marriage, as it has

---

25. Alter, *Hebrew Bible*, Gen 2:18–25.

26. Unfortunately Christians have often proved to be far too willing to overinterpret these passages and this metaphor so as to justify patriarchy, misogyny, and bigotry against queer people. We maintain that any such interpretation does violence to the text and to the fundamental dignity of all persons.

been practiced, is far from the ideal that we are exploring. Spousal abuse is real and horrific. Controlling and abusive marriages are traumatic. However, like with sexual intimacy, the horrors of its abuse and misuse speak to its potential for beauty. The fact that something can be misused does not negate its positive uses.

And that first section of the Genesis 2 passage does point us back to what healthy existence ought to look like. The human is alone and that is not good; the human needs a suitable companion—a "sustainer" in Robert Alter's translation of the text—someone who is with that human but is not that human: another human who will be the same and also different, distinct. And so, in this myth, God draws on the stuff of the human and creates an independent, new, distinct, *other* human out of the human-stuff: the human's rib. And the human recognizes this new other as the same as himself while also not-himself: "bone of my bones and flesh of my flesh."[27] And already we see the recognition of a desire which we hold in tension: the desire to be (re)joined with while also remaining distinct. One alone was not good; neither are two alone good, since they are then merely one alone and also another one alone. But two together, two-who-are-one-flesh, that is good.

Marriage is, of course, only one of many ways that humanity joins individual *me*'s into *we*'s; in the birth and adoption of children we grow our families; when we discover and invest in deep friendships, our I's become Us's. We have been speaking here on how engaging in the sacrament of marriage, both as participants and as witnesses, can be a eucontaminative calisthenic. But marriage is not a Christian requirement or duty. Unfortunately an allosexual normativity and amatonormativity[28] has pervaded views of marriage in the church that marginalizes and problematizes individuals who remain unmarried despite the fact that St. Paul can easily be read as asexual and quite explicitly speaks of the benefits of not marrying (1 Cor 7:7–8). The church would also do well

---

27. *Myth* here should not be read as a denial of the truth of this story but as a recognition of the genre and genre conventions of the text it appears in. As Lewis and Tolkien would be quick to remind us; there are true myths. See Lewis, *Miracles*, and his essay "Myth Become Fact" in Lewis, *God in the Dock*, and Tolkien's essay "On Fairy Stories" and his poem "Mythopoeia" in Tolkien, *Tree and Leaf*, for a full exploration of this.

28. The term "amatonormativity" was coined by Elizabeth Brake, who defines it as "the assumptions that a central, exclusive, amorous relationship is normal for humans, in that it is a universally shared goal, and that such a relationship is normative, in that it *should* be aimed at in preference to other relationship types." See Brake, "Amatonormativity."

to rediscover some of our older ceremonies and liturgies of joining and uniting individuals into a beautiful tapestry of us-and-we-who-are-one overwhelming disgust's individuation with intimacy and love, sexual or platonic.

In order to engage marriage and weddings as eucontaminating calisthenics, we need to fall back once more on mindfulness and intimacy. As with the Eucharist where we recommend attending to the disgust-inducing nature of the act, with marriage and weddings, try attending to both the way that this union of two into one is a violation of our desire to avoid a loss of an imagined bounded-self and, at the same time, celebrate the way in which all of that reticence tends to fall away in the presence of love and intimacy.

BAPTISM

The final corporate eucontaminating calisthenic we want to explore here is the sacrament of baptism. And just like we did with marriage and with the threefold communion service, we want to suggest that the keys to experiencing this sacrament as a eucontaminating calisthenic—the way to form ourselves away from over-developed disgust reactions—is to approach this practice with mindfulness and intimacy at the forefront.

Upon examination, baptism turns out to also hold a great depth of practical and experiential insight into the eucontaminating gospel. Baptism is a boundary-crossing sacrament. In baptism, we declare our commitment to, and membership in, the church—the body of Christ.[29] Looked at from another perspective, baptism is the sacrament by which we welcome other people into our shared corporate and spiritual body. When we celebrate a baptism, we are celebrating our own corporate eucontamination by that person. When we participate as congregants and church members and parishioners in the liturgy of baptism, we are declaring not only our willingness, but our enthusiasm to have our collective body transformed by the inclusion of this new soul. Paralleling the way that our physical bodies are biochemically transformed by the substance of the Eucharist, each baptism socially and spiritually transforms our corporate body. We are no longer the same after we have incorporated you into us!

---

29. Or we are declared members of the body of Christ depending on your theology.

If we have not yet been formed in the eucontaminating Way of Jesus, it is possible that celebrating a baptism with this at the forefront of your mind might bring up some uneasiness. Is this really a person you want to have as part of our spiritual body, as part of our community? How do you feel about saying that this person is a part of "us"?

Among online progressive type Christians, there is a sort of standing, low-key, usually background disagreement over whether or not people whom we sharply disagree with about morally and ethically important topics are *really* Christians. For those of us who are post-evangelical, we have probably had the accusation of not being a real Christian thrown at us so many times that it can feel good to turn it around. "If you don't affirm God's queer children then you aren't even a real Christian," or "given everything Jesus had to say about caring for 'the least of these' you can't be a real Christian if you support a politics of protecting the privileged and the wealthy" can feel really good. But while there may well be legitimate theological reasons to conclude that someone's understanding of who God is and what God is like ultimately amounts to a different religious tradition altogether, there may also be less legitimate reasons for the assertion. An unwillingness to share participation in the body of Christ with people who hold to sinful and harmful theologies and beliefs[30] can instead depend on the idea that we have to keep our corporate body free from contamination; that Christ's body has a minimum threshold for flawed and harmful members. That is to say that it depends on a refusal to recognize the power of Jesus to eucontaminate his own body. This is not something new to the church either. In Acts 18, we read what seems to be a strange side-story about the young church struggling around the distinction between John's baptism and a baptism of the Holy Spirit. One (though definitely not the only) way to understand the significance of this theological issue comes back to eucontamination. John the Baptist preached a baptism of repentance to help prepare the person and community for the coming messiah. It helped you get yourself in order so that God would commune with you. The baptism of the Holy Spirit, however, is radically different. The Holy Spirit enters believers as they are. She does not wait for us to get our act together. She eucontaminates us and is not

---

30. Again, please do not over apply this point by pressuring people to enter into spaces or be around those who are not safe or who will oppress them. It is entirely possible to acknowledge that another person is both a fellow member of the body of Christ and deeply flawed, abusive, cruel, unsafe and should not be anywhere near vulnerable, oppressed, or marginalized members of that same body.

at risk of being polluted by our humanity. St. Paul and his followers knew this was crucial for the young church to embrace. God eucontaminates us and does not wait for us to clean up first.

It's also crucial to hold tightly to baptism's connection to death. In Col 2:12–13 St. Paul mentions baptism as a participation in Jesus's death and resurrection, saying:

> When you were buried with him in baptism, you were also raised with him through faith in the power of God, who raised him from the dead. And when you were dead in trespasses and the uncircumcision of your flesh, God made you alive together with him, when he forgave us all our trespasses. (NRSVUE)

As we discussed in chapter 7, death is very much something we tend to want to keep *out* of our experience; and yet the Way of Christ leads to eternal life, the "life of the ages" only *through* death. When we celebrate a baptism—ours or anyone else's—we are congregated and celebrating a funeral or maybe a wake. In baptism we recognize the turn in a person's story, that critical moment in their narrative, when their trajectory shifted and came under the influence, the gravity, of the Way of Jesus. In God's eternal story, there is a crisis. At one moment in space-time, the God of all existence cried out *Eloi Eloi Lama Sabachthani*, and then God died. At the incarnation, God's story fused itself together with the story of humanity, and at the cross that fused story, the God-man Jesus, wove death into himself. Driven by love and a desire for union with us (Lovers delight in their union) Jesus chose to embrace death itself into his being. And on Easter Sunday, Jesus broke the power of death. The Christian story of reality is one in which death has been transformed from an ending into a door. And in baptism we embrace death—we re-enact it—but through that death we also enact Jesus's victory over death: his eucontamination of death itself.

And this had to be that way. Life comes through death. This is perhaps most evident in food, but all around us, the death of one brings life elsewhere. Psychologically, Christ is calling for us to let our bullshit selves, our egos, die. Remember, life is found in facing the death of who we think we are. Freud's death drive actually points to life in resisting the suffocation of comfort and what we think we want. In the death of baptism, we can let those desires of the flesh die because they aren't really us. We are freed to love when we are free to die. Only by letting my false, imaginary self die can I ever hope in the resurrection of more. My (Paul) ego is trapped in the isms of this world and how I've been marked: whiteness, misogyny, sexism, classism, nationalism, and on and on. Christ offers us hope that when we allow our sense of self to die, we can find resurrection. You are not your ego. You can face the full shame of who you have been, what your image has cost others, the world, and you. Christ has freed us! Thanks be to God!

10

Further Up and Further In!

This is the land I have been looking for all my life, though I never knew it till now.... Come further up, come further in.
—C. S. Lewis, *The Last Battle*

WE'VE COVERED A LOT of ground in these past few chapters. Disgust plays a central role in shaping our understanding of ourselves as individual and corporate beings. We rarely recognize it as such, but disgust mechanisms exert their influence on us all the way from small, internal reactions up through shaping how we vote. The Christian narrative does not deny this. Instead, it invites us further into this process, subverting disgust's default operations to help us learn to love. The incarnation of God through the person of Jesus was just such a subversion. Jesus interacts directly with our disgust mechanisms and uses its logic to invert and thereby subvert its operation. The Holy and Divine irrupted into sinful humanity so as to redeem us. Light overcomes darkness, righteousness cleanses sin. God does not fear our imperfection but eucontaminates us into the bride of Christ. Instead, God dares us to continue striving to live as if this is true.

By entering this world as the Divine, Jesus dares us to allow his Spirit to eucontaminate us into God. Jesus offers us himself as Truth, as Life, and as the Way to help us live out this radical scandal. Our hope in this text has been to spark and perhaps stir more thoughts and possibilities within each of you around what it may mean to take the incarnation of Christ seriously. What if Truth is actually a person? What if Life isn't bound by what is comfortable? What if the Way of Jesus woos us from a place of deep desire?

Eucontamination points to a Truth which is not a static set of propositions or facts one can possess. Truth is not about our bullshit egos and the certainty we cling to in its defense. Truth is a person. Truth calls to us from beyond our imaginations into a relationship. Paradoxically, it is both the cynic and the idealist who reduce their worlds to the immediate and refuse the possibility of a Truth beyond their understanding.[1] Communally, Truth helps us live in the tension between the immanent and the transcendent. Instead of a belonging that requires the scapegoating and exclusion of an other, Truth offers us a unity around our shared non-belonging.

As the Life, Jesus eucontaminates our understanding of health and joy. Shame is not the enemy, but an invitation towards grieving false images of who we were in order to move towards a more full reality of who we are. Instead of needing to prop up an image of ourselves in the eyes of everyone else, we are free to experience the life of passing through the death of our "old selves." The eucontamination of Life liberates us from the gaze of a racist, capitalist, patriarchal big Other for whom we are never good enough. Instead of endlessly trying to avoid the shame of our own failure, the Life of Jesus invites us into the folly of our own freedom and belovedness. It is the impossible joy of the marginalized that bears witness to a Life beyond our limited, bullshit worlds—beyond our shame.

The Way of Jesus then, is a playful act of subversive and defiant freedom. The Way refuses to let us hide from our desires. We are terrifyingly free to pursue our desires, freed from the dictates of an imaginary big Other we've projected into the heavens. This freedom is found in the eucontaminating defiance of our egos and the way *they* say we should be. It is not merely resistance to something, but truly freedom from it. "For freedom, Christ has set us free." The Way is an invitation into play, and life, and joy. The Way of Jesus leaves love, joy, peace, patience, kindness, goodness, gentleness, faithfulness, and self-control in its wake. In this wild embrace of desire, we also find the space to love—fully love— one another. In the recognition of our own lack and vulnerability, the

---

1. See McGowan, *End of Dissatisfaction*.

eucontaminating Way of Jesus woos us to face the lack in each other. Instead of objectifying one another into tools for our own image, we can rejoice with those who rejoice and weep with those who weep. We can be the Bride of Christ.

The Way, the Truth, and the Life are dangerous, unstable, and wild. Once touched, they will not leave you the same. Jesus continually disturbs our comfortable worlds and forever invites us to play with the unimaginable and the not quite yet. We believe that it is through these vectors of eucontamination that we find connection with ourselves and with each other. Truth, beauty, and goodness are not found in bullshit worlds, protected by disgust, but in the wilderness of the other that won't leave you alone. Silence, comfort, a reticence to make a scene or stand out, and the desire to just get along are all powerful draws that can keep us trapped in an insulated cycle of disgust wherein we repeatedly push off anything that would threaten our status quo. But we can't encounter what we really want till we have died to what we think we need. The silence of comfort is not the peace we long for.

SOME THOUGHTS FOR THE CHURCH IN THIS MOMENT: THE CYCLE OF DISGUST

What role can the church play in helping us to hear the music and draw us out of our bullshit solitary safety? Well, we want to suggest that it means learning to break the cycle of disgust—how disgust is experienced and then enacted upon a marginalized other for the comfort of the majority. The following steps are rough outlines of how disgust is often marshaled socially to scapegoat and soothe. Through the stages of nausea, trigger, expel, and rationalize, groups create bullshit images of themselves at the cost of others. It is through the Truth, Life, and Way of Jesus that the church can recognize and then resist and subvert at each step so as to be a stubborn stumbling block to scapegoating. It is the church's mission to be a community of Love in this world. As such, we must offer not just resistance, but something much more beautiful than an image of purity belonging.

Stage One—Nausea

Nausea is the most common "default" stage for societies and communities because it accounts for the state of affairs before any big actions have taken place. The nausea stage is where the social negotiation around whether or not a given person, idea, or group can be incorporated into the community's understanding of itself is taking place.

At this stage, the community is being encouraged to imagine a particular type of person or group as a threat to the identity of the community (it is always in the abstract at this point, though particular "representative" individuals are often used as propaganda to inculcate the nausea). This is necessarily done through propaganda[2] which simultaneously encourages a particular understanding of what the *true* community is like while presenting the targeted group as incompatible with—in fact a threat to—that identity. The "us"/"them" boundary is reinforced and a blended sense that the targeted group is both a threat to the community and is inferior to the community is inculcated.[3] Importantly with disgust, this nausea is not interpreted as a problem on the side of the majority experiencing the nausea but on those who are marked as nauseating or disgusting.[4] This is where the dehumanizing can be seen as those in the targeted groups are imbued with the power of contaminants and objectified as pollutants instead of fellow humans.

At this stage in the process, the nature and limits of the community's bullshit image of itself is still being negotiated. Since all identities are constructed and ultimately fail, the discussion itself isn't actually about Truth; it is instead always and necessarily a negotiation around power (who has the authority to define "who we are") and politics. So long as the "debate" about the group remains a live one, nausea will increase over time until the excluders manage to create a successful triggering event.[5] More than

---

2. For a thorough breakdown of how propaganda affects the consciousness and influences political and social negotiations of who is and is not "us" see Jason Stanley's *How Propaganda Works* and *How Fascism Works*.

3. Hannah Arendt's documentation in *The Origins of Totalitarianism* of the way that this process was executed in the form of rising anti-Semitism in the nineteenth and twentieth centuries is paradigmatic for this process at its worst.

4. See Ahmed, *Cultural Politics*, loc. 1980: "Disgust is about an object, such that one's feelings of sickness become attributed to the object ('I feel sick, you have sickened me, you are sickening')."

5. Over the last decade or so it has become common for LGBTQIA+ people to become exasperated with the framing of the recurring and intensifying discourse around the legitimacy of our existence *as* queer people. Frequently LGBTQIA+ folx will say,

at any other stage, the discourse at this point tends to focus on facticity and misinformation regarding the target group. Reason, logic, and facts are marshaled with varying degrees of efficacy against propaganda.

While this use of propagandistic bullshit is a defining element within fascist movements, Liberal and Leftist politics are not free from its powerful allure. We documented several instances of its use by the authoritarian and Christian Nationalist right in chapter 3, and in the summer of 2024 this could be seen in the conversation around the false claim that JD Vance had used a couch for sexual enjoyment.[6] In many left-leaning circles the veracity of the claim was irrelevant because it *felt* like it could be true. To the production of nausea, reason and truth are irrelevant.

Stage Two—Trigger

While it is possible for the social nausea towards a given group to grow to the point that no individual trigger is necessary, more often particular events are used to justify moving from a feeling of dis-ease about the targeted group, to their expulsion. Once a "sufficient" degree of nausea towards the targeted community has taken root—so as to become normalized in the minds and bodies of the majority—a significant portion of the population imagine the targeted groups itself as a threat to the community's identity, the stage is set for a catalyzing event to prompt an excessive response. The event can be based in some real infraction on the part of one or more members of the targeted group but it can also be fabricated wholly or in part. All that is necessary is for *something* to shift the community from thinking something "ought" to be done about them, to a sense of urgency that something *must* be done.[7] Highlighting the perceived or real misdeed of a member of the targeted community is generally sufficient to trigger expulsion or oppression, just as the slightest

---

in exasperation, "My existence, my rights, are not a *debate* to be had; this is my life!" In doing so we are highlighting the threat represented by the social situation of our legitimacy as debatable, contested, and ultimately a source of increasing nausea within a queerphobic church and society.

6. See Joffe-Block, "What the JD Vance Couch Jokes."

7. We need to note that the disgust cycle in many ways recapitulates the cycles of activism and revolution. The pattern of building frustration and anger at injustice culminating in a precipitating event which tips an oppressed population into action is in many ways a more just counterpart of the disgust cycle. Noting the power dynamics and the presence or degree of dehumanization involved can be key in distinguishing the two.

whiff of a bad smell or particle of food or even spit caught in your throat is enough to trigger vomit when you already feel nauseous. Perhaps the most well-known and infamous example of a nausea trigger taking place would be the pogroms of Kristallnacht, which were both the culmination of the Nazi nausea-building campaign of anti-Semitism leading up to November 9, 1938, and the opening of the next move into explicit violence and genocide by the Nazis. Kristallnacht was ostensibly triggered by the assassination of Ernst vom Rath by Herschel Gynszpan as a reaction to the deportation and extreme mistreatment of his family, but the assassination was in fact only a pretext used by the Nazis as justification for the next step in their campaign of violent exclusion.[8]

While a society can experience nausea for a broad variety of reasons (think about the social anxiety that results from increased populations of unhoused people, from economic strain, from changing social mores, from a fear of waning power and privilege), the triggering event will tend to focus on a particular target group and make them into scapegoats under the corporate belief that their expulsion will relieve the total tension that the community is experiencing. What may be an important differentiation between a healthier form of this nausea that can lead to change as opposed to one that leads to oppression is the difference in the degree of complicity people are able to find in themselves. If the system is broken and I live within it, then my advocacy to change that system necessarily implicates me as well. I must be looking in the mirror and finding my part in the problem. In contrast, what we are outlining here is when people are encouraged to see the other as the sole problem—the scapegoat—as a way to protect themselves from any experience of guilt or shame. The majority dumps their responsibility and agency on the target group to protect themselves from a more painful Truth about who they are. If the nausea is already firmly established, no amount of reason or pleading will be able to prevent stage three: vomiting/expulsion.

Most recently, the right wing misinformation insisting that Haitian immigrants in Ohio were actually consuming pets[9] can be seen as an example of a false claim intended to trigger an expulsion. The inaccuracy of the claim was irrelevant because the idea fit a pre-existing narrative that immigrants are a threat to the community and thus deserving of deportation. The underlying nausea towards immigrants fueled the belief

---

8. See "Kristallnacht."
9. See Gomez et al., "How a Fringe Online Claim."

in the story and subsequent threats made against local schools and other institutions,[10] regardless of acknowledged, shared facts.

Stage Three—Vomit/Expel

At this point, the community will act to rid itself of the targeted group. This may happen in any number of forms ranging from official redefinitions of the group's identity designed expressly to exclude members of the targeted community (e.g., the Nashville Statement or more recently the Congressional bathroom ban on trans people) all the way to act of genocide and/or ethnic cleansing. In the wake of the Obergefell decision, the advent of the Nashville Statement, which successfully attempted to redefine Conservative Evangelicalism as structurally and essentially exclusionary of LGBT people, identities, and relationships, would be an example on one end of this spectrum of exclusion, while on the other end, the inquisition and the Holocaust are horrific examples of how violent and prolonged this stage can be.

Beyond direct, oppositional resistance to the expulsion process and protection of the targeted community and of those associated with them, few options remain to resist. In the same way that a vomiting body acts to expel everything it experiences as a contaminant, a vomiting society will expel everything and everyone that it associates with the targeted group. The line between allies and members of the targeted group will disappear or be drastically diminished (usually through the use of terms like "race traitor," "heretic," or "accomplice") in the minds of the nauseous community.[11] However, individual community members who are less fully in the grip of the nausea may still retain a greater degree of sympathy for and capacity to hear from allies. In the throes of an expulsion event, reason is almost entirely useless as institutional power is marshaled to enact the expulsion and its very use becomes a self-referential endorsement of

---

10. See Aftoora-Orsagos and Rubinkam, "Ohio State Police."

11. For more on how disgust is "sticky" and attaches to all who are associated with what is already experienced as disgusting, see chapter 4 of Ahmed, *Cultural Politics*, loc. 2044: "Disgust hence operates as a contact zone; it is about how things come into contact with other things . . . . While disgust involves such a metonymic slide, it does not move freely: it sticks to that which is near it; it clings. Furthermore, an object can become disgusting because it resembles another object that is disgusting (Rozin and Fallon 1987: 30; Angyal 1941: 397). Hence, disgust can move between objects through the recognition of likeness. Disgust binds objects together in the very moment that objects become attributed with bad feeling, as 'being' sickening."

the act—"they wouldn't be doing this if it wasn't necessary." The greatest violence and weight of the expulsion will generally (though not necessarily—"traitors" and "apostates" are never popular) be reserved for identified members of the targeted community.

Stage Four—Rationalize

Only after a vomiting/expulsion event will the community begin to reflect on what it has just done. But that reflection will not be based in careful reason, and the community will almost certainly not conclude that it was in the wrong. At most, there may be some recognition that the vomiting was unpleasant and that "in a few cases" things may have gotten a little out of hand. The goal of the rationalization phase is not honest self-analysis but the justification of what has already happened. Having expelled the targeted group, tearing apart its old identity in the process—remember that up until the vomiting event the targeted group was still part of the community as a matter of material fact—the community will now search for bullshit stories, theories, or explanations to cover over and soothe the traumatized edges of its new identity. This is a process not of truth and reconciliation but of soothing and patching. This is not the work of poetry or prophecy but propaganda and bullshit. It is about creating an impression and feeling better, not about facing reality.[12] Here in the United States one of the most well recognized stage four rationalization efforts is represented by the emergence and acceptance of the "Lost Cause Myth" in the wake of the Civil War. This was a way of using bullshit to help white Americans avoid confronting our identity as a structurally racist nation.[13] A second example of stage four rationalization is the embrace of "Manifest Destiny" both in the moment and as a historical myth in order to absent ourselves from confronting our identity as a nation built on colonial ethnic cleansing and genocide.[14]

---

12. For a thorough examination of how society re-tells and mythologizes its history and what purpose that revision serves, see Stanley, *Erasing History*.

13. See Kendi, *Stamped from the Beginning*; Wilkerson, *Caste*; Hoard, "Beyond Fragility"; and Jones, *White Too Long*, to begin exploring the intricacy and effects of this dynamic.

14. See Charles and Rah, *Unsettling Truths*; Augustine, *Land Is Not Empty*; Brown, *Bury My Heart*; and Dunbar-Ortiz, *Indigenous Peoples' History*, for a fuller explication of America's origins in ethnic cleansing and genocide of Native American Peoples.

Here is where poets and prophets come to the fore. Poets and prophets speak from and to the Truth of the trauma that the collective body just inflicted on itself and refuse to play along with the group's desire to rationalize its past actions and new exclusionary identity. Their job is to disrupt or inhibit the community's ability to rationalize what it has done or justify what it has become. They hold a merciless mirror of Truth in front of the community and show it the trauma it is trying to deny, not letting it look away. This task is necessarily difficult and dangerous (many prophets were killed) as the prophets are trying to cause the community to see and accept what it does not want to see and accept. At the same time, this task is essential because the recognition of the Truth of what a group has done leads necessarily to the death of the community's current understanding of itself. It points to the possibility of Life on the other side of this corporate death, a life freed from the weight of denial and rationalization. As the nausea decreases due to the successful expulsion of the targeted (eu)contaminating group and the felt need to negotiate the community's identity passes, there is an opportunity for prophets to do their work inviting the community to "dream God's dream anew";[15] to expand its imagination of itself by reckoning with what it has done and opening itself up to being healed by the re-incorporation of the originally scapegoated community through a posture of humility and lament. However, a key point here is the distinction between a dissociative avoidance of the past that whitewashes the horrors to create the image of reunion, and the painful acknowledgment of harm through facing the shame and grief of what has happened.

And as we have said, this is a *cycle*, which means that while all of this is taking place, the community or society is already re-entering into the nausea phase regarding some other group(s), idea(s), or individual(s), and the ongoing resolution or disruption of the rationalization stage will have an impact on the shape and outcome of existing nausea phases. Societies and communities which accept, grieve, and integrate the shame of their complicity in scapegoating groups in the past are more likely—though not at all guaranteed—to resist the nausea-inducing propaganda that seeks to restart the cycle.

---

15. Haugen, "All Are Welcome."

WHAT CAN OUR CHURCHES DO?

As Christians we are called to be on the side of Truth, to embrace Life, and seek to follow in the Way of Jesus. It is vital for churches to work to disrupt this disgust cycle both internally and within the societies, communities, and nations in which we sojourn so as to embody the love of God in the world. Churches would be well served to think through the disgust cycle and work to recognize what stage of it they are experiencing at any given time. Most of our time is spent in the first and fourth stages (*nausea* and *rationalize*) and those are areas where many churches already have well developed tools and practices that can help. During stages two and three (*triggering* and *vomiting*) however, the church is both urgently needed and too often unprepared. Throughout this, we should keep in mind that the Truth, Life, and Way of Jesus are eucontaminants, that can both increase nausea in a society (when that society feels threatened by the Truth) and decrease it (when society accepts the Truth as corrective to the propaganda and bullshit that were generating nausea in the first place). A core vocation of the church is to stand in solidarity with the stigmatized and disgusting—remembering that it is not the people who are disgusting, but society who is disgusted. Like our Lord, we should be "reckoned with the lawless" (Luke 22:37) such that at every stage of the disgust cycle, the church is standing with the stigmatized and is leveraging any power, privilege, or influence it has on their behalf, fully knowing that this means casting our lot in with a targeted and scapegoated community.

During Stage One—Nausea

During the nausea stage, the church is best able to combat the disgust cycle in two ways. First, the church needs to stand as a counter-witness to all dehumanizing and nauseating propaganda. Jesus spoke powerfully and directly to this calling as his central message in the Sermon on the Mount: we are taught to love our enemies and to pray for those who persecute us. The vocation of every Christian and of the church as a whole is to stand always against the dehumanization of any person or group. Even when we rightly understand a group or person to be a legitimate threat or to be engaging in active harm, we are tasked with never losing sight of their humanity, their possession of the *imago Dei*, and the unconditional and undying love that God has for them. Beyond that, the church has been taught to embrace an "upside down" view of the social order wherein those that our community deems least worthy of honor and dignity—the oppressed, poor, and marginalized—are understood to be the very people whom we are most honored to count as members of our body.

Second, the church must stand as a prophetic witness to the ultimate falseness and failure of its own self-image and of its society's self-image. The church's humanizing call to be a counter-witness against the dehumanizing propaganda of nausea is a form of harm reduction. It says "they are also our neighbor," "facts matter," "here is how God calls us to treat the foreigner, the widow, the orphan, and the 'least of these.'" Without letting up on that message, the church must also be hospitable to the prophets who call the world's attention to the fact that the identity itself is bullshit, to the existence of those who have already been cast out. To put this in familiar Christian language, the primary task of the church during the nausea stage is to follow Jesus's taught and lived behavior towards neighbors and enemies. Jesus continually expanded our understanding of neighbor and he commands us to love our enemies. Within these instructions lies a powerful subversive message around how we hold boundaries and view others. Remember, loving your enemy is the only way to disrupt the enemy-making system.

Internally, this means that the church works during the nausea stage to reinforce within itself an understanding of the marginalized *other* as members worthy of greater honor (1 Cor 12:23). We can do this in myriad ways ranging from the practices we described as *calisthenics of eucontamination*, to our teaching, communing, and hospitality. Themes of enemy love and of valuing the "least of these" ought to abound at all times and especially in the nausea stage.[16]

Externally, the church bears a responsibility to stand as a public witness against all dehumanization. It is vital that this witness should be public and visible. By saying loudly and to the world that all are loved by God and deserving of human dignity and respect, by advocating on

---

16. Christians who find themselves in stage one and are working to untangle the complexity of standing firmly on the side of the oppressed while living out Jesus's exhortation to love our enemy will be well served by Melissa Florer-Bixler's *How to Have an Enemy*. Florer-Bixler rigorously explored this tension and concludes that "this is where Jesus draws the line—where he invites us to set up our lives and welcome others to the liberatory and disruptive good news of upended social convention. This is where a new people is made from those who were hungry and thirsty, who waste away in prisons, and who linger in sick wards. Jesus cares about what we do with our lives. If there are people who will not join this work, who harm the witness of the good news, we shake the dust and return to the work given us to do" (154).

behalf of the marginalized and oppressed, and by leveraging whatever privilege and moral weight available, the church is supporting the primary task of mitigating society's nausea. Then by following that first message with prophetic denunciation of the city's, state's, or nation's injustice, oppression, and violent laws and structures, the church can work to fulfill its vocation as a city on a hill.[17]

Always and always the church will, in doing all of this, be acting as a eucontaminant both towards the minds of its own individual members and within society—risking its own expulsion as the price of a chance to participate in the sanctification of society.

During Stage Two—Triggering

The triggering stage is generally very short lived relative to the first and fourth stages, and for that reason it is important that the church (or churches) be preparing for it while still in the nausea stage. There won't be enough time to determine policies and establish denominational stances once the triggering stage begins. At this point the urgent work of the church is to counter bullshit with facts and love. When people are in crisis and required to make immediate decisions with heavy consequences, those who navigate the crisis successfully are those whose training has prepared them best. A congregation that has been steeped in the vital call of Jesus to love our neighbor and our enemy, to pursue truth, and to live out the self-sacrificing Love of Jesus will react to a triggering event out of that training. In contrast, a congregation steeped in an overapplied purity metaphor, concerned with keeping itself apart from any potential (eu)contamination by outside people, thoughts, cultures, or customs will react out of that training. The former love-formed congregation will be far more resistant to scapegoating, stereotyping, and fear mongering. It will be ready with counter-messaging that cuts through the bullshit. The latter purity-formed congregation will be far more vulnerable to the Triggering bullshit and will likely either stand aside or join in with the scapegoating of the targeted group. Every voice raised in opposition to bullshit

---

17. The phrase "city on a hill" has a long history of colonial and even genocidal misuse on the part of white Christian Americans. Jesus used the phrase in Matt 5:14 just after the beatitudes and before teaching his followers to love our enemies and to "turn the other cheek"; rather than a commendation of violent power over the other, it is meant to be an exhortation to act in the Way of Jesus's eucontaminating self-sacrifice and love for one another.

matters in moments of triggering, from the pastoral voice reminding all that these people too are our neighbors, to the prophetic voice calling out the very urge to scapegoat in the first place.

During Stage Three—Vomit/Expulsion

When vomiting or expulsion is taking place, the first job of the church is to stand so close to the targeted group that they cannot be expelled unless the church is expelled along with them. If it is society, the state, or the nation doing the expelling, then it is the calling of the church to provide material and vocal aid to those being targeted to such a degree that the powers enacting the expulsion will be forced to expel the church as well. As with stage two, the way the church behaves and the way each person behaves during a vomiting/expulsion event is going to depend primarily on the way in which the church was formed beforehand. To the congregation that has been formed in Jesus's command to love everyone from neighbor to enemy, total solidarity with the oppressed may well be frightening but it will also be natural and instinctive. In this we ought to read Jesus's teaching in Luke 6:44–46 (NRSVUE) as both warning and encouragement:

> For each tree is known by its own fruit. For people do not gather figs from thorns, nor do they pick grapes from a bramble bush. The good person out of the good treasure of the heart produces good, and the evil person out of evil treasure produces evil, for it is out of the abundance of the heart that the mouth speaks. Why do you call me "Lord, Lord," and do not do what I tell you?

The time of crisis is a time when our hearts reveal their fruit of what is already there—what we have planted, tended, and nurtured. These are the moments of fire: "Now if anyone builds on the foundation with gold, silver, precious stones, wood, hay, straw—the work of each builder will become visible, for the day will disclose it, because it will be revealed with fire, and the fire will test what sort of work each has done" (1 Cor 6:12–13 NRSVUE). In these times, the congregation that is rooted in Jesus's Way of Love will be the one providing housing, cover, material aid, shelter, and support to the scapegoated community. The congregation formed in the Way of Jesus will be scapegoated along with their neighbors in defiance of the cycle of disgust. A church or congregation which finds itself in stage three would do best to take the German Confessing Church[18] during the Nazi era or the American Black Church (throughout America's history but especially at the height of slavery and Jim Crow[19]) as models for how to exist and resist in the context of ongoing stage three expulsion.

During Stage Four—Rationalize

In January of 2023, a video of a Severna Park high school student mocking, belittling, threatening, and using slurs against a special needs classmate went viral on social media.[20] This led to a significant uproar in the local community and pressure on the school and the local district to ensure that something was being done about bullying and hate speech at the high school (one of the most prestigious in the district). In a public statement, the school's principal stated, "That's not who we are," and "I will not tolerate it moving forward." The line is a popular one with leaders who are addressing scandals and embarrassments that come to life because it is nearly always well received and serves a useful purpose. Despite being patently false, grade A bullshit (leaders only ever say "this is not who we are" to communities whose members have just shown that "this" is precisely "who they are"), the phrase papers over a potential gash in the image of the group. Reminding folks that "we" are not "this" helps keep the problem on a few lone, problematic individuals (now being reduced to a *this* instead of a more human *they*) and not on the collective *we*. It also implicitly expels the perpetrators from the group, leaving the collective feeling pure again so the problematic, embarrassing behavior won't be more broadly attributed to the group, but remain on the lone individuals. It alleviates the tension.[21] This same line and reasoning can

---

18. David Gushee's *Righteous Gentiles* read in tandem with Bonhoeffer's *Cost of Discipleship* and Cones, *Cross and the Lynching Tree*, would make excellent Christian reading leading up to and during stage three.

19. See Tisby, *Spirit of Justice*, for particular examples and inspiration from these voices and movements.

20. See Patton, "Severna Park High School"; and Asbury, "Severna Park High," for details of the account.

21. Notably, the phrase is also most frequently deployed when the perpetrator of the incident is a member of a relatively privileged, socially normative, group within society. When minorities commit acts of violence and cruelty the public is (re)assured that "something is being done about them," but when upper middle class white boys are caught in scandal, the community wants to hear from their leaders that the behavior is not representative of any larger problem within the community, much less of the character of the community as a whole.

be seen in the oft-used excuse of a "few bad apples" as in when police officers are caught abusing Black Americans or the horrific abuses and torture techniques by American soldiers were exposed. Blaming a few bad actors helps to alleviate a desire for justice while keeping the culture and system that helped cause that behavior intact.[22]

So too, in the wake of stage three, the rationalization begins; society is hungry to hear precisely that they are not the sort of society that would do what they just did. The bullshit mills fire up and everyone is eager to buy because the tear in their self-image is painful. It hurts to experience a gap between who we think we are and who we have been shown to be. It is destabilizing to our sense of self—shameful. Patching up that gap with avoidance and denial is a much easier solution (if actually far more costly to our humanity) than deconstructing and reconstructing the image of who we are. In the context of stage four, the church has an enormous opportunity to extend its reach and its audience. After an expulsion event, a significant percentage of the population is in a place of searching for comfort and a way to ease their consciences. The church (if it has survived stage three) is seen as an institution with the authority to pronounce innocence and dispense grace. The public is likely to show up at the church doors begging for bullshit and will richly reward those churches willing to dispense it to them. This is the great temptation of churches and of church leaders in the stage four contexts: that they will be willing to dispense what Dietrich Bonhoeffer famously described in *The Cost of Discipleship* as "cheap grace":

> Cheap grace means grace sold on the market like cheapjacks' wares. The sacraments, the forgiveness of sin, and the consolations of religion are thrown away at cut prices. Grace is represented as the Church's inexhaustible treasury, from which she showers blessings with generous hands, without asking questions or fixing limits. Grace without price; grace without cost![23]

This temptation is one that a eucontaminated and eucontaminating church must resist at all costs. We have every theological excuse to follow it and all the pragmatic justifications in the world if we yield to it. But as we have seen, cheap grace is nothing but bullshit and is anathema to the eucontaminating Truth, Life, and Way of Jesus Christ. Stage four is the time for the prophets.

22. See Zimbardo, *Lucifer Effect*.
23. Bonhoeffer, *Cost of Discipleship*, 45.

During stage four, the church is called to very nearly the same things that it is called to in stage one only with the emphases reversed. To a society in the throes of stage one, pastoral voices which work to remind us of each person's value and to form us in the love of our neighbors is vital as a form of harm reduction. Participating in the social negotiation of the role of the marginalized in our self-images is vital. Meanwhile, the prophetic voices calling out the system that erects stronger barriers between "neighbor" and "enemy" need to be hosted and amplified. But in stage four the urgent need is for a prophetic voice from the church which holds the powerful, the bystanders, and the excluders to account for what they have done. During stage four the church is tasked with refusing to let us look away from the harm we have done because it is here in this moment that the redemptive work of Jesus lies. Jesus did not come for the healthy but the sick. The beauty of the gospel is that we can finally tell the truth about our bullshit self-images and the pain that we have perpetrated. We don't need to hide from it, avoid it, or deny it. The Love of Jesus is the very thing that sustains us in the grief, lament, and trauma of not just of what's happened to us but of what we have done. The expulsion has shown that this is *exactly* who *we* are—a people willing to sacrifice and scapegoat others to protect our own bullshit self-image—and somehow God's love remains. Stage four is a time that calls for Nathans saying to the King Davids "you are that man" (2 Sam 12:7) who raped and murdered. For those who show any willingness to be eucontaminated by the Truth, and follow the Way of Love, Life (costly grace) lies on the other side of the death of our bullshit identities. We are truly free!

LOCATING OUR THOUGHTS

Our reflections in this book are by no means either a beginning nor a final word on this. As our footnotes and references suggest, we believe we are standing on the shoulders of so many others who have risked listening to and following the dare of Christ. We are also bound by our own location, beautifully limited by our life experiences. May you find the edges of what's thinkable to us and resist those unnecessary limitations, pushing us to dream more. We pray you will be empowered to follow the foolish call of Christ and wooing of the Spirit wherever she may lead you.

It has been such a joy to be on this journey with my sister, Billie. I (Paul) am so grateful for an opportunity to discuss, argue, collaborate, and create with her. And while I believe we have experienced a taste of the age to come, writing as siblings also forecloses what's possible in our imaginations. We can't imagine what you may have to teach us about ourselves and about the eucontaminating work of the Spirit. We are trapped within the bodies, cultures, families, and social imaginations of Hoard siblings living on different coasts of the US in the 2020s. We both imagine ourselves to be white and have been marked as such our entire lives. We strive to listen and learn from the stories and experiences of bodies of color, but are unable fully see through their eyes. We are both able-bodied and, as such, are often insulated from the reality of our world that our disabled siblings experience. We are both allosexual individuals in monogamous marriages. We have much to learn from our aro and ace siblings and the rest of the queer community as to what love, relating, and community can hold.

We note these limitations for a number of reasons. Firstly, we want to de-center our own perspectives. Too often the voice of the author/s is taken as authoritative, representative, and generalizable. However, we are unable to see past our own experiences. These reflections we have offered are only valuable if contextualized to our lives and social locations. Secondly, our limitations are the significant barriers that create the possibility of contextualizing. One of the less noted, deeply insidious myths of modernity is the fantasy of truth and knowledge that can exist free of context—disconnected from any knower.[24] Knowledge, as we talked about in chapter 4, is always located in a person, context, and community. By stating ours, we hope to allow our reflections to have a home and thus be a gift from our location to wherever you find yourself. We don't know your context, we haven't lived your life, we are not in your situation. Please play with our ideas, wrestle with them, and reimagine what they may be able to offer you in your context. Contextualizing our thoughts will hopefully assist in the necessary interpretive task you must now perform to recontextualize them for your context. We cannot know what following the Way of Jesus looks like in your life. We pray that we have given you some helpful considerations as you too follow the dare of Jesus.

Finally, we highlight these limitations because we want to underscore, earmark, and repeat how important your (eu)contamination of us is. Many of our social identifiers (white, able-bodied, allosexual) place both of us in a more central social location. We do not merely tolerate the

---

24. See Meek, *Loving to Know*.

existence and presence of those from different locations, but recognize our desperate hope for your eucontaminating impact on us. We cannot be truly ourselves without the blessing of your difference. In this book we have noted the beautiful blessing that is Billie's queerness in her and my (Paul's) life. I do not love her and merely *tolerate* her transness. No, I am not fully me without her full inclusion and eucontamination in my life. I, as a straight, cis man cannot be my full self without her. Her queerness is an invitation to the queering of my own identities. Instead of seeing myself as a man within a heteronormative masculinity defined by its adherence to a stereotypical fantasy of maleness that cannot tolerate any hint of femininity, I am free to be a man who identifies with a maleness that is not at constant threat of contamination. I don't need to fear the loss of my masculinity because it is a robust maleness. Billie's story of coming out offered me a chance to question and query my own identity. How did I know I wasn't also gender queer or non-binary? Why hadn't I questioned my own heterosexuality? My straightness isn't "normal"; it is merely the unique way God created me. What a beautiful gift it has been to no longer fear queerness but trust in my own sense of self. I can freely cry at movies, hate sports, and show my affection for those I love without any of those actions threatening my being a "real man." Because I am free from the oppression of that image of maleness. That toxic form of masculinity in modern society continues to grow more restrictive each year because it defines itself in opposition to the other (the feminine). Toxic masculinity is nothing but the failed attempt to be "not feminine." A position that is fueled by a disgust that forever dehumanizes the "man" who imagines himself one along with everyone else in his life out of the attempt to prop up a fantasy that can't ever be true. We are all messier than we think. What a beautiful contradiction it is to be human!

Here, we also want to reiterate a caution about mishearing us. By highlighting the beauty of eucontamination, we are not advocating the abandonment of boundaries. Recognizing the problems of disgust does not mean that threats no longer exist. Instead, we hope that recognition allows one to hold effective and humane boundaries. We are inviting you to resist the lure of dehumanization that comes from disgust, not asking you to ignore all boundaries. Dangers exist in the world. Not all people can be trusted. Power dynamics are real and must be taken into consideration. As you do though, notice how disgust may sometimes be used to make holding those boundaries easier. Jesus continually calls us back to see the image of God in everyone, even while holding them accountable.

We also want to reiterate that a posture of eucontamination requires that you also be open to transformation. The life of the Spirit within you is more robust than the evil that exists in the world, but this does not turn you into the savior. It instead invites you into a posture of being (eu)contaminated. Growing up, we saw the way missionary churches are more often colonizing outposts than communities of Christ. The good news of Jesus has far too often been used as a license for empire.[25] If we are to proclaim the good news of Jesus's eucontamination into the world, we must do so from a posture of perpetual openness to eucontamination ourselves. Those of us from Western contexts have too often followed the models of empire and corporation in spreading franchised churches instead of listening to what others may have to teach us.[26] The posture of eucontamination is not the "white magic" of modernity that uses power and process to homogenize outcomes and standardize experience. It is instead the "wild magic" of a fully enchanted world that whispers what it will and irrupts when it wants.[27] Or again, from Lewis, it is not tame.

FURTHER UP AND FURTHER IN

And so with this taste of heaven we have glimpsed in our collaboration, we say in chorus with Lewis, "further up and further in!" That call, repeated and repeated in *The Last Battle*, is shaped by the protagonists' discovery that the further up and further in they go along the Way of Aslan, the bigger and more complex reality becomes. Worlds they thought lost are found in their True form, now bigger, more enticing and interconnected with ever branching and expanding Reality.

This is the staggering Truth of heaven and of our desire for it: that the further up and further in we go, the larger and more real it becomes. There is a wildness, an untamed, uncultured, unmanageable quality to heaven and to our desire for it that defies our bullshit-loving egos. Each time we manage to let prophetic truth in to dismantle our little bullshit imaginary realities is a step further into "deep heaven." And each step along this Way of Jesus is another step through the death of our old image

25. See Charles and Rah, *Unsettling Truths*.

26. There is a whole book to be written about the history of a purity-oriented church from Constantine through the Crusades, the Reformation and Counter-Reformation, and the Homogenous Church Growth movement through to the Christian Nationalists of today. We hope someone will write it soon.

27. See Altimont, "Rewilding," paras. 2–7, 17.

of ourselves into a new, slightly-less-false image of who we are, and of reality as it is. We will all die a thousand small deaths in pursuit of the haunting melody of Life that calls to us each time from the margins of the new bullshit world we are only just putting the finishing touches on. And each battle for Life and Joy will be a battle for and against reality itself, and will be a death.

As we follow in the Way of Jesus, we hold with joy the tension between his promise that "my yoke is easy and my burden is light"[28] and his instruction to take up our cross and follow him. That Jesus's "easy yoke" and "light burden" are a cross lies at the center of what it means to be his follower, his disciple. How can a cross be an easy yoke and a light burden? It is a cross, an instrument of our own deaths. Even Jesus acknowledged and grieved the weight of the cross in Gethsemane. The answer, the great secret of God, is the call of Joy from the other side of the grave, of a thousand, thousand graves. It was "for the Joy what was set before him" that Jesus "endured the cross, disregarding its shame" and it was on the other side of that cross, drawn by that Joy that Jesus had "taken his seat at the right hand of the throne of God";[29] it is the call of heaven—of more, ever more true reality—that renders our cross easy and light.[30]

It is an easy mistake to think of following the Truth along the Way towards Life as a bounded journey towards a discrete and comprehensible end point. The reverse is true; what is, is so much more than what we are tempted to imagine must be. As we, together and alone, pursue Truth we find ourselves living a Life and lives we could not have imagined, and in the living of that Life we begin to find that the strains of Joy which have been calling to us all along are drawing us along a Way that is itself a destination: branching out infinitely and yet contained in the One who is the Truth, the Life, and the Way.

The eucontaminating work never ends. There is always more to taste, more to enjoy, more to embrace. The beauty of Truth is never exhausted. The Life of Jesus never dies. The Way of the Spirit has no end!

---

28. Matt 11:30 NRSVUE.

29. Heb 12:2.

30. In *The Great Divorce* the character of George MacDonald explains to the narrator that "both good and evil, when they are full grown, become retrospective. . . . The good man's past begins to change so that his forgiven sins and remembered sorrows take on the quality of Heaven: the bad man's past already conforms to his badness and is filled only with dreariness" (Lewis, *Great Divorce*, 69).

Let us embrace the love, joy, and goodness that Christ offers as we join together and keep pursuing him.

> It was the Unicorn who summed up what everyone was feeling. He stamped his right fore-hoof on the ground and neighed and then cried,
>
> "I have come home at last! This is my real country! I belong here. This is the land I have been looking for all my life, though I never knew it till now.... Come further up, come further in!"[31]

---

31. Lewis, *Last Battle*, 150–51.

Appendix

Liturgy of Eucontamination

Dwight Friesen

INVOCATION

. . . Welcoming One Another as G-d in Christ Welcomes All

Cheers—Officiant 1

Offers a toast to open the proceedings

Gathering—Officiant 1

- Light Candle
- Sound Singing Bowl

Wash Before Dinner—Officiant 2

- Participants are invited to wash one another's hands and to reflect on the questions "who is *me*" and "who is *we*" in this space.
    - Provide space for diners to name how they experience themselves as a threat to the space! Or from the space, or from other

diners. How do we reclaim this as a shift to Eucontaminant—a good contamination.

Welcome—Officiant 1

One: The Peace of Christ is with you.

Many: **And also with you.**

Litany of Contamination—Officiant 1

One: At the beginning of each day in the first creation myth of Genesis G-d contaminates what is. The Divine sings difference into being, inviting a new relationship. Without the other, we'd be left with chaos. What Is encounters Other . . . and something new emerges. "Let there be light!" is sung into the formless void. Separating light from dark.

Many: **G-d names the variant "day" and declares it "good!"**

One: On day two, G-d infects the primordial waters of Earth with space.

Many: **G-d names the variant "sky" and declares it "good!"**

One: G-d continues creational Eucontamination day after day, until on the sixth day, G-d introduces mammals and caps the day by introducing humans in all our protein diversity.

Many: **G-d names the variant "image bearers," and declares it "very good!"**

One: The Divine does not shame day one for not being day two, nor condemn day five for not being day six. New life emerges when something Other is brought into relationship with what is, thus reality evolves to reflect its Creator.

Many: **All this makes G-d smile, and rest into the goodness of difference living in harmony. Amen.**

Officiant 1 briefly introduces themself then invites diners to welcome each other at their tables

WORD

... Finding Ourselves in G-d's Story of Shalom for All & Everything

Litany for Followers of the Transgressive One—Officiant 1

One: When the time came for Mystery to be known, Creator became Creation, revealing G-d as WITH... Emmanuel! G-d is with us!

Many: **The Living Word became flesh and moved into the neighborhood.**

One: "If you have seen me, you have seen the One who sent me," said Jesus of Nazareth.

Many: **So, who is Jesus? And what does Jesus do?**

One: Because Jesus is G-d, the Incarnate One does not consider equality with G-d something to grasp or cling to, but surrenders divinity in order to discover a way of symbiotic love with you, me, and all of creation.

Many: **If Christ is willing to give up G-dness in pursuit of loving relationship, what might that invite of us ... of me?**

One: Jesus the Christ dined with the wrong people, embraced the unclean, flipped the tables of the powerful, welcomed the children, forgave his murderers, and called us friends.

Many: **Is this what Shalomic life looks like? Could it be, that the Kindom of G-d welcomes all and everything? Could it be that Jesus' new commandment "To love one another, as Jesus has loved us" fulfills all prior commandments?**

One: For G-d did not send Christ into the world to condemn the world but to reconcile all and everything through Emmanuel.

Many: **Teach us, O G-d, to welcome the widow, the orphan, and the stranger; guiding us to live justly, to love mercy, and to walk humbly with the G-d who is WITH. Cheers.**

Introduction of Food—Officiant 2

- Offer a few words about fermentation as a form of eucontamination
- Introduce the meal

Contaminated Unto the Good—Teacher

Note that this section can be replaced with open time for participants to eat and enjoy one another's company.

- Teacher(s) unpack Eucontamination

TABLE

... Discovering Christ in the Everyday Things & People of Life

Litany of the Table—Officiant 1

One: Who is welcome at Christ's table?

Many: **All are welcome and loved by G-d!**

One: Even me?

Many: **Yes. Even you!**

One: But I'm so hungry, and thirsty, and weary.

Many: **Come as you are, this table is lovingly prepared for you, and for all.**

One: But I feel so I afraid, and lonely . . . I ache.

Many: **At Christ's table you are not alone. It is here we discover communion.**

One: Then let's welcome each other.

Many: **Yes, let's become a welcoming people! Cheers to the open table Christ sets!**

Practicing Peace with Your Neighbor—Officiant 1

One: The presence and peace of Christ is with you!

Many: **And also with you.**

Invite participants to "take a few moments, stand and stretch, walk around as you are able, welcoming those you haven't met, greeting those you already know, and bringing our next course to your table."

Love Feast—Officiant 1

- (Sound singing bowl to invite people to sit together and eat.)
- Friends, before you are the gifts of G-d for all of humanity, all who hunger for G-d's grace are welcome.
- *Raise a fork full, to offer thanks in a way that makes sense for you; as you eat hold gratitude for the body of Christ*
- Now raise your cup . . . Cheers, to the abundant life in and through Jesus the Christ.
    - Friends, the table has always been a place and a practice of joining.
        - Christ sets it,
        - Christ is the host,
        - Christ is its substance, and
        - Christ opens the table to all who are hungry or thirsty, all!
- As you break bread and drink from the cup, hold and offer gratitude for the gift of the Other in your life and in this room.

BENEDICTION

. . . Sending Each Other to Learn & Practice Faithful Presence

Litany of Mutual Sending—Officiant 1

One: The table is the intimate place where friends and family gather to make sense of life, to discover a way of Christ-like love, and to rehearse how to live an alternative narrative in our fragmented world, filled with hurt, fear, and loneliness.

Many: **Send us out into our lives, as followers of Jesus, open to being contaminated unto the common good.**

One: What will we do when we feel afraid?

Many: **We will remind each other that Jesus goes before us, wooing us to discover an ever more courageous way of love.**

One:	What will we do when we feel alone?
Many:	**We will remind each other that we've got each other's back. That G-d is with us. That we are loved. And we are not alone. Cheers.**

Sending—Officiant 1

Jesus once said, "The kin-dom of G-d is like a pinch of yeast or a bread starter that a baker works into a mass of flour and water until integrated throughout the dough." Once contaminated it finds new life, starts to grow, and becomes one, from many. Offering nourishment for all.
(And so, friends as we send each other out of this place and beyond, we dare ourselves and one another . . .)

One:	As Jesus touched persons with leprosy and contaminated them with wholeness and health,
Many:	**Embolden us to move toward "the unclean" within our respective cultural contexts.**
One:	As Jesus engaged persons marginalized by empire and religion,
Many:	**Embolden us to welcome all and everyone, especially those who have been marginalized by oppressive systems whom we've been tricked into fearing.**
One:	As Jesus welcomed children and those without voice or standing,
Many:	**Embolden us to stand in awe of the gift of the other.**
One:	Go now, in Christ's peace and love. You are not alone.
Many:	**Thanks be to G-d! We are not alone!**

Bibliography

Aftoora-Orsagos, Patrick, and Michael Rubinkam. "Ohio State Police to Protect Schools After Furor over Haitian Immigrants in Springfield." AP News, September 17, 2024. https://apnews.com/article/trump-vance-haitian-immigrants-springfield-ohio-threats-d74b7ff56f9a45d9389d8ebee4af1652.

Ahmed, Sara. *The Cultural Politics of Emotion*. New York: Routledge, 2014.

Alexander, Michelle. *The New Jim Crow: Mass Incarceration in the Age of Colorblindness*. New York: New Press, 2010.

Allen, Amy, and Mari Ruti. *Critical Theory Between Klein and Lacan: A Dialogue*. New York: Bloomsbury Academic, 2021.

Alter, Robert. *The Hebrew Bible: A Translation with Commentary*. New York: Norton, 2019.

Altimont, Lauren. "Rewilding Virginity, Birthing Magic, and Resurrecting the Fermented Christ." Substack. https://substack.com/home/post/p-145244548.

American Psychiatric Association. *Diagnostic and Statistical Manual of Mental Disorders*. 5th ed., text rev. American Psychiatric Association, 2022.

Anselm, and Gaunilo. *Proslogion: With the replies of Gaunilo and Anselm*. Translated by Thomas Williams. Indianapolis: Hackett, 2001.

Anyabwile, Thabiti. "The Importance of Your Gag Reflex When Discussing Homosexuality and 'Gay Marriage.'" The Gospel Coalition, October 6, 2020. https://www.thegospelcoalition.org/blogs/thabiti-anyabwile/the-importance-of-your-gag-reflex-when-discussing-homosexuality-and-gay-marriage/.

Arendt, Hannah. *The Origins of Totalitarianism*. Introduction by Anne Applebaum. New York: Mariner Books Classics, 2024.

Arnsdorf, Isaac. "Trump Makes Demonizing Immigrants a Core Message with 'Blood' Refrain." *The Washington Post*, December 22, 2023. https://www.washingtonpost.com/politics/2023/12/22/trump-campaign-immigrants-mass-deportations/.

Asbury, Nicole. "Severna Park High Students Disciplined in Bullying Incident of Peer with Special Needs." *The Washington Post*, January 13, 2023. https://www.washingtonpost.com/education/2023/01/13/severna-park-school-bullying-video/.

"The Athanasian Creed." In *The Book of Common Prayer and Administration of the Sacraments*, 769–71. Huntington Beach, CA: Anglican Liturgy, 2019.

Atlas, Galit. *The Enigma of Desire: Sex, Longing, and Belonging in Psychoanalysis*. London: Routledge, Taylor & Francis, 2016.

Augustine. *Saint Augustine's Confessions*. Translated by Henry Chadwick. Oxford: Oxford University Press, 2011.

Augustine, Sarah. *The Land Is Not Empty: Following Jesus in Dismantling the Doctrine of Discovery*. Harrisonburg, VA: Herald, 2021.

Bader, Michael. *Arousal: The Secret Logic of Sexual Fantasies*. London: Virgin, 2003.

Bailly, Lionel. *Lacan: A Beginner's Guide*. Oxford: Oneworld, 2009.

Baldwin, James. *The Fire Next Time*. New York: Vintage International, 2016.

Ball, James. *Post-Truth: How Bullshit Conquered the World*. London: Biteback, 2018.

Barfield, Owen. *Poetic Diction: A Study in Meaning*. Middletown, CT: Wesleyan University Press, 1984.

Beck, Richard. *Unclean: Meditations on Purity, Hospitality, and Morality*. Eugene, OR: Cascade, 2012.

Bell, John L., and Graham Maule. *Will You Come and Follow Me (The Summons)*. © 1987 WGRG, Iona Community, Scotland. Chicago: GIA Publications, 1987.

Berzoff, Joan, et al. *Inside Out and Outside In: Psychodynamic Clinical Theory and Psychopathology in Contemporary Multicultural Contexts*. New York: Rowman & Littlefield, 2022.

Bonhoeffer, Dietrich. *The Cost of Discipleship*. New York: Touchstone, 2018.

Boothby, Richard. *Death and Desire: Psychoanalytic Theory in Lacan's Return to Freud*. London: Routledge, 2015.

———. *Embracing the Void: Rethinking the Origin of the Sacred*. Evanston, IL: Northwestern University Press, 2023.

———. *Freud as Philosopher: Metapsychology After Lacan*. New York: Routledge, 2001.

———. *Sex on the Couch: What Freud Still Has to Teach Us About Sex and Gender*. New York: Routledge, 2014.

Boyd, Gregory A. *The Myth of a Christian Nation: How the Quest for Political Power Is Destroying the Church*. Grand Rapids: Zondervan, 2006.

Brake, Elizabeth. "Amatonormativity." Elizabeth Brake, October 9, 2023. https://elizabethbrake.com/amatonormativity/.

Brinker, Jennifer. "Mass of Reparation Atones for Sins of Clergy Sexual Abuse." Archdiocese of St. Louis, March 28, 2019. https://web.archive.org/web/20240521071341/https://www.archstl.org/mass-of-reparation-at-cathedral-basilica-atones-for-sins-of-clergy-sexual-abuse-2940.

Bromberg, Philip M. "Shrinking the Tsunami: Affect Regulation, Dissociation, and the Shadow of the Flood." *Contemporary Psychoanalysis* 39 (2003) 379–96.

Brother Maverick. "Gay Pastor Brandan Robertson Gets Absolutely DISMANTLED by Voddie Baucham." YouTube, April 10, 2024. https://www.youtube.com/watch?v=j7Yc-ZN4eL4.

Brown, Brené. *Daring Greatly: How the Courage to Be Vulnerable Transforms the Way We Live, Love, Parent, and Lead*. New York: Gotham, 2012.

Brown, Dee. *Bury My Heart at Wounded Knee: An Indian History of the American West*. New York: Henry Holt, 2022.

Brueggemann, Walter. *The Prophetic Imagination*. Philadelphia: Fortress, 1999.

Brumm, Joe, dir. *Bluey*. Season 1, episode 5, "Shadowlands." Aired October 5, 2018, on ABC Kids.

Buber, Martin. *I and Thou*. Translated by Walter Kaufmann. New York: Charles Scribner's Sons, 1970.

Cambridge English Dictionary. "Contamination." *Cambridge English Dictionary*. https://dictionary.cambridge.org/us/dictionary/english/contamination.

BIBLIOGRAPHY

Caputo, John D. *The Folly of God: A Theology of the Unconditional*. Salem, OR: Polebridge, 2015.

———. *Hermeneutics: Facts and Interpretation in the Age of Information*. London: Pelican, 2018.

———. *Philosophy and Theology*. Nashville: Abingdon, 2006.

Celenza, Andrea. *Erotic Revelations: Clinical Applications and Perverse Scenarios*. London: Routledge, Taylor & Francis, 2014.

Charles, Mark, and Soong-Chan Rah. *Unsettling Truths: The Ongoing, Dehumanizing Legacy of the Doctrine of Discovery*. Downers Grove, IL: InterVarsity, 2019.

Chesterton, G. K. *Orthodoxy*. New York: John Lane, 1908.

Claiborne, Shane. *The Irresistible Revolution: Living as an Ordinary Radical*. Grand Rapids: Zondervan, 2006.

Coates, Ta-Nehisi. *Between the World and Me*. New York: Spiegel & Grau, 2015.

Cone, James H. *The Cross and the Lynching Tree*. Maryknoll, NY: Orbis, 2022.

———. *God of the Oppressed*. Rev. ed. Maryknoll, NY: Orbis, 1997.

Cooper-White, Pamela. *Braided Selves: Collected Essays on Multiplicity, God, and Persons*. Eugene, OR: Cascade, 2011.

———. *The Psychology of Christian Nationalism: Why People Are Drawn In and How to Talk Across the Divide*. Minneapolis: Fortress, 2022.

Copjec, Joan. *Read My Desire: Lacan Against the Historicists*. Cambridge, MA: MIT Press, 1994.

The Council on Biblical Manhood and Womanhood. "The Nashville Statement." https://cbmw.org/the-nashville-statement/.

Creed, Barbara. *The Monstrous-Feminine: Film, Feminism, Psychoanalysis*. London: Routledge, 1993.

Crenshaw, Kimberlé. *On Intersectionality: Essential Writings*. New York: The New Press, 2022.

Croasmun, Matthew. *The Emergence of Sin: The Cosmic Tyrant in Romans*. Oxford: Oxford University Press, 2017.

Cushman, Philip. *Travels with the Self: Interpreting Psychology as Cultural History*. New York: Routledge, 2019.

Daniels, Brandy. "Queer Theory." In *Religion: Embodied Religion*, 289–308. New York: Macmillan Reference, 2016.

Dante Alighieri. *The Divine Comedy: Paradiso*. Translated by Robin Kirkpatrick. London: Penguin, 2007.

Dawsey, Josh. "Trump Derides Protections for Immigrants from 'Shithole' Countries." *The Washington Post*, January 12, 2018. https://www.washingtonpost.com/politics/trump-attacks-protections-for-immigrants-from-shithole-countries-in-oval-office-meeting/2018/01/11/bfc0725c-f711-11e7-91af-31ac729add94_story.html.

Day, O'Donnell. "The Birthing of a Mind." *The Other Journal* 38 (2024). https://theotherjournal.com/2025/01/the-birthing-of-a-mind/.

Descartes, René. *Meditations on First Philosophy: In Which the Existence of God and the Distinction of the Soul from the Body Are Demonstrated*. Translated by Donald A. Cress. Indianapolis: Hackett, 1993.

DeYoung, Patricia A. *Understanding and Treating Chronic Shame: Healing Right Brain Relational Trauma*. 2nd ed. New York: Routledge, 2021.

DiAngelo, Robin. *White Fragility: Why It's So Hard for White People to Talk About Racism*. Boston: Beacon, 2018.

Doctor, Pete, dir., *Inside Out*. Burbank, CA: Walt Disney Studios, 2015.

Dolan, Eric. "Scientists Revist Solomon Asch's Classic Conformity Experiments—and Are Stunned by the Results." *Psypost*, December 6, 2023. https://www.psypost.org/skeptical-scientists-revisit-solomon-aschs-classic-conformity-experiments-and-are-stunned-by-the-results/.

Du Mez, Kristin Kobes. *Jesus and John Wayne: How White Evangelicals Corrupted a Faith and Fractured a Nation*. New York: Liveright, 2020.

Dunbar-Ortiz, Roxanne. *An Indigenous Peoples' History of the United States*. Boston: Beacon, 2015.

Eckhart, Meister. *Meister Eckhart: The Essential Sermons, Commentaries, Treatises, and Defense*. Edited and translated by Edmund Colledge and Bernard McGinn. New York: Paulist, 1981.

Ellis, Albert. *Reason and Emotion in Psychotherapy*. New York: Lyle Stuart, 1962.

Fanon, Franz. *The Wretched of the Earth*. Translated by Richard Philcox. New York: Grove Press, 2004.

Ferguson, Trey. *Theologizin' Bigger: Homilies on Living Freely and Loving Wholly*. Grand Rapids: Lake Drive, 2024.

Fernandez, Eleazar S. *Reimagining the Human: Theological Anthropology in Response to Systemic Evil*. St. Louis: Chalice, 2004.

Fink, Bruce. *The Lacanian Subject: Between Language and Jouissance*. Princeton, NJ: Princeton University Press, 1997.

Finkin, Matthew W., and Robert C. Post. *For the Common Good: Principles of American Academic Freedom*. New Haven, CT: Yale University Press, 2009.

Five Iron Frenzy. "Someone Else's Problem." Track 5 on *Engine of a Million Plots*. New York: Singing Serpent, 2013.

Florer-Bixler, Melissa. *How to Have an Enemy: Righteous Anger and the Work of Peace*. Harrisonburg, VA: Herald, 2021.

Fors, Malin. *A Grammar of Power in Psychotherapy: Exploring the Dynamics of Privilege*. Washington, DC: American Psychological Association, 2018.

Frankfurt, Harry G. *On Bullshit*. Princeton, NJ: Princeton University Press, 2005.

Franzen, Axel, and Sebastian Mader. "The Power of Social Influence: A Replication and Extension of the Asch Experiment." *PLOS ONE* 18 (2023) e0279562.

Freud, Sigmund. *Beyond the Pleasure Principle*. Translated by James Strachey. The Standard Edition of the Complete Psychological Works of Sigmund Freud 18. London: Hogarth, 1955.

———. "Remembering, Repeating and Working-Through (Further Recommendations on the Technique of Psycho-Analysis II)." In *The Standard Edition of the Complete Psychological Works of Sigmund Freud*, edited and translated by James Strachey, 12:145–56. London: Hogarth, 1958.

Gafney, Wilda. "Wisdom's Table Is God's Table." *The Rev. Wil Gafney, Ph.D., Womanists Wading in the Word*™, November 19, 2020. https://www.wilgafney.com/2018/09/19/wisdoms-table-is-gods-table/.

———. *Womanist Midrash: A Reintroduction to the Women of the Torah and the Throne*. Louisville, KY: Westminster John Knox, 2017.

Gaztambide, D. "A Preferential Option for the Repressed: Psychoanalysis Through the Eyes of Liberation Theology." *Psychoanalytic Dialogues* 25 (2015) 700–713.

Girard, René. *Things Hidden Since the Foundation of the World*. London: Bloomsbury Academic, 2016.

Gomez, Henry, et al. "How a Fringe Online Claim About Immigrants Eating Pets Made Its Way to the Debate Stage." NBC News, September 13, 2024. https://www.nbcnews.com/politics/donald-trump/trump-fringe-online-claim-immigrants-eating-pets-debate-trump-rcna170759.

Greenberg, Gary. *The Book of Woe: The DSM and the Unmaking of Psychiatry*. New York: Blue Rider Press, 2013.

Gushee, David. *Righteous Gentiles of the Holocaust: Genocide and Moral Obligation*. New York: Paragon, 2003.

———. *Still Christian: Following Jesus Out of American Evangelicalism*. Louisville, KY: Westminster John Knox, 2017.

Guthrie, Lee. "Senator Calls LGBTQ+ People 'Filth,' Says Most Don't Want Them Here." *Tahlequah Daily Press*, February 23, 2024. https://www.tahlequahdailypress.com/news/senator-calls-lgbtq-oklahomans-filth-says-constituents-dont-want-them/article_c8979398-d260-11ee-9823-973bf20c3730.html.

Haidt, Jonathan. *The Righteous Mind: Why Good People Are Divided by Politics and Religion*. New York: Pantheon, 2012.

Halperin, David M. *One Hundred Years of Homosexuality: And Other Essays on Greek Love*. London: Routledge, 1990.

Hansen, Suzy. *Notes on a Foreign Country: An American Abroad in a Post-American World*. New York: Farrar, Straus and Giroux, 2017.

Hart, David Bentley. *The New Testament: A Translation*. New Haven, CT: Yale University Press, 2023.

———. *That All Shall Be Saved: Heaven, Hell, and Universal Salvation*. New Haven, CT: Yale University Press, 2019.

Haugen, Marty. "All Are Welcome." Hymnary.org. https://hymnary.org/text/let_us_build_a_house_where_love_can_dwe#authority_media_flexscores.

Hennessy-Fiske, Molly. "Okla. Nonbinary Teen Died After School Fight amid Reported Bullying." *The Washington Post*, February 21, 2024. https://www.washingtonpost.com/nation/2024/02/21/oklahoma-teen-lgbtq-nex-benedict-died/.

Hoard, Paul. "Beyond Fragility: Interpassive White Rage." *The Other Journal* 35 (2023) 3–12.

———. "On Pleasure and Games." *The Other Journal* 37 (2024). https://theotherjournal.com/2024/07/on-pleasure-and-games/.

Hoard, Paul, and Billie Hoard. "Eucontamination: Enacting a Centered-Set Theology in a Multicultural World." *Journal of Psychology and Theology* 52 (2023). https://doi.org/10.1177/00916471231173201.

———. "Queering as Eucontaminant Reorganization." *The Other Journal* 34 (2022).

Hoard, Paul, and Earl Bland. "'How Am I Responsible?' Evangelical White Rage and Moral Injury in the Interpassive Perpetration of White-Body Supremacy." *Psychoanalytic Dialogues* 33 (2023) 653–70.

Hoard, Paul, and Tim Suttle. "Lacanian Virtue Ethics? Cultivating Virtue Through Failure." *The Other Journal* 35 (2023). https://theotherjournal.com/2023/06/lacanian-virtue-ethics-cultivating-virtue-through-failure/.

Hoffman, Donald D. *The Case Against Reality: How Evolution Hid the Truth from Our Eyes*. New York: Norton, 2019.

Howard-Brook, Wes. *"Come Out My People!" God's Call Out of Empire in the Bible and Beyond*. Maryknoll, NY: Orbis, 2010.

Huang, Betsy. "The Audacity of Kamala Harris' Laughter—and the Racist Roots of Trump's Derision." *The Conversation*, September 26, 2024. https://theconversation.com/the-audacity-of-kamala-harris-laughter-and-the-racist-roots-of-trumps-derision-238189.

Jacobs, Lynne. "Learning to Love White Shame." *Journal of Race, Ethnicity, and Society* 10 (2020) 45–67.

Jennings, Willie James. *After Whiteness: An Education in Belonging*. Grand Rapids: Eerdmans, 2020.

Joffe-Block, Jude. "What the JD Vance Couch Jokes Say About Social Media This Election Season." *NPR*, August 1, 2024. https://www.npr.org/2024/07/31/nx-s1-5055854/vance-harris-social-media-rumors-jokes.

Jones, Robert P. *White Too Long: The Legacy of White Supremacy in American Christianity*. New York: Simon & Schuster, 2021.

Kaur, Harmeet. "Archdiocese of New York Condemns the Funeral of a Trans Activist at St. Patrick's Cathedral." *CNN*, February 19, 2024. https://www.cnn.com/2024/02/19/us/cecilia-gentili-funeral-trans-activist-cec/index.html.

———. "Trans Icon Cecilia Gentili Is Honored at a Famous Cathedral." *CNN*, February 17, 2024. https://www.cnn.com/2024/02/17/us/cecilia-gentili-funeral-st-patricks-cathedral-cec/index.html.

Kendi, Ibram X. *Stamped from the Beginning: The Definitive History of Racist Ideas in America (a Summary)*. New York: Bold Type, 2020.

Kohut, Heinz. *How Does Analysis Cure?* Chicago: University of Chicago Press, 1984.

"Kristallnacht." United States Holocaust Memorial Museum, October 18, 2019. https://encyclopedia.ushmm.org/content/en/article/kristallnacht.

Kubrick, Stanley, dir. *The Shining*. Burbank, CA: Warner Bros., 1980.

Kuhn, Thomas S. *The Structure of Scientific Revolutions*. 2nd ed. Chicago: University of Chicago Press, 1970.

Lacan, Jacques. *The Four Fundamental Concepts of Psychoanalysis*. Edited by Jacques-Alain Miller and translated by Alan Sheridan. New York: Norton, 1998.

Lavietes, Matt. "Some Democrats Blame Party's Position on Transgender Rights in Part for Harris' Loss." *NBC News*, November 8, 2024. https://www.nbcnews.com/nbc-out/out-politics-and-policy/democrats-blame-partys-position-transgender-rights-part-harris-loss-rcna179370.

Lebrecht, Norman. *Mahler Remembered*. New York: Norton, 1987.

Lee, Cindy S. *Our Unforming: De-Westernizing Spiritual Formation*. Minneapolis: Fortress, 2022.

Lester, Dave, and Zach Malm, hosts. "112: Dr. Matt Warner Was Canceled at a Conservative College (With Dr. Paul Hoard)." *Veterans of Culture Wars*, June 4, 2024. https://podcasts.apple.com/us/podcast/112-dr-matt-warner-was-cancelled-at-a-conservative/id1537732624?i=1000657770310.

Leupin, Alexandre. *Lacan Today: Psychoanalysis, Science, Religion*. New York: Other Press, 2004.

Levine, Peter A. *In an Unspoken Voice: How the Body Releases Trauma and Restores Goodness*. Berkeley: North Atlantic, 2010.

Levitan, Monica. "Rapper Parody Costs 3 Their Jobs at Grace College and Seminary." *Diverse: Issues In Higher Education*, June 20, 2017. https://www.diverseeducation.com/campus-climate/article/15100763/rapper-parody-costs-3-their-jobs-at-grace-college-seminary.

Lewis, C. S. *The Four Loves*. New York, New York: Harcourt; Brace, 1960.
———. *God in the Dock*. Grand Rapids: Eerdmans, 1970.
———. *The Great Divorce*. San Francisco: HarperCollins, 2003.
———. *The Last Battle*. New York: Macmillan, 1995.
———. *Mere Christianity*. New York: HarperOne, 2009.
———. *Miracles*. New York: HarperCollins, 2009.
———. *Perelandra*. New York: Macmillan, 1965.
———. *Surprised by Joy: The Shape of My Early Life*. New York: Harcourt Brace, 1995.
———. *Till We Have Faces*. San Diego: Harcourt Brace, 1984.
———. *The Weight of Glory and Other Addresses*. New York: Harper One, 2001.
MacDonald, George. *Unspoken Sermons. Series I, II, and III*. New York: Start Publishing LLC, 2012.
Malaparte, Curzio. *The Skin*. Translated by David Moore. Introduction by Rachel Kushner. New York: New York Review Books, 2013.
McGilchrist, Iain. *The Master and His Emissary: The Divided Brain and the Making of the Western World*. New Haven, CT: Yale University Press, 2009.
McGowan, Todd. *Capitalism and Desire: The Psychic Cost of Free Markets*. New York: Columbia University Press, 2016.
———. *The End of Dissatisfaction? Jacques Lacan and the Emerging Society of Enjoyment*. Albany: State University of New York Press, 2004.
———. *Enjoying What We Don't Have: The Political Project of Psychoanalysis*. Lincoln: University of Nebraska Press, 2013.
———. *Enjoyment Right and Left*. Brooklyn: Sublation, 2022.
———. *Emancipation After Hegel: Achieving a Contradictory Revolution*. New York: Columbia University Press, 2019.
———. "The Lust for Power and Logic of Enjoyment." *Crisis and Critique* 6 (2019) 205–24.
———. *Psychoanalytic Film Theory and the Rules of the Game*. New York: Bloomsbury Academic, 2015.
———. *The Racist Fantasy: Unconscious Roots of Hatred*. New York: Bloomsbury Academic, 2022.
———. *The Rules of the Game: Psychoanalysis and the Logic of Capitalism*. Albany: State University of New York Press, 2016.
———. *Universality and Identity Politics*. New York: Columbia University Press, 2020.
McGrath, S. J. "Sexuation in Jung and Lacan." *International Journal of Jungian Studies* 3 (2009) 41–56.
McLuhan, Marshall. *Understanding Media: The Extensions of Man*. New York: McGraw-Hill, 1964.
McNeil, Derek. "White Rage: In Discourse with Paul Hoard." *The Other Journal* 35 (2023). https://theotherjournal.com/2023/05/white-rage-in-discourse-with-paul-hoard/.
McWilliams, Nancy. *Psychoanalytic Diagnosis: Understanding Personality Structure in the Clinical Process*. New York: Guilford, 2011.
———. "Psychoanalytic Reflections on Limitation: Aging, Dying, Generativity, and Renewal." *Psychoanalytic Psychology* 34 (2017) 50–57.
Meek, Esther L. *Loving to Know: Introducing Covenant Epistemology*. Eugene, OR: Cascade, 2011.
Menakem, Resmaa. *My Grandmother's Hands: Racialized Trauma and the Pathway to Mending Our Hearts and Bodies*. Las Vegas: Central Recovery Press, 2017.

———. *The Quaking of America: A Guide to Understanding and Healing Trauma*. New York: Flatiron, 2021.

Mitchell, Stephen A., and Margaret J. Black. *Freud and Beyond: A History of Modern Psychoanalytic Thought*. New York: Basic, 1995.

Morris, Shane. "Heresy at the Heart of Derek Webb's 'Boys Will Be Girls.'" The Gospel Coalition, June 29, 2023. https://www.thegospelcoalition.org/article/heresy-boys-girls-webb/.

Mullins, Rich. "Promenade." Track 4 on *Brother's Keeper*. Nashville: Reunion, 1995.

———. "We Are Not as Strong as We Think We Are." Track 5 on *Songs*. Nashville: Reunion, 1995.

Nevins, Jake. "Cecilia Gentili Is Looking for God in Her New One-Woman Show." *Interview Magazine*, November 1, 2023. https://www.interviewmagazine.com/culture/cecilia-gentili-is-looking-for-god-in-her-new-one-woman-show#:~:text=They%20made%20it%20very%20clear.

Ng, Leonard, trans. *Tao Te Ching*. February 12, 2016. https://leonard-ng.com/tao-te-ching/.

Nolan, Christopher, dir. *Inception*. Warner Bros., 2010.

Noll, Mark A. *The Scandal of the Evangelical Mind*. Grand Rapids: Eerdmans, 1994.

Nussbaum, Martha Craven. *From Disgust to Humanity: Sexual Orientation and Constitutional Law*. New York: Oxford University Press, 2010.

Nutter, David, dir. *Game of Thrones*. Season 3, episode 9, "The Rains of Castamere." Aired June 2, 2013, on HBO.

Ogden, Thomas H. "On Holding and Containing, Being and Dreaming." *The International Journal of Psychoanalysis* 80 (1999) 1349–64.

Patton, Mark. "Severna Park High School, County Address Bullying." *Severna Park Voice*, February 17, 2023. https://www.severnaparkvoice.com/stories/aacps-addresses-bullying-students-respond,54946.

Peele, Jordan, dir. *Nope*. Universal City, CA: Universal Pictures, 2022.

Pfaller, Robert. *On the Pleasure Principle in Culture: Illusions Without Owners*. Translated by Lisa Rosenblatt. London: Verso, 2014.

Pidcock, Rick. "Offense Taken: Parsing the Uproar over the Olympics Opening Ceremony." *Baptist News Global*, July 29, 2024. https://baptistnews.com/article/offense-taken-parsing-the-uproar-over-the-olympics-opening-ceremony/.

Plato. *Phaedrus*. Translated by Benjamin Jowett. The Internet Classics Archive. http://classics.mit.edu/Plato/phaedrus.html.

Post, Kathryn. "Grace College Professor Ousted After Online Commentators Flag 'Woke' Social Media Posts." *Religion News Service*, May 8, 2024. https://religionnews.com/2024/05/08/grace-college-professor-ousted-after-online-commentators-flag-woke-social-media-posts/.

PRRI Staff. "A Christian Nation? Understanding the Threat of Christian Nationalism to American Democracy and Culture: Findings from the 2023 PRRI/Brookings Christian Nationalism Survey." PRRI, February 8, 2023. https://www.prri.org/wp-content/uploads/2023/02/PRRI-Jan-2023-Christian-Nationalism-Final.pdf.

Reed, Peyton, dir. *The Break-Up*. Universal City, CA: Universal Pictures, 2006.

Reitherman, Wolfgang, dir. *The Sword in the Stone*. Burbank, CA: Walt Disney Studios Motion Pictures, 1963.

Rise Against. "Rules of Play." Track 11 on *Nowhere Generation*. Fort Collins, CO: The Blasting Room, 2021.

Rollins, Peter. *The Idolatry of God: Breaking Our Addiction to Certainty and Satisfaction.* New York: Howard, 2013.

Rowson, Jonathan. *Moves That Matter: A Chess Grandmaster on the Game of Life.* London: Bloomsbury, 2019.

Rozin, Paul, and April E. Fallon. "A Perspective on Disgust." *Psychological Review* 94 (1987) 23–41.

Rusnak, Josef, dir. *The Thirteenth Floor.* Columbia Pictures, 1999.

Sartre, Jean-Paul. *Being and Nothingness: An Essay on Phenomenological Ontology.* Translated by Hazel E. Barnes. New York: Philosophical Library, 1956.

Saturday Night Live. "2024 Pre-Election Cold Open." YouTube, November 3, 2024. https://www.youtube.com/watch?v=e6Funs6yyEw.

Scheff, Thomas J. "Shame in Self and Society." *Symbolic Interaction* 26 (2003) 239–62.

Sellers, Tina Schermer. *Sex, God, and the Conservative Church: Erasing Shame from Sexual Intimacy.* New York: Routledge/Taylor & Francis Group, 2017.

Serano, Julia. *Excluded: Making Feminist and Queer Movements More Inclusive.* Berkeley, CA: Seal, 2013.

———. *Sexed Up: How Society Sexualizes Us, and How We Can Fight Back.* New York: Seal, 2022.

———. "Should Democrats Throw Trans People Under the Bus?" *Switch Hitter,* November 11, 2024. https://substack.com/home/post/p-151474290.

———. *Whipping Girl: A Transsexual Woman on Sexism and the Scapegoating of Femininity.* Berkeley, CA: Seal, 2016.

Seuss, Dr. *How the Grinch Stole Christmas.* New York: Random House, 2021.

Sharp, Isaac B. *The Other Evangelicals: A Story of Liberal, Black, Progressive, Feminist, and Gay Christians, and the Movement that Pushed Them Out.* Grand Rapids: Eerdmans, 2023.

Siegel, Daniel. *The Developing Mind: How Relationships and the Brain Interact to Shape Who We Are.* 3rd ed. New York: Guilford, 2020.

Simon, Paul. "Hurricane Eye." Track 9 on *You're the One.* Burbank, CA: Warner Bros., 2000.

Smith, James K. A. *You Are What You Love: The Spiritual Power of Habit.* Grand Rapids: Brazos, 2016.

Spencer-Helms, Tamice. *Faith Unleavened: The Wilderness Between Trayvon Martin and George Floyd.* Middletown, DE: KTF Press, 2023.

Stack, Liam. "N.Y. Archdiocese Condemns Funeral of Transgender Activist at Cathedral." *New York Times,* February 17, 2024. https://www.nytimes.com/2024/02/17/nyregion/cecilia-gentili-st-patricks-cathedral.html.

Stanley, Jason. *Erasing History: How Fascists Rewrite the Past to Control the Future.* New York: One Signal, 2024.

———. *How Fascism Works: The Politics of Us and Them.* New York: Random House, 2020.

———. *How Propaganda Works.* Princeton, NJ: Princeton University Press, 2017.

Steinmetz, Katy. "Kimberlé Crenshaw on What Intersectionality Means Today." *TIME,* February 20, 2020. https://time.com/5786710/kimberle-crenshaw-intersectionality/.

Suits, Bernard. *The Grasshopper: Games, Life and Utopia.* 3rd ed. Peterborough, CAN: Broadview, 2014.

Summit Ministries. "About Summit Ministries." https://www.summit.org/about/.

Tisby, Jemar. *The Spirit of Justice: True Stories of Faith, Race, and Resistance.* Grand Rapids: Zondervan, 2024.

The Longest Johns. "Ashes." Track 6 on *Cures What Ails Ya.* Nashville: Decca Records, 2020.

Thompson, Curt. *The Soul of Shame: Retelling the Stories We Believe About Ourselves.* Downers Grove, IL: InterVarsity, 2015.

Thurman, Howard. *Jesus and the Disinherited.* Boston: Beacon, 2022.

Tolkien, J. R. R. *The Fellowship of the Ring.* Boston: Clarion, 2004.

———. *Tree and Leaf.* London: HarperCollins, 2001.

Tolstoy, Leo. *The Kingdom of God Is Within You.* Translated by Constance Garnett. N.d.: Kshetra, 2016.

Tomlinson, Hugh. "The Two Sentences That Doomed Kamala Harris's Campaign." *The Times,* November 15, 2024. https://www.thetimes.com/world/us-world/article/kamala-harris-trans-gender-democrat-election-campaign-kvzqz9d6c.

Tonstad, Linn Marie. *Queer Theology: Beyond Apologetics.* Eugene, OR: Cascade, 2018.

Tufekci, Zeynep. *Twitter and Tear Gas: The Power and Fragility of Networked Protest.* New Haven, CT: Yale University Press, 2017.

Tyson, Phyllis, and Robert L. Tyson. *Psychoanalytic Theories of Development: An Integration.* New Haven, CT: Yale University Press, 1990.

Van der Kolk, Bessel. *The Body Keeps the Score: Brain, Mind, and Body in the Healing of Trauma.* New York: Viking, 2014.

Verhaeghe, Paul. "From Impossibility to Inability: Lacan's Theory of the Four Discourses." *The Letter: Irish Journal for Lacanian Psychoanalysis* 22 (2001) 91–108.

Volf, Miroslav. *Exclusion and Embrace: A Theological Exploration of Identity, Otherness, and Reconciliation.* Nashville: Abingdon, 2019.

Wachowski, Lana, and Lilly Wachowski. *The Matrix.* Warner Bros., 1999.

Waitz, Carl, and Theresa C. Tisdale. *Lacanian Psychoanalysis and Eastern Orthodox Christian Anthropology in Dialogue.* New York: Routledge, 2022.

Watkins, Mary, and Helene Shulman. *Toward Psychologies of Liberation.* Houndmills, UK: Palgrave Macmillan, 2010.

Welcher, Rachel Joy. *Talking Back to Purity Culture: Rediscovering Faithful Christian Sexuality.* Downers Grove, IL: InterVarsity, 2020.

Wells, H. G. *The Island of Doctor Moreau.* New York: Norton, 2023.

West, Cornel. *The Cornel West Reader.* New York: Basic Civitas, 1999.

Whitehead, Andrew L. *American Idolatry: How Christian Nationalism Betrays the Gospel and Threatens the Church.* Grand Rapids: Brazos, 2023.

Wilkerson, Isabel. *Caste: The Origins of Our Discontents.* New York: Random House, 2023.

Willard, Dallas. *The Divine Conspiracy: Rediscovering Our Hidden Life in God.* New York: HarperCollins, 2009.

Wilson, Jason. "Revealed: US Conservative Thinktank's Links to Extremist Fraternal Order." *The Guardian,* March 11, 2024. https://www.theguardian.com/us-news/2024/mar/11/claremont-institute-society-for-american-civic-renewal-links.

Wilson, Ken, et al. *A Letter to My Congregation: An Evangelical Pastor's Path to Embracing People Who Are Gay, Lesbian, Bisexual and Transgender into the Company of Jesus.* Canton, MI: Read the Spirit, 2016.

Winnicott, Donald. *Home Is Where We Start From: Essays by a Psychoanalyst*. New York: Norton, 1986.
Wu, Tim. *The Attention Merchants: The Epic Scramble to Get Inside Our Heads*. New York: Knopf, 2016.
Zimbardo, Philip G. *The Lucifer Effect: Understanding How Good People Turn Evil*. London: Rider, 2019.
Žižek, Slavoj. *How to Read Lacan*. New York: Norton, 2007.
———. *Looking Awry: An Introduction to Jacques Lacan Through Popular Culture*. Cambridge, MA: MIT Press, 1991.
———. *The Sublime Object of Ideology*. London: Verso, 2009.

www.ingramcontent.com/pod-product-compliance
Lightning Source LLC
Chambersburg PA
CBHW022009220426
43663CB00007B/1023